KERRY MARIE
AZARIAH
CONBOY

Saintly Solutions
to Life's Common Problems

CONFIRMATION DAY
MAY 9th, 2003

" COME HOLY SPIRIT! "

COME BY MEANS OF THE POWERFUL
INTERCESSION OF THE
IMMACULATE HEART OF
MARY,
YOUR WELL BELOVED SPOUSE!!
—AMEN

Fr. Joseph M. Esper

Saintly Solutions
to Life's Common Problems

— from Anger, Boredom, and Temptation
to Gluttony, Gossip, and Greed

SOPHIA INSTITUTE PRESS®
Manchester, New Hampshire

Sophia Institute Press®
Box 5284, Manchester, NH 03108
1-800-888-9344
www.sophiainstitute.com

Library of Congress Cataloging-in-Publication Data

Esper, Joseph M.
    Saintly solutions to life's common problems : from anger, boredom, and temptation to gluttony, gossip, and greed / Joseph M. Esper.
        p.   cm.
    Includes bibliographical references.
    ISBN 1-928832-37-7 (pbk. : alk. paper)
    1. Christian life — Catholic authors. 2. Christian saints. I. Title.

BX2350.3 .E86 2001
241 — dc21   2001049618

02 03 04 05 06 07 08 09 10 9 8 7 6 5 4 3 2

Contents

Saintly Solutions to
Life's Common Problems

⌒

Appendix

Remember,
O most gracious Virgin Mary,
that never was it known
that anyone who
fled to thy protection,
implored thy help,
or sought thy intercession
was left unaided.
Inspired with this confidence,
I fly unto thee,
O Virgin of virgins,
my Mother;
to thee do I come,
before thee I stand,
sinful and sorrowful.
O Mother of the Word Incarnate,
despise not my petitions,
but in thy mercy
hear and answer me. Amen.

St. Bernard

Introduction

It can safely be said that Christians today — faced by a society that constantly works to undermine or discredit their moral values and beliefs — have more than enough moral problems and life challenges, but far too few spiritual role models. We are more technically knowledgeable and proficient than ever before, but perhaps less aware of life's central issues, and more confused and uncertain in our response to them than at any time in recent history. This book represents a modest attempt to address this imbalance by drawing attention to those people who are uniquely qualified to teach us how to cope with the problems and difficulties of life: the saints.

By their spiritually successful lives, the saints can inspire us, encourage us, and give us practical wisdom and examples on how to cope with and overcome life's challenges.

Some of the saints demonstrated the worst human traits and behavior, including anger, greed, lust, and numerous other sins — but, with the help of divine grace and through their own honesty, humility, and hard work, they became the best of people.

Contrary to what many of us usually assume, holiness did not as a rule come easily to the saints; it was an ongoing challenge and struggle, sometimes marked by failures and setbacks. Even as they were increasingly remade in the image of Christ, they remained all too human, with faults and quirks, temptations and weaknesses, and unique outlooks and personalities; they all had problems to solve, temptations to overcome, and difficulties and irritations to endure.

In other words, they were just like us . . . with one difference: they strove, in everything they did, to discover Jesus and to live as signs and servants of His Presence.

As the saints focused on the Cross, their rough edges were gradually smoothed out and polished, their faults overcome and transformed into virtues, and their human nature cleansed and renewed and glorified. This is the process that all of us must undergo if we are to enter into the perfection of Heaven. The saints, who have already traveled this path, are happy to help show us the way. This is most especially true of the Virgin Mary, our spiritual mother who constantly intercedes on our behalf. The Church urges us to turn to her in all our needs, no matter how great or small, for she, more than anyone else, is eager to help us to know and follow her Son, Jesus, and she — as Queen of All Saints — is able to obtain for us all the treasures of divine love and mercy.

In this book I have included many sins, temptations, problems, challenges, and life situations commonly experienced by people today, along with inspiration and practical advice from the example of the saints. Their holy example in facing life's challenges will allow us to follow in their footsteps on the path to Heaven.

But the saints not only help us by their example; they also intercede for us. Scripture tells us that "we are surrounded by so great a cloud of witnesses,"[1] the holy men and women of every age who have gone before us and who, like the angels, now watch over us from Heaven and intercede on our behalf. St. Thérèse of Lisieux, known to us as the Little Flower, once wrote, "I believe that the blessed in Heaven have a great compassion for our wretchedness;

[1] Heb. 12:1.

they remember that when they were frail and mortal like us, they committed the same faults, endured the same struggles, and their fraternal love becomes greater even than it was on earth, which is why they do not cease to protect us and pray for us." One of the underappreciated riches of the Catholic Tradition is the veneration it gives the saints and the encouragement it offers us to seek their prayers and assistance. St. Thérèse, who had stated that she would spend her Heaven doing good for those on earth who requested her help, is perhaps a spokesperson for the entire heavenly court in this regard. God is glorified when His creatures demonstrate true love for each other — and the saints are now, like the angels, capable of doing this in the most wonderful way, and they rejoice when we give them this opportunity.

So, in your daily struggle with your sins, weaknesses, and problems, do not merely rely on the inspiration and example the saints have left you, but pray to them, too, so that they may intercede for you before the throne of God.

The French author Leon Bloy wrote, "There is really only one tragedy in life: not to have been a saint." In other words, if we do not travel the path of holiness — even if it begins only with our last breath on earth — we cannot experience salvation and eternal happiness. On Judgment Day everyone will be revealed as being completely and perfectly committed to Christ, or as wholly and unalterably opposed to Him. There will be no middle ground, and as the saints realized, each day we spend here on earth has eternal significance. Scripture urges us not to be "sluggish, but imitators of those who through faith and patience inherit the promises."[2] This is vitally important advice — and I pray that this book will make it easier to follow.

Rev. Joseph M. Esper

[2] Heb. 6:12.

As You Read This Book

As you read this book, whether you wish to learn about the saints for your own edification or entertainment or whether you seek help or advice for a particular problem or life situation you're experiencing, keep in mind the following:

• *Remember that, whatever you're facing, you're not alone.* Jesus has promised to remain always with those who trust in Him,[3] offering strength and refreshment to those who are burdened or weary[4] — and all the saints have experienced this divine help first-hand. The stories contained in these chapters remind us that the saints, too, had to struggle with life's problems, and their example of perseverance and trust may inspire you to remain faithful to your own efforts to answer the Lord's call.

• *Cultivate a devotion to particular saints* — those who experienced the same weaknesses or temptations you do and those whose lives illustrate the corresponding virtues. It's natural and fitting that you feel a particular attraction to those saints who had similar occupations, difficulties, or life

---

[3] Matt. 28:20.
[4] Matt. 11:28-29.

experiences as your own; they have a special understanding of your needs, and are particularly eager to assist you if you ask for their help.

• *Don't assume that traveling the path of perfection was easy for the saints, but will be impossible for you.* By and large, these holy men and women were not *born* saints; they became saints as a result of their willingness to cooperate with God's grace.

• *In seeking to overcome your personal weaknesses, choose only one area, or at most two, to work on at a time.* As the saints discovered, overcoming faults requires not only divine assistance, but humble dedication and perseverance. Don't attempt to do too much at once; after all, as long as you're honestly trying to come closer to the Lord, He'll be very patient with you.

• *If you don't see immediately the changes you seek — either in your personality or in your life — don't grow discouraged.* Some of the saints were recipients of miracles, and others underwent dramatic conversions, but most of them, using God's grace, overcame their faults or problems one day at a time. Even the holiest of saints — our Lady excepted — if asked whether they were holy, would have insisted on their own sinfulness. Nevertheless, God's grace was at work in them in a wonderful manner. In the same way, your openness to God allows Him to bring about beneficial changes in you, even though you're unaware of them.

• *Read each of the points in each chapter under "For Further Reflection."* One or more of these quotes, ideas, or suggestions may offer you insight, inspiration, or encouragement. Ask the Holy Spirit to make you receptive to whatever message you need to hear.

• *Consider the advice given in under "Something You Might Try."* If this isn't practical and useful to you now, continue reflecting and praying about your situation for at least several days, asking particular saints of your choice to help you find the answer.

• *Read the Scripture passages suggested in each chapter under "Further Reading."* Ask the Lord to speak to you through His Word, and to give you an openness to His truth as it applies to your life right now.

• *Pray the prayer given at the end of each chapter.* If necessary, make it your own, modifying it to fit your situation; if you wish, write out your own prayer on this subject, and begin praying it each day.

The saints are those men, women, and children who have successfully arrived home at our heavenly Father's kingdom, and — eternally rooted as they are in the love of Jesus Christ — they are eager to help us and rejoice with us as we, too, seek to complete our own lifelong journey.

Saintly Solutions
to Life's Common Problems

Anger

Let every man be quick to hear, slow to speak, slow to anger,
for the anger of man does not work the righteousness of God.

James 1:19-20

Do you have a fierce temper? If so, you're in good company: some of the saints were known for this personality defect — a characteristic that, with God's help, they overcame. The Gospels tell us that Jesus nicknamed the brothers Sts. James and John the "sons of thunder"[5] — perhaps because of their impetuous nature, as when they wanted Him to call down fire from Heaven to destroy an inhospitable town.[6] Other saints known for expressing anger include St. Basil the Great, whose hot-blooded temperament made it difficult for him to exercise tact in his dealings with others; St. Cyril of Alexandria, whose early years as a bishop were marked by quarreling, intolerance, and even violence; and the brilliant Church scholar and bishop St. Augustine, who was very unappreciative of opposition. A more contemporary example is the nineteenth-century French religious brother St. Benildus, who once remarked of his difficulties as a teacher, "I imagine that the

[5] Mark 3:17.
[6] Luke 9:51-56.

angels themselves, if they came down as schoolmasters, would find it hard to control their anger." The saint admitted that it was only with the Virgin Mary's help that he managed to keep from murdering some of his most ill-behaved students (which proves two things: saints have tempers, and they're allowed to exaggerate, as the rest of us do).

When it comes to a reputation for anger, few would argue that St. Jerome deserves anything other than first place. This great Scripture scholar had a brilliant but prickly personality and was famous for his arguments with other Church figures, including St. Augustine, conducted through letters that were often vitriolic or sarcastic. St. Pammachius, a former Roman senator, corresponded with Jerome, and tried to get him to tone down his language, without notable success; the Roman widow St. Marcella also corresponded with Jerome, sometimes challenging his ideas and once scolding him for his trigger-quick temper. It should be noted on Jerome's behalf, however, that in addition to being gentle with the poor and downtrodden, he was well aware of his weaknesses and performed great acts of penance (such as living in a cave) because of them.

Some saints who are known to us for their gentle nature — notably the great bishop St. Francis de Sales and the holy French priest St. Vincent de Paul — had to work very hard to overcome their tendency toward anger and contentiousness. St. Vincent said that, without the grace of God, he would have been "hard and repulsive, rough and cross," and St. Francis once claimed that it took him more than twenty years to learn to control his temper.

St. Remigius, when asked how he maintained an even temper, responded, "I often consider that my guardian angel is always by my side."

In the fourteenth century, Bl. John Colombini was a rather greedy merchant, particularly known for his bad temper. He flew into a rage one day because dinner wasn't ready when he arrived home. Hoping to shame him into better behavior, his wife handed him a book about the saints. John threw the book onto the floor, but then — ashamed of his temper — he picked it up and began to read. He became so engrossed in reading about the saints that he forgot his dinner; indeed, he was completely converted by the experience. He subsequently gave away most of his wealth, turned his home into a hospital, and personally cared for a suffering leper. When his wife urged him to be prudent in his charities, John — who was no longer easily offended by rebukes — gently reminded her that she was the one who had hoped for his conversion (to which she is supposed to have responded, "I prayed for rain, but this is a flood").

Learning to control our temper takes time and patience — and some of the saints were willing to make extreme efforts in this regard. For instance, when a storm interfered with his harvest, St. Nathalan angrily complained against God. Immediately repenting, he vowed to gain control of his anger and took a radical step to remind himself of this vow: he bound his right hand to his leg with an iron lock and threw the key into a river, promising that it would never be unlocked until he made a penitential pilgrimage to Rome. Years later Nathalan arrived in Rome; he purchased a fish from a boy there, and inside the fish's stomach was a key — which, of course, opened the lock.

Although the Lord probably doesn't expect such unusual efforts from us, He does want us to control our anger, and He gives us opportunities to do this — especially in daily life: bearing patiently with others' annoying habits, correcting others' mistakes with kindness and courtesy, refraining from blaring the horn when someone cuts us off in traffic, refusing to yield to the temptation to judge others' motives rashly.

When we have to speak to someone with whom we're angry, we should first pray for the Lord's guidance and help. It's often more effective to speak in terms of asking favors, rather than making demands or giving orders (for example, "May I ask a favor? Will you please pick up your clothes, rather than tossing them on the floor? Thank you; that will really help me"). Asking the Holy Spirit to give us the right words can help defuse a potentially explosive situation.

St. Thérèse of Lisieux advises us, "When you are angry with someone, the way to find peace is to pray for that person and ask God to reward him or her for making you suffer." We don't usually think of it this way, but those people who anger us are doing us an unintentional favor by allowing us to grow in patience, so we should try to be gentle with them.

Similarly, says St. Alphonsus Liguori, "When it happens that we commit some fault, we must also be gentle with ourselves. Getting at ourselves after doing something wrong is not humility but a subtle form of pride. . . . To be angry at ourselves after the commission of a fault is a greater fault than the one just committed, and it will lead to many others."

Thus, God wants us to control our tempers — even when we ourselves are their target. His healing mercy and peace are offered to everyone, but we'll miss out on them if we allow our anger to get in the way.

For Further Reflection

"Anger is a desire to revenge. 'To desire vengeance in order to do evil to someone who should be punished is illicit,' but it is praiseworthy to impose restitution 'to correct vices and maintain justice.' If anger reaches the point of a deliberate desire to kill or seriously wound a neighbor, it is gravely against charity; it is a mortal sin." — *Catechism of the Catholic Church*, par. 2302 (*Thus, depending on the circumstances and our motivation for it, anger can be righteous and justified, or gravely sinful. We must take care to control sinful anger and strive to keep even righteous anger from becoming morally offensive.*)

"Dismiss all anger, and look into yourself a little. Remember that he of whom you are speaking is your brother, and, as he is in the way of salvation, God can make him a saint, in spite of his present weakness." — *St. Thomas of Villanova*

"The lion can be tamed and made obedient, but your own wrath renders you wilder than any lion." — *St. John Chrysostom*

Something You Might Try

♦ St. Francis de Sales advises that, to avoid the sin of anger, you must quickly ask God to give peace to your heart when you're angered and then turn your thoughts to something else. Don't discuss the matter at hand, or make decisions, or correct another person while you're angry. When a person angers you, St. Francis advises, consider the person's good qualities, rather than the words or actions you find objectionable.

♦ If you wish to control your temper, become aware of the circumstances in which you're most likely to be angry: in certain settings (such as rush-hour traffic), with certain people (perhaps a particular neighbor or acquaintance), or at certain times of the day (maybe just before the end of the workday, when you're scrambling to clear your desk). Once you've learned from experience what things can anger you, prepare for these moments with a short, silent prayer — for instance, "Lord, help me avoid losing my temper," or "Dear Jesus, let me stay calm."

♦ It's also helpful to recall, when you're in a peaceful mood, a recent situation when you lost your temper. Ask yourself, "Was my anger justified? How will I respond to this situation in the future?" You can even "practice" responding properly by pretending this situation is repeating itself; by letting yourself feel angry when you're alone, you can rehearse possible responses and evaluate which ones might help you.

Further Reading

Scripture: Proverbs 19:11; Matthew 5:22; 1 Corinthians 13:5; Ephesians 4:26-31.

Classics: St. Francis de Sales, *An Introduction to the Devout Life;* St. Alphonsus Liguori, *The Practice of the Love of Jesus Christ.*

Contemporary Works: Rudolf Allers, *Self-Improvement.*

Father of saints and sinners,
there are times when I become very angry and upset,
times when I disappoint You and myself by losing my temper.
I am sorry; I ask for Your forgiveness and Your assistance.
Help me to follow the example of St. Francis de Sales
in persevering in my struggle against anger.
I wish, like Your Son, to be angry only
when I see injustice and hatred;
I wish, like Your saints, to be forgiving when
I see repentance and contrition.
Give me humility, compassion, and right judgment,
so that everything I do and everything I experience
will add to the glory of Your holy name. Amen.

Anxiety

Have no anxiety about anything, but in everything by prayer and
supplication with thanksgiving let your requests be made known to God.
And the peace of God, which passes all understanding,
will keep your hearts and your minds in Christ Jesus.

Philippians 4:6-7

Some saints were as prone to worry and anxiety as the rest of us are. But, by placing their trust in the Lord's presence and care, they were able to overcome their fears. Some of these fears were relatively minor ones, as faced by Bl. Helen of Udine, who, during a period of distress, was terrified even of loud noises. Others were serious fears, as faced by St. Augustine of Canterbury, the abbot of a monastery in Rome. In the year 596, he was chosen by Pope St. Gregory the Great to lead a group of forty monks on a missionary journey to England. (There were some scattered Christian communities there, but the island as a whole was pagan and uncivilized.) Augustine and his companions set out, but on reaching France, they were frightened by stories of the dangerous waters of the English Channel and the fierce temperament of the Anglo-Saxon tribes. Leaving his companions there, Augustine hurried back to confer with the Pope. Gregory encouraged the worried missionary and sent him back on his way, after telling him, "He

who would climb a lofty height must go by steps, not by leaps."
Augustine returned to the other missionaries; they crossed over
into England and there experienced great success in spreading the
Gospel.

It's said that the words "Be not afraid" appear in Scripture 366
times — one for each day of the year (leap years included). Certainly we need this sort of ongoing reminder and encouragement;
life can be difficult and is often filled with anxieties, great and
small. Jesus told St. Martha that, unlike her sister Mary, she was
"anxious and troubled about many things."[7] Martha took this
correction to heart and learned to trust in the Lord — so much so
that later, even as she grieved the death of her brother Lazarus,
she was able to acknowledge Jesus as the Resurrection and the
life.[8] Martha's sister St. Mary Magdalene likewise acknowledged
Christ's power on this occasion; she was one of the few followers
of Christ who, on Good Friday, dared to proclaim her loyalty to
Him publicly by standing beneath His Cross,[9] and for her courage
and devotion she was rewarded by being the first witness of the
Resurrection.[10]

All Christians are called to be a source of strength and courage
to others. One who understood this was St. Catherine of Siena,
who — centuries before women were acknowledged as equal to
men — used her tremendous influence to guide the affairs of popes
and kings. The papacy had found Rome to be hostile and unpleasant and had taken refuge in the French city of Avignon. This
"temporary" arrangement dragged on and on, to the detriment of
the Church. Catherine finally persuaded a timid Pope Gregory XI
to leave Avignon and return to Rome.

---

[7] Luke 10:41.
[8] John 11:24-27.
[9] John 19:25.
[10] John 20:11-18.

Another woman of strength and courage was the early third-century martyr St. Perpetua, a young noblewoman (and presumably a widow) who had recently given birth to an infant son. After being arrested as a Christian with some companions, she kept a diary in prison. She wrote, "What a day of horror! Terrible heat, owing to the crowds! Rough treatment by the soldiers! To crown all, I was tormented with anxiety for my baby. . . . Such anxieties I suffered for many days, but I obtained leave for my baby to remain in the prison with me, and being relieved of my trouble and anxiety for him, I at once recovered my health, and my prison became a palace to me and I would rather have been there than anywhere else."

St. Perpetua, her companion St. Felicity, and several other Christians were mauled by wild animals and then put to death by the sword; according to legend, the executioner was so shaken by Perpetua's brave demeanor that she herself had to guide his sword to her neck.

Compared with what the martyrs suffered, the things we worry about may seem trifling, but God offers us the same gifts of courage and strength that sustained the martyrs in their trials.

There's a saying that "Courage is fear that has said its prayers." Prayer is indeed the key to overcoming or coping with anxiety, for it reassures us of God's presence and reminds us of our need to rely on His strength, not on our own. As St. John Vianney said, "God commands you to pray, but He forbids you to worry."

This attitude of confidence applies even to our encounters with evil, for St. Teresa of Avila notes that every time evil spirits fail to terrify us or dissuade us from doing good, "they lose strength, and the soul masters them more easily. If the Lord is powerful and they are His slaves, what harm can they do to those who are servants of so great a King and Lord?" Nothing can happen to us without our Father's knowledge and permission, and He is able to arrange all things for our good. We, for our part, however, must avoid useless speculation; as St. Francis de Sales tells us, "It will be quite enough to receive the evils that come upon us from time to time, without anticipating them by the imagination."

According to St. Jerome, facing our fears and doing our duty in spite of them is an important way of taking up our cross; thus, we can reassure ourselves that in our efforts to be brave, we are actually serving Christ.

One who understood this was St. Thomas More, who from his prison cell wrote to his daughter, "I will not mistrust Him, Meg, although I shall feel myself weakening and on the verge of being overcome with fear. I shall remember how St. Peter at a blast of wind began to sink because of his lack of faith, and I shall do as he did: call upon Christ and pray to Him for help. And then I trust He shall place His holy hand on me and in the stormy seas hold me up from drowning."

As this English saint notes, we must keep our focus on Christ, not on ourselves; once we turn to Jesus in trust, we are ready to follow the advice of St. Francis de Sales: "If you earnestly desire to be delivered from some evil, or to attain to some good, above all things, calm and tranquilize your mind, and compose your judgment and will; then quietly and gently pursue your aim, adopting suitable means." Jesus offers us His peace;[11] if we accept it and use His grace, nothing shall overcome us.

For Further Reflection

"Let nothing disturb you, nothing cause you fear. All things pass; God is unchanging. Patience obtains all. Whoever has God needs nothing else; God alone suffices." — *St. Teresa of Avila*

"Stop listening to your fears. God is your guide and your Father, Teacher, and Spouse. Abandon yourself into the divine bosom

---

[11] John 14:27.

of His most holy good pleasure. Keep up your spiritual exercises and be faithful in prayer." — St. *Paul of the Cross*

"Anxiety is the greatest evil that can befall the soul — sin only excepted. . . . When our heart is troubled and disturbed within itself, it loses the strength necessary to maintain the virtues that it had acquired. At the same time, it loses the means to resist the temptations of the enemy, who then uses his utmost efforts to fish, as they say, in troubled waters." — St. *Francis de Sales*

Something You Might Try

♦ St. Paul of the Cross advises us, "When you notice that your heart is moving away even the tiniest bit from that inner peace that comes from the living faith-experience of the divine presence in the soul, stop and examine what the cause of this anxiety might be. Maybe it is some worry concerning your house or children, or some situation you cannot change at present. Bury it in God's loving will." Remind yourself that nothing can happen without the Lord's knowledge and permission — and as a loving Father, He will never abandon or forget you.

♦ Sometimes anxiety is not merely a spiritual problem, but is caused by a mental disorder. If you suffer from a severe case of anxiety or from panic attacks, consult your doctor, who can suggest homeopathic or natural remedies or prescribe a medication for you. You might also consult the Anxiety Disorders Association of America.

Further Reading

Scripture: Matthew 6:25-27, 34; 1 Corinthians 7:32.

Classics: St. Ignatius of Loyola, *Spiritual Exercises*; St. Francis de Sales, *An Introduction to the Devout Life*.

Contemporary Works: Carlos G. Valles, *Let Go of Fear*; Brother Daniel Korn, *A Way of the Cross for Anxious Times*.

Almighty God,
who knows our necessities before we ask,
and our ignorance in asking:
Set free Your servants from all anxious
thoughts for the morrow;
give us contentment with Your good gifts;
and confirm our faith so that,
according as we seek Your kingdom,
You will not suffer us to lack any good thing,
through Jesus Christ our Lord. Amen.

St. Augustine

Argumentativeness

*Do not argue about a matter which does not concern you,
nor sit with sinners when they judge a case.*

Sirach 11:9

True or false: Because of their great holiness, saints never get into arguments with other people — least of all other saints.

False. This perfect harmony will be`true for all followers of Christ when they arrive in Heaven, and it *should* be true here on earth, but because of human weakness, it isn't — not even for the holiest people. Indeed, saints have even been known to argue (sometimes charitably, sometimes less so) with other saints.

St. Paul describes how he publicly rebuked St. Peter for going back on an earlier agreement that Gentile converts to Christianity should be treated equally with those of a Jewish background.[12] Paul was never one to shy away from controversy; having been commissioned by God to preach the Gospel, the message of truth and life, he wouldn't allow anything to interfere with the fulfillment of this responsibility. We can admire this sort of forceful determination in a just and holy cause; as it happens, however, not all disputes involving saints had such an honorable motivation.

[12] Gal. 2:11-14.

The great scholars St. Jerome and St. Augustine had a deep respect for each other's learning and intelligence, but they didn't
seem to like each other personally, as their correspondence (especially Jerome's) makes clear. Jerome had a habit of equating disagreement with his writings with disloyalty to the Church.

Other disputes among saints involved St. Finnian of Moville
and the great Irish missionary St. Columba, who argued fiercely
over whether Columba had the right to copy a manuscript belong-
ing to Finnian; and the eighth-century abbot St. Sturm and the
bishop St. Lull, who conducted a long dispute regarding proper jurisdiction over Sturm's abbey. An argument over a seemingly less
important issue involved the twelfth-century English hermit St.
Bartholomew of Farne and a fellow monk named Thomas. The
subject of their disagreement: how much food to eat each day. It
seems that Thomas couldn't get by with as little nourishment as
Bartholomew, and when he wondered whether Bartholomew was
secretly supplementing his own rations, the saint — greatly offended at being accused of hypocrisy — went off in a huff. Thomas
apologized, but it wasn't until a year later that reconciliation occurred (and only after the local bishop ordered St. Bartholomew
to return).

The Church has had her share of controversial leaders, many
of whom seemed to enjoy a good argument. For instance, on being
appointed bishop, St. Cyril of Alexandria behaved like the pro-
verbial bull in a china shop. In his zeal to defend the true Faith, he
closed the churches of schismatics (Christians who had broken
away from the authority of the Church), drove the Jews of Alexandria out of the city and confiscated their property, fought with
government officials, and antagonized local monastic groups. Eventually Cyril learned to control his temper and to exercise leadership in a more restrained way.

Another colorful figure was Pope St. Callistus, who was once a
slave in a leading Roman household. After losing some money

entrusted to his care, he fled, but was recaptured and imprisoned; after his release, he caused a disturbance in a Jewish synagogue — perhaps by trying to recover money from some Jews who were in his debt. This time Callistus was sentenced to work in the salt mines in Sardinia, but, freed through the influence of a Christian member of the imperial court, he became a deacon and papal advisor in Rome and was himself eventually elected Pope. His own stormy past may have given him greater than usual sympathy toward Christians who renounced their Faith during times of persecution, for he allowed them to return to the Church after they had given sincere signs of repentance. This generous policy in turn provoked a controversy with St. Hippolytus, a severe and demanding figure who felt Callistus was being much too lenient.

The fourteenth-century bishop and papal emissary St. Andrew Corsini had a knack for helping resolve quarrels — perhaps because he understood argumentative persons very well, having himself been bad-tempered as a youth.

Jesus said, "Blessed are the peacemakers,"[13] and Christians are called to live in this spirit. Sadly, many, including some saints, have at times failed to respond to this call. Quarreling comes easily and naturally to many of us — but it contradicts the message of the Gospel and undermines our membership in God's family.

To overcome argumentativeness, we must first, in the words of St. Vincent de Paul, "love our neighbor as being made in the image of God and as an object of His love." We would not dare speak disrespectfully to Jesus Himself, so we must remind ourselves that He dwells in other people — even those with whom we're angry.

St. John Vianney says, if we wish to avoid being hypocritical in God's eyes, we must have "universal charity for everyone — for the good and the bad, for the poor and the rich, and for all those who do us harm as much as for those who do us good." This doesn't

---

[13] Matt. 5:9.

mean we should never disagree with people, but that we should consider carefully the circumstances and means of doing so.

St. Louis of France advises us, "In order to avoid discord, never contradict anyone except in case of sin or some other danger to a neighbor, and when it is necessary to contradict others, do it with tact and not with temper." Error must be opposed with truth, but in a loving way. According to St. John of Kanty, "Fight all false opinions, but let your weapons be patience, sweetness, and love. Roughness is bad for your own soul and spoils the best cause."

Sometimes people are merely looking for an excuse to argue with us. In such cases, we must remain charitable. Calmly and patiently stating our position — more than once, if necessary — will usually be more effective than engaging in an argument; as the saints knew, a strong and peaceful spirit serves us well.

Many saints have been involved in mediating conflicts and serving as calming influences. At times, their peacemaking roles were in matters as broad and important as a religious controversy, as when St. Robert Bellarmine attempted to sway minds through gentleness rather than harsh invective. At other times, they involved simpler matters, as when a youthful St. Dominic Savio ended a fight between two boys by insisting that they direct their aggression at him, instead of at each other. An important part of peacemaking is promoting racial harmony, and one patron saint of such an effort might be Bl. Pierre Toussaint, a nineteenth-century black family servant in New York City; he personally encountered much racism, but helped spread the Gospel by always responding with gentleness and charity. This is the ultimate Christian response: not only to turn the other cheek, but to work for peace while upholding the truth in a spirit of genuine love and compassion.

For Further Reflection

"Tolerance is an important part of charity. Without it, it is difficult for two persons to get on together. Moreover, tolerance is the bond of all friendship and unites people in heart and opinion and action, not only with each other, but in unity with our Lord, so that they may really be at peace." — *St. Vincent de Paul*

"Some may say that it is unreasonable to be courteous and gentle with a reckless person who insults you for no reason at all. But St. Francis de Sales replies, 'We must practice meekness, not only with reason, but against reason.' . . . We must do what St. Francis de Sales did: 'I have made a pact with my tongue,' he wrote, 'not to speak when my heart is disturbed.' " — *St. Alphonsus Liguori*

"Our life and our death is with our neighbor. If we gain our brother, we have gained God, but if we scandalize our brother, we have sinned against Christ." — *St. Anthony*

Something You Might Try

♦ In the *Dialogue* of St. Catherine of Siena, Jesus says, "Love of me and [love] of neighbor are one and the same thing, and, so far as the soul loves me, she loves her neighbor, because love toward him issues from me." Thus, when you're tempted to quarrel with someone, remind yourself that it's actually Jesus Himself who stands before you.

♦ Arguments and disagreements are sometimes necessary, but before engaging in them, ask yourself these questions:
  • Is this issue important enough to argue over?
  • Is this the best time and setting to discuss the matter, or might the other person be more receptive and agreeable at a later time or in a different location?
  • If someone were approaching *me* to argue over this point, what approach would I want him or her to use? What would I consider respectful?

• Is there someone who can serve as a mediator or who can help me make my point calmly and fairly?

• Am I looking at this argument in terms of winning and losing, or am I truly seeking a "win/win" situation?

Giving careful thought to these and similar questions before expressing disagreement can make it much easier to prevent or resolve arguments.

Further Reading

Scripture: Sirach 28:8-11; Philippians 2:14.

Classics: St. Catherine of Siena, *Dialogue*; St. Francis de Sales, *An Introduction to the Devout Life*; St. Alphonsus Liguori, *The Practice of the Love of Jesus Christ*.

⌖

Lord, make me an instrument of Your peace.
Where there is hatred, let me sow love.
Where there is injury, pardon.
Where there is discord, vision.
Where there is doubt, faith.
Where there is despair, hope.
Where there is darkness, light.
Where there is sadness, joy.
O divine Master,
grant that I may not so much seek
to be consoled as to console;
to be understood as to understand;
to be loved, as to love;
for it is in giving that we receive,
it is in pardoning that we are pardoned,
and it is in dying that we are born to eternal life.

St. Francis of Assisi

Boredom

It is full time now for you to wake from sleep.
For salvation is nearer to us now than when we first believed.

Romans 13:11

One of the most important conversions in the history of the Church occurred partially as the result of a problem that most of us have faced: boredom. It's the story of the founder of the Jesuits: St. Ignatius of Loyola.

The youngest of eleven children, Ignatius was born in 1491 at the castle of Loyola in Spain of an ancient and noble family. As a young man, he dreamed of winning military glory and of making a name for himself. During a war with France, while Ignatius and other Spanish soldiers were defending the city of Pamplona, a cannonball injured his leg, and Ignatius was sent home to recuperate. Confined to bed, he understandably experienced boredom, and he requested something to read — preferably a book of romantic stories. Nothing was to be found except a book of the lives of the saints — hardly what Ignatius was interested in. Yet he began reading, at first just to pass the time, and as he read, he found himself more and more interested, and then inspired, by the lives of the saints. His dreams of military glory and courtly honors were soon replaced by an ardent desire to become a soldier for Christ — and eventually, after many trials and much spiritual growth, Ignatius of Loyola became one of the Church's greatest saints and the founder of one of her most important religious orders.

A little bit of boredom changed history. This should not surprise us, for God is able to use virtually any experience to help us grow in holiness, no matter how simple or mundane. The saint who understood this truth perhaps better than any other was St. Thérèse of Lisieux, known to us as the Little Flower. The nine years she spent in the convent until her death in 1897 at age twenty-four were uneventful and ordinary, yet also heroic — for she did everything, and suffered everything, with as much love as possible. Thérèse called this her "little way." She recognized that greatness in God's eyes comes not from performing heroic deeds, but from opening ourselves to love as fully as possible. Everyone, no matter how "boring" his life, has this potential to become a saint.

The best way to avoid boredom is to use our lives well, not only in our work, but also in our entertainment. The wrong forms of entertainment, and the misuse of leisure time, can easily lead us into sin; the widely known saying "Idleness is the Devil's workshop" contains much wisdom. This truth was particularly well understood by St. John Bosco, the nineteenth-century Italian priest who spent his life working with delinquent boys. It wasn't enough, he knew, to provide them with education and work; it was also necessary to make these things — including religious education — interesting and attractive. He and his companions went to great lengths to provide wholesome, enjoyable activities for the boys in their care.

A similar approach was used by one of St. John Bosco's contemporaries, the Spanish priest Bl. Emmanuel Domingo Y Sol. As part of his work with youths, he built a theater and sports arena for recreation — for he knew that interesting, wholesome activities allow sin and temptation much less influence in our lives.

This insight remains true today; whether we are in charge of others or only of our own souls, we should seek to do only those things which will help — or at least not hinder — our spiritual growth. Our lives in Heaven will certainly not be boring, and — as long as we place the Lord's will first — God is pleased when we also find life on His earth interesting and enjoyable.

For Further Reflection

"Few souls understand what God would accomplish in them if they were to abandon themselves unreservedly to Him and if they were to allow His grace to mold them accordingly." — *St. Ignatius of Loyola*

"Those who love God will find pleasure in everything; those who do not love God will never find true pleasure in anything." — *St. Alphonsus Liguori*

"Heaven will display far more variety than Hell." — C. S. *Lewis* (*Thus, the "forbidden fruits" that tempt us and that appear so appealing are not only spiritually dangerous; in the long run, they're actually less interesting and compelling than the glories and mysteries of God's kingdom.*)

Something You Might Try

◆ According to Archbishop Fulton J. Sheen, "If you will whatever God wills, you will always have exactly what you want. When you want anything else, you are not happy before you get it, and when you do get it, you do not want it. That is why you are 'up' today and 'down' tomorrow. You will never be happy if your happiness depends on getting solely what you want. Change the focus. Get a new center. Will what God wills, and your joy no man shall take from you." Thus, you can find fulfillment (and, in fact, healthy excitement) only by shifting the focus from yourself and your desires to God.

◆ When you live within yourself, cut off from other people, it's no surprise that you become bored. Oftentimes a remedy for boredom is to think of others instead of yourself — to do a favor, to lend a hand, or to surprise someone in a caring way.

Further Reading

Scripture: Isaiah 50:4; Matthew 11:28.

Classics: St. Alphonsus Liguori, *Conformity to the Will of God;* St. Ignatius of Loyola, *Spiritual Exercises.*

Lord, when I'm bored,
help me to think of You
with gratitude and joy,
and to think of others
with appreciation and concern.
Let me not be self-centered,
but open to the beauty of Your creation.
May all my experiences,
no matter how routine,
bring me to a deeper awareness
of Your presence
and to a greater sense of
thankfulness for Your gifts. Amen.

Broken Friendships

I have called you friends, for all that I have heard
from my Father I have made known to you.

John 15:15

Friendships can be a source, not only of spiritual growth, but also of great enjoyment and satisfaction — and thus, the ending of a friendship on bad terms can be the cause of considerable pain and sorrow. Arguments, disagreements, or misunderstandings can end relationships that had been life-giving and enriching. If this has happened to you, take heart; some of the saints had this unhappy experience.

The foremost example of friendship's coming to an end involves Jesus Himself — for one of His own disciples betrayed Him. When Judas Iscariot led the temple guard into the Garden of Gethsemane to arrest our Lord, Jesus addressed him as "friend"[14] — not ironically or sarcastically, but genuinely and lovingly. The Lord was willing to forgive Judas for what he was doing, but Judas refused; the relationship came to a tragic end — not because Jesus willed it so, but because Judas gave in to despair after his act of betrayal and hanged himself.

[14] Matt. 26:50.

Several instances of strained friendships among the saints have been recorded. St. Paul and St. Barnabas were close friends; indeed, it was Barnabas who introduced Paul to St. Peter and the other Apostles. Barnabas's acceptance of Paul helped the other early Christians overcome their suspicion of this former persecutor of the Church, and the two apostles were chosen by the Holy Spirit to go forth together as missionaries. Barnabas had his young cousin St. Mark accompany them; however, during the journey, Mark turned back for some unknown reason,[15] which angered Paul. When the two apostles were preparing for another missionary journey, Barnabas again wanted to take Mark along, but Paul, remembering the youth's earlier inconstancy, would not permit it, and this led to a temporary falling out between the two friends.

In the fourth century, St. Heliodorus met St. Jerome in Italy, and became a disciple and eventually a friend of the great scholar; he even helped finance Jerome's translation of the Bible into Latin, the common language of the day. (This translation, requested by Pope St. Damasus, became known as the *Vulgate*.) When Jerome and his disciples went to the Holy Land, Heliodorus followed, although he refused to join them in a life of seclusion in the desert, because he felt that God wasn't calling him to that lifestyle. Jerome, who was known for his fierce temper, was very upset by this and rebuked Heliodorus in an impassioned letter. Heliodorus returned to Italy and was appointed bishop of the small town of Altino; from there he demonstrated a generous and forgiving nature by continuing to send financial support to Jerome.

Sometimes personality differences can strain friendships. The classic example of this involves the fourth-century saints Basil and Gregory of Nazianzus. Basil was outgoing, forceful, and determined; Gregory was sensitive, shy, and retiring. Both men had

---

[15] Acts 13:13 (Mark was also known as John Mark, or John).

been ordained priests — Basil very willingly, Gregory very reluctantly — and both retired to a monastery for a time. In 370, Basil was appointed Bishop of Caesarea, and he proved to be well suited for an active role in defending Church teaching against the heresies of the day. Two years later, he, in turn, appointed his reluctant friend Gregory Bishop of Sasima, but, instead of going there, Gregory remained in Nazianzus to help his father, who was bishop there (in the early days of the Church, celibacy was not required of clergy). This greatly angered Basil, who was perhaps used to getting his own way in such matters. Eventually, however, the two friends were reconciled, and had this reconciliation not happened during their earthly lives, we can be sure it would have happened in Heaven.

Friendship is a gift from God; indeed, according to St. Aelred of Rievaulx, "God is friendship." That's why St. Francis de Sales could say, "Friendships begun in this world will be taken up again, never to be broken off." This thought may be a consolation if you're saddened over the end of a once-satisfying friendship; you have the assurance that in the kingdom of God, all broken relationships will be healed and perfected. (If you *don't* want to reestablish a relationship with someone even in Heaven, you had better start praying for a change of heart — for the only way to avoid knowing and loving someone in eternity is for one or both of you to miss out on God's kingdom.)

Our friends are supposed to help us grow in holiness, and we're to do the same for them. Helping one another to grow in holiness may sometimes call for fraternal correction, although in this regard, St. Francis Xavier advises, "The better friends you are, the straighter you can talk, but while you are only on nodding terms, be slow to scold." Our concern for our friends' spiritual well-being always involves the risk that they'll be offended by us or upset with us, but every friendship — even a broken one — can prove to be a blessing when seen from the viewpoint of eternity.

For Further Reflection

"Particularly when I am worn out by the upsets of the world, I cast myself without reservation on the love of those who are especially close to me. I know that I can safely entrust my thoughts and considerations to those who are aflame with Christian love and have become faithful friends to me. For I am entrusting them not to another human, but to God, in whom they dwell and by whom they are what they are." — *St. Augustine*

"For those who live in the world and desire to embrace true virtue, it is necessary to unite together in holy, sacred friendship." — *St. Francis de Sales*

"If a person were to suffer insults, beatings, and imprisonment for one of his friends, how distressed he would be to know that his friend remembered nothing of it and did not even want to hear people talk about it. On the other hand, how gratified would he be to know that his friend always spoke tenderly about it and often thanked him for it. Thus Jesus Christ is greatly pleased when we recall with loving gratitude His pains and the sorrows and death that He suffered for us." — *St. Alphonsus Liguori* (*Each time we are treated badly by a friend, we might ask ourselves how we've been treating the greatest Friend of all.*)

Something You Might Try

◆ St. Augustine says, "When we are harassed by poverty, saddened by bereavement, ill, or in pain, let good friends visit us. Let them be persons who not only can rejoice with those who rejoice but can weep with those who weep. Let them be persons who know how to give useful advice and how to win us to express our own feelings in conversation." *You* should strive to be the good friend Augustine speaks of, even to your former friends — especially when they experience misfortune. This will be a sign of genuine Christian charity on your part, and, in the case of a broken friendship, it may even make reconciliation possible.

◆ It's important to maintain a charitable spirit toward former friends, even if they act unjustly toward you. When St. Thomas More was condemned to death for refusing to accept the invalid marriage of King Henry VIII, he said to his judges — some of whom had been friends and colleagues — "As St. Paul held the clothes of those who stoned Stephen to death, and as they are both now friends in Heaven and shall continue there as friends forever, so I truly trust and will most heartily pray, that although your lordships have now here on earth been judges to my condemnation, we may nevertheless hereafter meet in Heaven in everlasting salvation."

Further Reading

Scripture: Sirach 6:6-7, 14-17; Job 42:10; John 15:13.

Classics: St. Francis de Sales, *An Introduction to the Devout Life*.

Contemporary works: James A. Magner, *Mental Health in a Mad World*.

My Jesus, from all eternity,
You were pleased to give Yourself to us in love.
And You planted within us a deep spiritual desire
that can be satisfied only by You.
I may go from here to the other end of the world,
from one country to another,
from riches to greater riches,
from pleasure to pleasure,
and still I shall not be content.
All the world cannot satisfy the immortal soul.

*It would be like trying to feed a starving man
with a single grain of wheat.
We can be satisfied only by setting our hearts,
imperfect as they are, on You.
We are made to love You;
You created us as Your lovers.
It sometimes happens that the more we
know a neighbor, the less we love him.
But with You it is quite the opposite.
The more we know You, the more we love You.
Knowledge of You kindles such a fire in our souls
that we have no energy left for worldly desires.
My Jesus, how good it is to love You.
Let me be like Your disciples on Mount Tabor,
seeing nothing else but You.
Let us be like two bosom friends,
neither of whom can ever bear to offend the other.*

St. John Vianney

Business Difficulties

Provide yourselves with purses that do not grow old,
with a treasure in the heavens that does not fail,
where no thief approaches and no moth destroys.
For where your treasure is, there will your heart be also.

Luke 12:33-34

Like most Christians today, many saints had to earn a living in the everyday world, and some struggled with problems in their work. Their example and prayers can bring us aid and inspiration in our times of worldly difficulty.

First and foremost, we need to recall and honor St. Joseph the Worker, the humble carpenter whose hard work supported the Holy Family. Although he must have found it frustrating and worrisome that Jesus and Mary had to live in poverty in spite of his best efforts, he never complained. His honesty and dedication make him a fitting patron of all who work for a living.[16] During His

---

[16] In 1955 Pope Pius XII — to counteract the Communist conception of work as nothing more than a means of building up an earthly Marxist kingdom — declared May 1 ("May Day," the Communist workers' holiday) to be the feast of St. Joseph the Worker.

public life, Jesus Himself was proud to be identified as the son of a carpenter.[17]

It should also be remembered that, along with a tax collector, Jesus chose simple, hard-working men, mostly fishermen, to be His Apostles; He wanted not well-educated scribes and doctors of the law who were puffed up by their own religious knowledge, but ordinary people whose humility would allow the Holy Spirit to turn them into productive laborers in God's kingdom.

God promises His servants happiness in the next world, but not necessarily success in this one — and we see this borne out in the lives of numerous holy men and women. The Canadian religious brother Bl. Andre Bessette was unsuccessful at a number of trades, including baking, shoemaking, and blacksmithing.

St. Elizabeth Ann Seton, the first American-born saint, married a wealthy businessman, but eleven years later, both his business and his health failed, and Elizabeth had to shoulder heavy responsibilities. After Mr. Seton's death and her own conversion to Catholicism, she opened a school in Boston to support her five children.

St. Alphonsus Rodriguez was a wool merchant in sixteenth-century Spain. Although he was a capable businessman, an economic downturn created many financial difficulties for him. Taking this and other misfortunes as a sign from God, he finally sold his business to pursue a religious career.

Quite often, saints are no better at money-making or successful investing than the rest of us are. In the eleventh century, St. Guy of Anderlecht was persuaded by a merchant of Brussels to join other speculators in investing his small savings in a business proposition. Guy agreed for a noble purpose: the venture would gain him more money to give to the poor. The saint lost everything, however, when the ship carrying the investors' goods sank while

---

[17] Cf. Matt. 13:55.

leaving harbor. Guy blamed himself, for he had tried to secure money on his own, rather than trusting in God to provide.

A failed investment also affected the life of St. Lutgardis; her father lost the money intended for her dowry in a business speculation, so she ended up being sent to a convent — and only after seeing a vision of Christ did she adjust to religious life.

St. Joan Delanoue, who inherited her parents' business of selling cloths, crockery, and religious trinkets, primarily to pilgrims visiting a nearby shrine, was once a successful merchant. Initially, she sought to make as much money as possible, overpricing items, refusing to give credit, and — to the scandal of the parish — keeping her store open seven days a week. She also let pilgrims sleep overnight in her home — for an exorbitant fee.

Then Joan was touched by divine grace, and she repented. She took her first small step toward generosity by giving away a dress, and because of the satisfaction this brought her, she was soon giving away other items (secretly, whenever possible), sharing her meals and her home with those who could not pay, and devoting all her resources to the relief of the poor. As her income declined, it became necessary for her to take on additional work and even to beg from the rich. Through her generosity, St. Joan became a failure at business — but she stored up lasting wealth for herself in Heaven.

Worldly success is often fickle and elusive; only heavenly riches will never disappoint us.

For Further Reflection

"Economic life brings into play different interests, often opposed to one another. This explains why the conflicts that characterize it arise. Efforts should be made to reduce these conflicts by negotiation that respects the rights and duties of each social partner: those responsible for business enterprises, representatives of wage-earners (for example, trade unions), and public authorities when appropriate." — *Catechism of the Catholic Church*, par. 2430.

"May you consider truly good whatever leads to your goal and truly evil whatever makes you fall away from it. Prosperity and adversity, wealth and poverty, health and sickness, honors and humiliations, life and death, in the mind of the wise man, are not to be sought for their own sake, nor avoided for their own sake. But if they contribute to the glory of God and your eternal happiness, they are good and should be sought. If they detract from this, they are evil and must be avoided." — *St. Robert Bellarmine*

"The business of this life should not preoccupy us with its anxiety and pride, so that we no longer strive with all the love of our heart to be like our Redeemer and to follow His example." — *St. Leo the Great*

Something You Might Try

♦ If you're undergoing business difficulties despite your good, honest efforts, consider that those difficulties may in fact be a sign of God's favor. A certain merchant donated money to St. Teresa of Avila and asked for her prayers. Later she told him, "It has been revealed to me that your name is written in the Book of Life, and as a token of this, nothing in the future will go on prosperously with you." This soon came to pass; the man went bankrupt and entered a debtors' prison, but his creditors, knowing of his good character, set him free. He remained poor until his death, but considered himself rich in God's grace.

♦ St. Francis de Sales advises, "When you are occupied in ordinary business and occupations that do not require your closest attention, think more of God than of them; and if your business is sufficiently important to absorb your whole attention in doing it well, then from time to time look to God, just as the sailor on his homeward voyage looks more often to the sky than to the waves that carry him. So will God work with you, in you, and for you, and your labor will be followed with consolation." The holy bishop also suggests, "Be very careful and diligent in all such business as falls to your share, for God, who has allotted it to you, would have you do it well. But, if possible, avoid solicitude — that is to say, do not undertake your affairs with disquietude, anxiety, and worry, and do not hurry and excite yourself about them, for all excitement hinders reason and judgment, and prevents us from doing well that very thing about which we are excited." Thus, in all our labors we should strive to do our best, and in a spirit of gratitude, humility, and trust; if we do, we can be sure of having God's favor, even if we fall short by worldly measurements of success.

Further Reading

Scripture: Isaiah 3:10; Psalm 90:17; Matthew 10:10.

Classics: St. Francis de Sales, *An Introduction to the Devout Life*.

Contemporary Works: J. Murray Elwood, *Not For Sale: Saving Your Soul and Your Sanity at Work*.

*Lord, I am trying
to earn my keep in the world,
but it's not easy.
There are bills to pay, problems to solve,
rules to follow, and people to satisfy,
and I struggle with these
and other challenges day after day.
Sometimes it's so hard,
I'm not sure how I'll cope.*

Help me.
Through the intercession
of St. Joseph the Worker
and all the other saints of history
who toiled for a living, please assist me.
Guide me, encourage me, and
help me to trust in Your loving care.
Let me meet each day's challenges
with confidence, integrity, and trust,
and help me to remember that the way
to store up true and lasting treasure is
by being honest, generous,
and full of faith.
Bless my efforts;
bless those who work with me
and those who depend on me.
Give me a sense of courage and hope,
and never let me forget that
You are with me in all things. Amen.

Conception and Pregnancy Difficulties

*When a woman is in travail she has sorrow, because her hour
has come; but when she is delivered of the child, she no longer
remembers the anguish, for joy that a child is born into the world.*

John 16:21

On January 22, 1973, the United States Supreme Court struck down all state and federal restrictions on abortion, in effect allowing abortion on demand at any stage of pregnancy. The results have been a moral disaster for our nation, introducing what Pope John Paul II has called a "culture of death." Since the infamous Supreme Court decision, more than thirty million children have been murdered in the womb, the lives of millions of women (who were often themselves victims) have been wracked by physical and emotional suffering, and an ugly and abiding scar has been inflicted on the soul of America.

One of the alleged reasons for allowing abortion is that it's often supposedly safer than childbirth; even if this highly questionable assertion were true in a physical sense, it is certainly wrong — disastrously wrong — from a spiritual and moral perspective. Life is a precious gift from God, even in cases of a difficult pregnancy or birth — and those women who trust in Him in such cases become a source of blessing for themselves and their families.

Indeed, a number of saints have been involved in cases of difficult childbirth. In the year 203, St. Felicity, a slave far advanced in pregnancy, was arrested as a Christian, along with the noblewoman St. Perpetua and four other Christians. Felicity underwent a difficult labor in prison; she gave birth to a girl, who was fortunately adopted by another Christian — for Felicity and her companions were soon after executed.

A more contemporary case of heroic motherhood involves Bl. Joanna Beretta Molla, a Brazilian woman who was expecting her fourth child in 1962. The joy of her pregnancy was shattered by a diagnosis of a tumor in her uterus. Against medical recommendations, she and her husband refused an operation that would have saved her life at the expense of her unborn child. A daughter was born to them, but a few days later Joanna died of complications.

In addition to the physical sufferings associated with difficult pregnancy and childbirth, some expecting parents face emotional hardships. The contraceptive mentality that has taken hold of our society looks on pregnancy as a problem, and this negative attitude is often a cause of suffering to many married couples who have numerous children. In fact, some parents who have as few as three children face snide remarks from neighbors, coworkers, and even friends and family members who have adopted the modern world's view that children are a problem.

But Scripture is replete with references that portray children as a blessing from God. Children are compared to olive plants — that is, a valuable gift of life — around the table of the just man.[18] Incidents of childless couples' being unexpectedly blessed with children are seen frequently in the story of salvation. When the Lord visited Abraham, He promised that he and his wife, Sarah — although both were very old — would have a son within a year.[19]

---

[18] Ps. 128:3.
[19] Gen. 18:10.

This child was Isaac, through whom the Lord fulfilled His pledge to make Abraham the father of a great nation.

Isaac experienced the blessings of fatherhood after praying on behalf of his barren wife, Rebekah.[20] Rebekah's pregnancy was difficult, however, for the twins in her womb, Esau and Jacob, jostled with each other as a preview of their intense rivalry later in life.

Centuries later, a childless couple named Elkanah and Hannah prayed for a son, and God granted their request; their child, Samuel, became a great prophet. Elizabeth and Zechariah waited long for a child and were rewarded for their prayerful patience when they became the parents of another great prophet: St. John the Baptist. Sts. Ann and Joachim were also childless for many years before they were blessed with a daughter: the Blessed Virgin Mary.

Not all prayers for the joys of parenthood are answered. Some couples remain infertile; others experience the tragedy of miscarriage or the death of a child; still others undergo the ordeal of seeing their children die spiritually by rejecting God in their adult years. It's a hard truth that no one has an absolute *right* to have children; all human beings, including children, ultimately belong to God; their parents are merely stewards in His name. God alone has the authority to bestow life, even when this means that some loving, seemingly deserving married couples remain childless.

If you and your spouse desire children, you may, after praying for the Lord's guidance, seek medical assistance (as long as you use morally approved means) or employ techniques such as Natural Family Planning to aid your efforts to conceive. But if it becomes apparent that God's plan is for you not to have children of your own, you must do your best to accept and obey in a spirit of trust. In such a case, adoption can be a practical, and noble, alternative.

The Church teaches that human life begins at conception and that each unborn child possesses a soul created by God Himself. A

[20] Gen. 25:21.

guardian angel is assigned to every unborn human being, and there are saints to whom expectant mothers can turn for prayers and assistance. The patron saints of women in labor are St. Ann, the mother of the Blessed Virgin Mary, and the virgin and martyr St. Margaret. The eighteenth-century Redemptorist lay brother St. Gerard Majella is considered a patron of childbirth. Women preparing to give birth, particularly those undergoing a difficult pregnancy, may also — if they have already chosen names — pray to the patron saints of their unborn children. Childless couples can likewise turn to the saints, particularly Sts. Ann and Joachim, Sts. Elizabeth and Zechariah, and others who waited and prayed for children for many years, for their intercession.

For Further Reflection

"Make a frequent offering of the tiny creature to our Creator's eternal glory, since He has chosen you to cooperate with Him in forming your child. But take the greatest care of your health: don't put yourself out or force yourself to pray at present. You must treat yourself with the utmost gentleness." — *St. Francis de Sales* (in a letter to a new mother)

"Society is suffering acutely because of the lack of truly Christian mothers. Since society is based on the family, its very shape and fate is largely in the hands of women. If they were given a thorough Christian education and were well-grounded in Christian principles, the whole of society would rise regenerated in newness of life." — *Bl. Placid Riccardi*

A mother with two well-behaved and lovable children was visited by a friend. After the children welcomed her and then politely excused themselves to go out and play, the friend exclaimed, "Oh, I'd give my life to have two such wonderful children!" The mother answered in a soft but earnest voice, "That's exactly what it costs." Most mothers do not die giving birth to their children, but they give up their lives for them in the sense of setting aside their own personal aspirations and activities, being ever ready to respond to their children's needs, and ever willing to teach them, discipline them, and love them. Our society will never be healthy or whole until it is completely willing to recognize, encourage, and honor such a noble sacrifice.

Something You Might Try

♦ Expectant mothers have a moral obligation to take reasonable steps to ensure the health and safety of their unborn children, including avoiding dangerous activities and substances, and consulting with doctors or other medical personnel as needed. In addition to these obvious physical preparations for birth, there should be spiritual preparations. Seek the intercession of St. Ann, St. Gerard Majella, and other saints, and pray to the patron saints of your unborn baby; invite family members to take part in these prayers. Ask friends, fellow parishioners, and family members (children in particular) to pray for your baby; such persons may well be honored to share in this way in the coming of new life, and you will receive spiritual strength and support. Finally, ask relatives and friends to participate in a "spiritual baby shower," bringing as gifts not only traditional items, but also promises to offer specific prayers for you and your baby. Such a baby shower might well include a Rosary or a simple prayer service; invite your pastor to offer a blessing and a prayer for a safe delivery.

♦ The Poor Clares in America were founded by Ven. Mother Mary Magdalene Bentivoglio, and she and her sisters were fortunate to have a wealthy benefactor named Mr. Creighton. He once asked the sisters to pray for a childless couple who were friends of his, and Mother Mary Magdalene and the other sisters responded enthusiastically. Some time later, Mr. Creighton received from his friends a telegram that said, "Twins born! Call off the Poor

Clares." Prayer can indeed be very powerful. If you and your spouse are having difficulty conceiving, ask God for the blessing of a child, and ask others to pray for this intention. Methods such as Natural Family Planning can also help couples to discover when conception is most likely to occur. Your parish should be able to offer information on Natural Family Planning.

Further Reading

Scripture: Revelation 12:1-2, 5; Matthew 18:10; Mark 10:13-16.

Contemporary Works: Martha Sears, R.N., *25 Things Every New Mother Should Know*; Martha Manning, *All Seasons Pass: Grieving a Miscarriage*.

Blessing of a Mother Near the Time of Birth
Loving God, Your love for us is like that of a mother,
and You know the hard joy of giving birth.
Hold the hand of Your servant N. now and keep her safe;
put Your own spirit into her very breathing and into
the new baby, for whom we wait with awe and hope.
We ask this through Christ our Lord. Amen.

Prayer of a Mother
Lord God, You made us out of nothing and
redeemed us by the Precious Blood of Your Son.
Preserve the work of Your hands, and defend both me
and the tender fruit of my womb from all perils and evils.
I beg of You, for myself, Your grace,
protection, and a happy delivery.
Sanctify my child and make this child Yours forever.
Grant this through Christ our Lord. Amen.
From *Catholic Household Blessings and Prayers*

Concern for Departed Loved Ones

[Judas Maccabeus] took up a collection . . . to provide for
a sin offering. In doing this he acted very well and honorably,
taking account of the resurrection. For if he were not expecting
that those who had fallen would rise again, it would have
been superfluous and foolish to pray for the dead.

2 Maccabees 12:43-44

When loved ones die, many people experience, in addition to grief and loneliness, a concern over the state of those loved ones, particularly if those departed souls weren't the saintliest people in their lifetime or if they died sudden, unprovided deaths. What has become of these souls, those who are left behind wonder.

The Church has always taught the existence of Purgatory, a place or state of existence after death, where, if necessary, we're cleansed of any remaining effects of our sins and made ready to enter into Heaven. Moreover, as Scripture attests, our prayers and sacrifices can be of immense spiritual help to the persons undergoing this purification process; we can pray for specific persons, such as deceased loved ones, or for the souls in Purgatory in general.

The Church's teaching on Purgatory is logical. We know that God is perfect; that nothing imperfect can enter into His presence; that our sins harm and disfigure our character; that some or all of this harm can be healed by our good deeds and acts of love on earth; that not everyone who loves God completes this process during his or her lifetime; and that, because God loves us and wants us to be with Him in Heaven, there must be some opportunity for us to finish being healed, or purged of our sins, after death, should this be necessary.

This cleansing process is what we call Purgatory. The saints believed without reservation in this reality. They themselves, because of their immense love of God, were ready to enter Heaven immediately after death, but they were mindful of those who were not as fortunate; after all, this is one of the signs of true love: caring for those in need, whether that need be physical or spiritual.

St. Elizabeth of Portugal, who reigned as queen of that country at the beginning of the fourteenth century, had a much-loved daughter named Constance. The young princess died very suddenly after being married, causing Elizabeth and her husband, King Denis, much grief. Soon after this, a hermit came to the queen with a shocking story: while he was praying, Constance had appeared to him, beseeching him to take a message to her mother. She was suffering terribly in Purgatory and would remain there a very long time unless Mass was offered for her each day for a year. The courtiers ridiculed the hermit as a fool or an impostor, but Elizabeth considered his words carefully; then she asked Denis what he thought. The king responded, "I believe that it is wise to do that which has been pointed out to you in so extraordinary a manner. After all, to have Masses celebrated for our dear deceased relatives is nothing more than a paternal and Christian duty." Elizabeth accepted this advice, and arranged for the Masses to be said by a holy priest. One year later her daughter appeared to her, clothed in a brilliant white robe, and said, "Today, dear mother, I am delivered from the pains of Purgatory and am about to enter Heaven." St. Elizabeth gave thanks to God and expressed her gratitude by distributing alms to the poor.

A number of saints (plus other mystics and visionaries) have allegedly seen Purgatory (and also Heaven and Hell). St. Frances of Rome was granted such a vision; she said that it consists of three levels. The lowest level is like a vast burning sea, where the persons undergo various sufferings related to the sins they committed on earth. The middle level is less rigorous, but still unpleasant. The highest level of Purgatory is populated by those who are closest to being released. These persons suffer mainly the pain of loss: that of yearning for God and of not yet truly possessing Him.

There's consolation in all three levels, but especially in the highest. The souls in Purgatory know that, sooner or later, they'll be with God in Heaven and that all their present sufferings are valuable and redemptive. Other saints and visionaries confirm this description, adding that our prayers and sacrifices — because they're freely given — are immensely helpful to those in Purgatory, for God greatly values each one of our freely offered sacrifices, no matter how small. Some mystics have supposedly learned that when we pray for specific persons who are in Purgatory, they see us at that instant and are strengthened by the knowledge that we're remembering them.

Many of the saints are said to have had experiences that confirmed the Church's teaching on Purgatory. For instance, St. Louis Bertrand, a seventeenth-century priest, offered Masses, prayers, and sacrifices for his deceased father until finally he was granted a vision of his entry into Heaven. This happened only after eight years of prayer on his part. In the twelfth century, the famous Irish bishop St. Malachy learned that his sister was destined to suffer a long time in Purgatory, for she had lived a very sinful life before repenting; his prayers eased her sufferings, but did not significantly lessen her time there. In the fifteenth century, the sister of St. Vincent Ferrer appeared to him as she was about to enter Heaven and revealed that had it not been for the many Masses he offered on her behalf, her time in Purgatory would have been much longer.

A story is told about St. Teresa of Avila in this regard. A priest she knew had just died, and God revealed to her that he would remain in Purgatory until a Mass was said for him in the chapel of a new Carmelite house that was to be built. Teresa hurried to the site and had the workmen begin raising the walls of the chapel immediately, but as this would still take too long, she obtained permission from the bishop for a temporary chapel to be erected. Once this was done, Mass was celebrated there, and while receiving communion, Teresa saw a vision of the priest thanking her most graciously before entering God's kingdom.

Showing concern for the dead and the dying is a great sign of love. Bl. Raymond of Capua, the biographer of St. Catherine of Siena, wrote that she attended her father, Jacomo, during his final hours. Learning in a revelation that this holy man nonetheless would require some purification in Purgatory, Catherine begged God to let her suffer pains of expiation on his behalf so that he might enter Heaven immediately. God agreed; Jacomo, who had been suffering greatly, thereupon experienced a happy and peaceful death, while Catherine was seized with violent pains that remained with her for the rest of her life. Raymond witnessed her suffering, but he also took note of her incredible forbearance and patience, along with her great joy on her father's behalf.

An incident from the life of the Italian priest Bl. Padre Pio indicates that souls in Purgatory may request our prayers. One day in the 1920s, he was praying in the choir loft when he heard a strange sound coming from the side altars of the chapel. Then there was a crash as a candelabra fell from the main altar. Padre Pio saw a figure he assumed to be a young friar. But the figure told him, "I am doing my Purgatory here. I was a student in this friary, so now I have to make amends for the errors I committed while I was here, for my lack of diligence in doing my duty in this church." The figure said that he had been in Purgatory for sixty years, and after requesting Padre Pio's prayers, he vanished. Many other souls in

Purgatory are said to have asked for his assistance, including four deceased friars sitting around the fireplace in a state of great suffering; Padre Pio spent the night in prayer, securing their release.

Other saints are said to have had similar experiences, including St. Odilo, the eleventh-century abbot who began the practice of offering Mass for all the souls in Purgatory on what is now known as All Souls Day, the day after the feast of All Saints.

Our prayers for those who suffer there can be spiritually valuable to them (and to ourselves), whereas neglect of this important form of charity would be a major spiritual failing on our part. Because the saints believed in both sin and redemption, mercy and justice, they also acknowledged the existence of Purgatory and did everything possible to relieve those undergoing purification there. As the saints were far more conversant with the ways of Divine Providence than any of us could honestly claim to be, we would do very well to follow their example.

For Further Reflection

"All who die in God's grace and friendship, but still imperfectly purified, are indeed assured of their eternal salvation; but after death they undergo purification, so as to achieve the holiness necessary to enter the joy of Heaven." — *Catechism of the Catholic Church*, par. 1030

"It cannot be doubted that the prayers of the Church, the Holy Sacrifice, and alms distributed for the departed relieve those holy souls and move God to treat them with more clemency than their sins deserve. It is the universal practice of the Church, a practice that she observes as having received it from her forefathers — that is to say, the holy Apostles." — *St. Augustine*

"Many [Doctors of the Church] affirm with great probability that we should believe that God reveals our prayer to those holy souls so that they may pray for us. The souls in Purgatory, being beloved of God and confirmed in grace, have absolutely no obstacle to prevent their praying for us. If we desire the help of their prayers, it is only fair that we should remember to help them with our prayers and good works." — *St. Alphonsus Liguori*

Something You Might Try

♦ Reflect on this passage from the writings of St. Francis de Sales: "To assist the souls in Purgatory is to perform the most excellent of the works of mercy, or rather it is to practice in a most sublime manner all the works of mercy together: it is to visit the sick; it is to give drink to those who thirst for the vision of God; it is to feed the hungry, to ransom prisoners, to clothe the naked, to procure for poor exiles the hospitality of the heavenly Jerusalem; it is to comfort the afflicted, to instruct the ignorant — in fine, to practice all the works of mercy in one." Consider what you might do for those who've died: offer your sacrifices for the souls in Purgatory, have Masses offered for them, pray for your deceased loved ones, etc.

♦ In addition to praying for those now in Purgatory, think about how to avoid this experience yourself. After all, it may be presumptuous — or at least unduly optimistic — to assume you'll automatically enter Heaven as soon as you die. In his 1936 booklet *How to Avoid Purgatory*, Fr. Paul O'Sullivan offers the following suggestions:
  • Give up your sins as much as possible.
  • Do penance for the sins you've committed.
  • Offer up your sufferings as a sacrifice.
  • Regularly attend Mass and receive the sacraments.
  • Ask God for the grace to avoid Purgatory.
  • Practice holy resignation (that is, trustingly accept God's will in all things, especially in regard to the time and circumstances of your death).

• If and when appropriate, receive the Last Rites of the Church.

◆ Your own love for the souls in Purgatory — expressed by your prayers and sacrifices on their behalf — is received very favorably by God. If you find yourself in Purgatory after death, those whom you've previously helped release from there will not cease praying on your behalf until you join them in the kingdom of God. As St. John Vianney stated, "We must pray for them that they may pray for us."

Further Reading

Scripture: Matthew 18:34; Luke 12:58-59; 1 Corinthians 3:12-15.

Classics: St. Alphonsus Liguori, *The Way of Salvation and Perfection.*

Contemporary Works: Fr. Paul O'Sullivan, *How to Avoid Purgatory;* Stephen Foglein, *What Do We Know about Our Future? Heaven, Purgatory, and Hell;* Michael H. Brown, *After Life.*

⌒

O Eternal Father,
I offer Thee the Most Precious Blood of Thy Divine Son, Jesus,
in union with all the Masses said throughout the world today,
for all the holy souls in Purgatory and for sinners everywhere —
for sinners in the universal Church, for those in my own home,
and for those within my family. Amen.

St. Gertrude

(Jesus is said to have promised St. Gertrude that every time this prayer is recited, one thousand souls will be released from Purgatory and enter into Heaven, and two hundred sinners will receive the grace to repent. Because Christ's sacrifice is perfect and infinite, there's no limit to the number of times it can be offered to the Father, and thus, this prayer can be effective every time it's prayed.)

Criticism

There is a reproof which is not timely; and there is a man
who keeps silent but is wise. . . . There is one who by keeping silent
is found wise, while another is detested for being too talkative.

Sirach 20:1, 5

Which great saint, known and loved throughout the world (hint: especially in Ireland), was, during his lifetime, accused of being an "ambitious ignoramus"? Yes, St. Patrick — the beloved Apostle of Ireland, whose memory is revered on the Emerald Isle and everywhere else the Irish have settled. You might conclude that, if St. Patrick himself couldn't escape criticism, neither can anyone else, saints included — and you'd be right. The experience of being criticized (and also, for many of us, the experience of having to *give* criticism) is usually an unpleasant one — yet it's part of being a Christian.

Jesus once noted, with perhaps a touch of exasperation, that some people can always find a reason to criticize others: "To what, then, shall I compare the men of this generation, and what are they like? They are like children sitting in the marketplace and calling to one another, 'We piped to you, and you did not dance; we wailed, and you did not weep.' For John the Baptist has come eating no bread and drinking no wine; and you say, 'He has a demon.' The Son of Man has come eating and drinking; and you say, 'Behold, a glutton and a drunkard, a friend of tax collectors and sinners!' "[21] "Yet," Jesus remarked, "wisdom is justified by all her children"[22] — in other words, the value and validity of all criticism, or the lack thereof, will be made known at the end of time.

Being criticized is an unavoidable part of life, but we needn't give criticism more importance than it deserves. The fourth-century monk St. Macarius the Elder was once approached by a young man seeking spiritual counsel. The holy monk sent the youth to a nearby cemetery, telling him to speak aloud to the dead who were buried there: first criticizing and reproaching them, and then flattering and praising them. When the young man returned, St. Macarius asked what response the dead had made. "None," the youth answered. "Then," said the saint, "go and learn to be moved neither by abuse nor by flattery. If you die to the world and to yourself, you will begin to live for Christ."

A similar sense of detachment is recommended by St. Francis de Sales, who says, "To be pleased at correction and reproofs shows that one loves the virtues that are contrary to those faults for which he is corrected and reproved. And, therefore, it is a great sign of advancement in perfection." The saint also noted, "We can never please the world unless we lose ourselves together with the world. It is so whimsical that it is impossible to satisfy it."

Living for Christ will almost certainly involve some degree of verbal opposition or second-guessing. Some of the Church's greatest saints experienced criticism during their ministries on earth — for instance, St. Joseph Calasanz, for believing that poor children deserved an education; St. Margaret Mary Alacoque, for claiming to have received visions of Christ; St. Pius V, for implementing the reforms of the Council of Trent; St. Columban, for insisting on

[21] Luke 7:31-34.
[22] Luke 7:35.

Church discipline within religious monasteries; and St. Philip Neri, for founding a religious group that allowed laypeople to strive for holiness and whose members actually enjoyed themselves while serving God. As these examples show, criticism is often misguided; it may be the result of honest misunderstanding, jealousy, laziness, fear, selfishness, or many other motives. Indeed, critical words are often a tool of the Devil; Satan may try to interfere with God's work by prompting criticism of those trying to carry it out.

This is not to say that all criticism is wrong, however, nor does it imply that saints should be exempt from it. Sometimes critical words may contain an important truth or serve as a form of divine guidance. The seventeenth-century French priest St. John Eudes established a religious order for the education of priests and kept very busy with this and other activities. One day a woman who was caring for several reformed prostitutes reproached him, saying, "Where are you off to now? To some church, I suppose, where you'll gaze at the images and think yourself pious. And all the time what is wanted of you is a decent house for these poor creatures." Instead of defending himself (a very natural and justifiable reaction — especially for a saint), or responding angrily, John took these words to heart; recognizing them as a message from God (even if delivered rather inelegantly), he established a new religious order of sisters who actively cared for reformed prostitutes.

John Eudes was able to accept criticism and use it constructively, but not everyone has this ability. The monk Bl. Antony Grassi, for instance, greatly feared having harsh words directed at him and, when being corrected by a superior, would beg, "Please, Father, only a few inches of voice."

Many other holy men and women found it just as difficult to give criticism as to receive it. Jesus commanded His followers not to speak harshly toward one another.[23] Most of the saints were

[23] Matt. 5:22.

careful to follow this biblical injunction, even in difficult circumstances. St. John Baptist de La Salle observed, "Detraction, like fire borne onward by the wind, passes from mouth to mouth, and what it does not destroy, it blackens."[24] And St. Philip Neri advises, "If we wish to keep peace with our neighbor, we should never remind anyone of his natural defects."

It's very important to speak charitably, even when we have something important to say; above all, we must never use defense of the Gospel as an excuse for harsh words. The great Jesuit bishop St. Robert Bellarmine was a powerful defender of the Faith against the attacks of Protestantism; he preached very effectively against heresy, but without mentioning his opponents by name. Similar tact was shown by St. Hugh of Grenoble, who, when occupying a position of authority in a monastery, disliked making official reports in which he had to describe the shortcomings of other monks. "Why should I set down faults?" he asked.

Unfortunately, not all the saints were so consistently charitable and gentle in their words. In the thirteenth century, St. Boniface of Lausanne was known for great learning and integrity, but not for diplomacy and tact. A series of disputes at the University of Paris, where he taught, reached the point at which his students would no longer attend his lectures. Later Boniface was appointed Bishop of Lausanne, where he labored zealously for eight years, but his forthright style — such as denouncing the weaknesses of his clergy from the pulpit — made him many enemies, and at his own request he was relieved of his duties by the Pope.

Faults such as these can be overcome with divine grace. St. Mechtildis, like many people today, had a tendency to speak quickly, and often sharply, without thinking; she struggled against this weakness and eventually became a model of discretion.

---

[24] Detraction is the unjust damaging of a person's good name by revealing a fault or crime of his.

The great abbot St. Bernard of Clairvaux was at first very severe in the discipline he imposed on the monks under his authority, no doubt thinking this would greatly aid their growth in holiness; he was so strict, however, that the monks became discouraged and so afraid of his criticism that they almost lost sight of the need to continue pleasing God by growing in charity and mutual concern. When Bernard realized this, he disciplined himself for his fault — by maintaining a long period of silence. This, indeed, is perhaps the best remedy for a tendency to criticize others: a silent tongue.

For Further Reflection

"People who change their way of life and begin to think about making spiritual progress also begin to suffer from the tongues of detractors. Whoever has not yet suffered this trial has not yet made progress." — *St. Augustine (Thus, being criticized is an inescapable part of the process of growing closer to God.)*

"Take pains to refrain from sharp words. If they escape your lips, do not be ashamed to let your lips produce the remedy, since they have caused the wounds." — *St. Francis of Paola*

"One is often carried away over the sins and shortcomings of others. It would be far better to talk *less* about them and to pray *more*." — *St. John Vianney*

Something You Might Try

♦ St. Thérèse of Lisieux gives us an example of how to give correction, and her fellow sister shows us how to receive it. In her role as novice mistress, Thérèse once had to correct a sister to whom she was very close. She prayed beforehand, asking for words that would be gentle but full of conviction. As she later described the encounter, "There were tears in my voice, and I spoke with such tender expressions, made my affection for her so clear, that her tears were soon mingling with mine. Very humbly, she admitted the truth of all I said, promised to begin a new way of life, and asked me as a favor always to warn her of her faults. In the end, when we parted, our affection for one another had reached an entirely spiritual level; it wasn't a human thing any longer."

♦ Humor is often a helpful means of coping with criticism. St. Mary Soledad, the nineteenth-century foundress of the Handmaids of Mary Serving the Sick, was — like most founders of religious orders — subject to many complaints. One of her nuns, sympathizing with Mother Soledad, wryly noted that she would be well-symbolized by an anvil — for it's something that was always being hit.

Further Reading

Scripture: Sirach 19:9; Sirach 41:22, 24; 1 Peter 3:9.

Classics: St. Thérèse of Lisieux, *The Story of a Soul*; St. Francis de Sales, *An Introduction to the Devout Life*; St. Alphonsus Liguori, *The Practice of the Love of Jesus Christ*.

Contemporary Works: Rudolf Allers, *Self-Improvement*.

⌒

God of mercy and truth,
You gave us the ability to speak
so that we might glorify You and
encourage our brothers and sisters.
Help me overcome my tendency to
speak unkindly about others
and to criticize those around me.
Teach me instead to praise, to encourage, to defend,
and to say only those things I myself would
want to hear from someone else.

Form within me the habit of praying for help
in overcoming those faults I observe and of
speaking respectfully to those with whom I disagree.
Please give me also the courage to accept criticism
from others by responding calmly,
while honestly considering whether their remarks
contain wisdom and truth.
May all my words be pleasing to You
and beneficial to those who hear them. Amen.

Depression

I am utterly spent and crushed; I groan because of the tumult
of my heart. Lord, all my longing is known to Thee;
my sighing is not hidden from Thee.

Psalm 38:8-9

Depression can often have a physiological aspect, which means
that an examination by a physician will frequently be a good starting point in addressing the situation and any underlying problems.
Severe, ongoing depression isn't something we should become resigned to or attempt to cope with alone; professional assistance
should generally be obtained, usually after a doctor has ruled out a
physical or chemical cause.

But almost everyone suffers from a mild form of depression from
time to time, and in such situations, the experiences of some of the
saints may be able to help and encourage us.

Is it possible that a saint — someone who has tasted the wonder and richness of divine love far more deeply than the rest of us
have — could be troubled by a melancholy, restless spirit? Most
definitely. For instance, the fourteenth-century virgin St. Flora of
Beaulieu, after a normal childhood, refused to cooperate with her
parents' attempts to find her a husband; instead, she announced
that she was dedicating herself to God and entered a convent.

This, however — even though it was her calling — precipitated an intense and prolonged period of depression, affecting her behavior in a way that greatly irritated the other sisters. Eventually, with the help of an understanding confessor, Flora weathered this period and made great spiritual progress because of it.

Two seventeenth-century French saints in particular suffered greatly from depression — for very different reasons. The Jesuit priest St. Noel Chabanel was one of the North American Martyrs; he worked among the Huron Indians with St. Charles Garnier. Missionaries often become very sympathetic toward those to whom they minister, but this was not the case for Fr. Noel; he felt a strong repugnance for the Indians and their customs. This, along with difficulty in learning their language and similar challenges, caused him a lasting sense of sadness and spiritual suffocation. How did he respond? By making a solemn vow never to give up or to leave his assignment — a vow that he kept until the day of his martyrdom.

A different form of heroic sanctity was practiced by St. Jane Frances de Chantal. She was happily married to Baron de Chantal for eight years; when her husband died, her father-in-law — a vain, stubborn old man — forced Jane and her three children to move in with him. It's not surprising that Jane became very depressed. What is perhaps surprising (at least to our society, in which people make a high art of complaining and of claiming "victimhood" status) is how Jane responded: she chose to remain cheerful and to respond to the unkindnesses of her father-in-law with charity and understanding. Much later in life, even after forming a warm and holy friendship with the great bishop St. Francis de Sales and working with him to establish a religious order for older women, Jane still experienced times of suffering and trial — but she continued to respond by remaining cheerful and active.

Keeping busy also proved to be a lifeline amid the seas of depression for St. Augustine, one of the greatest figures of the

Church — and, indeed, of Western civilization. His mother, St. Monica, no doubt merited great graces simply by patiently bearing her brilliant son's moodiness and unpredictability. Augustine was searching for truth, but on his own terms, and it was many years before — assisted by his mother's innumerable prayers and his admiration for the great bishop St. Ambrose — he finally surrendered to God and accepted Baptism. Soon afterward his mother died and then his own son, and during the more than forty years that followed, his powerful personality — sanctified but not erased by divine grace — often manifested itself in a tendency toward both intense anger and severe depression. St. Augustine rose above these shackles through prayer, sacrifice, and work. Indeed, his responsibilities as bishop and his writings in defense of the Church kept him very busy.

Another powerful personality — one also given to feelings of deep restlessness and grief — was possessed by St. Ignatius of Loyola. In his autobiography (written in the third person), Ignatius stated, "The things he saw strengthened him then and always gave him such strength in his faith that he often thought to himself: if there were no Scriptures to teach us of these matters of the Faith, he would be resolved to die for them, only because of what he had seen." This sense of certainty and conviction had not come easily; after his conversion to the Faith, Ignatius had to struggle with a period of scrupulosity (in which he was tempted to despair of ever being worthy in God's sight), followed by a depression so severe that he actually considered suicide. Of course, he persevered, and God drew him out of the dark pit of inner suffering, through which he had been prepared to do great things on behalf of Christ and His Church.

St. Ignatius experienced first-hand what he was later to refer to as *desolation* in his *Spiritual Exercises*. Much akin to depression, desolation is a state in which we feel restless, irritated, uncomfortable, unsure of ourselves and our decisions, assailed by doubts, and unable to persevere in our good intentions. According to Ignatius, God cannot cause desolation, although He may allow it for His own purposes — such as to remind us of our profound need for Him, or to "shake up" a sinner so as to bring about repentance. Feelings of desolation, Ignatius notes, are often caused or provoked by the evil one, especially after we've taken practical steps to grow in holiness or to discern and follow God's will. Based in part on his own experience, St. Ignatius of Loyola offers three very important pieces of advice to anyone undergoing desolation:

- *Don't change an earlier good resolution,* for after you've made a decision that's pleasing to God, the Devil may try to make you have second thoughts.

- *Intensify your religious activities* — that is, spend more time in prayer, meditation, and good deeds. For if Satan's temptations merely cause you to increase your efforts to grow in holiness, he'll have an incentive to leave you alone.

- *Persevere in patience,* for the Devil's authority and ability to assault you is strictly limited by God, meaning that you'll be relieved of your spiritual sufferings if only you hold out long enough.

As Ignatius discovered, depression can be a great spiritual challenge — and also a great opportunity for growth. Let us keep this in mind whenever we suffer from depression and turn to the saints for their intercession.

For Further Reflection

St. Philip Neri, known for his constant cheerfulness, used to pray, "Let me get through today, and I shall not fear tomorrow."

"Refresh yourself with spiritual songs, which have often caused the tempter to cease his wiles; as in the case of Saul, whose evil spirit departed from him when David played upon his harp be-fore the king.[25] It is also useful to be actively employed, and that with as much variety as may be, so as to divert the mind from the cause of its sadness." — *St. Francis de Sales*

"I don't know what your destiny will be, but one thing I know: the only ones among you who will be really happy are those who have sought and found how to serve." — *Albert Schweitzer*

Something You Might Try

◆ Keep things in perspective. As St. Augustine notes, "Every morning you put on your clothes to cover your nakedness and to protect your body from the inclement weather. Why don't you also clothe your soul with the garment of Faith? Remember every morning the truths of your creed, and look at yourself in the mirror of your Faith. Otherwise, your soul will soon be naked with the nakedness of oblivion." In a sense, Augustine is pointing out the importance of beginning the day with prayer. If this prayer helps us remember that we have received all good things from our loving Father, who also offers us an eternity of joy and fulfill-ment, it will be easier to fight depression and keep things in proper perspective.

◆ Merely identifying your problems can help you feel better about them. Make a list of all the things that depress you. Di-vide the items into two categories: those you can't do anything about and those you can. Take the former and place them in God's hands; then take the latter and, starting with the easiest one, do something!

◆ If you suffer from severe or ongoing depression, contact your doctor or the National Institute of Mental Health.

[25] 1 Sam. 6:23.

Further Reading

Scripture: Proverbs 12:15; Proverbs 15:15; Psalm 77:1-14.

Classics: St. Francis de Sales, *An Introduction to the Devout Life*.

Contemporary Works: Andrew Paige, *Emerging from Depression*; Earnie Larsen, *Overcoming Depressive Living Syndrome*; William Burke, *Protect Us from All Anxiety*; Rachel Callahan and Rea McDonnell, *God is Close to the Brokenhearted*.

⌒

My strength fails;
I feel only weakness, irritation, and depression.
I am tempted to complain and to despair.
What has become of the courage I was so proud of,
and that gave me so much self-confidence?
In addition to my pain, I have to bear the
shame of my fretful feebleness.
Lord, destroy my pride; leave it no resource.
How happy I shall be if You can teach me
by these terrible trials, that I am nothing,
that I can do nothing, and that You are all!

Archbishop François Fenelon

Dishonesty

*Speaking the truth in love, we are to grow up in every way
into Him who is the head, into Christ. . . . Therefore, putting
away falsehood, let everyone speak the truth with his neighbor,
for we are members one of another.*

Ephesians 4:15, 25

One day the holy fifteenth-century Polish priest St. John of Kanty
was walking down a country road when he was stopped by some
robbers; they took the money in his bag and demanded to know
whether he had any more. John said no, and the robbers departed.
Immediately after this, however, John remembered that he had
some coins sewn into his cloak, so he hurried after the highway-
men, caught up with them, and, apologizing for his error, handed
over the additional coins. The robbers were so amazed by his honesty that they returned everything they had taken from him.

The type of holy and absolute honesty demonstrated by St.
John of Kanty is very surprising to us today — perhaps, in part, because our society has made honesty a relative thing. "It was only a
little white lie"; "I don't cheat on my taxes as much as most people
do"; "If I told my boss what I *really* think of her idea, I'd never get
that promotion, and that would be bad for my family." The Seventh Commandment does not say, "You shall not steal *unless it's*

something you really need or want." The Eighth Commandment does not say, "You shall not bear false witness *unless you have a really good reason.*" These commandments call us to be honest, for, as God's children, we are meant to imitate our Father — and no falsehood will ever be found in Him.

John's actions certainly went above and beyond the call of duty, for while we're expected to be honest, there are certain limits. For instance, we're not morally required to reveal information to people who have no legitimate authority or right to ask it of us, and — while outright lying should be avoided — we're entitled to use mental reservations in answering unjust questions. For instance, when asked by robbers whether we have any money, we may add to our negative response the unspoken statement "At least, not any that I wish to give to you."

St. Athanasius practiced this sort of "silent honesty" or "holy deception" when he was being pursued down a river by some enemies who didn't know him by sight. From his boat, he turned back toward them, and when they asked, "Have you seen Athanasius the bishop?" he responded truthfully, "It's only a short time since he passed this very spot, going up the river." By practicing our Lord's advice to be as clever as snakes and innocent as doves,[26] Athanasius managed to escape.

Deceptions, of course, can also serve selfish purposes. Before her conversion, St. Joan Delanoue was quite concerned with becoming rich and very unconcerned with the plight of the poor. She would deliberately wait until almost suppertime to send her niece out to purchase food for the household's evening meal; that way, if beggars came to her door earlier in the day, she could truthfully tell them, "There's no food in the house." This ruse — in which honesty was turned into an illegitimate servant of greed — was common knowledge to Joan's neighbors; they were disedified

[26] Cf. Matt. 10:16.

by her stinginess, but, after her conversion, they were amazed by her newfound generosity.[27]

Jesus praised honesty, while also encouraging those who had fallen short of this ideal, as we see in the story of Zacchaeus. As the chief tax collector of Jericho, Zacchaeus was a very wealthy man, and the implication is obvious: he acquired most of his wealth by cheating people and by accepting kickbacks from the other tax collectors under his supervision. This is why people murmured in shock and disapproval when Jesus invited Himself to Zacchaeus's house — a gentle, non-threatening way of calling a known sinner to a change of heart. This most unpopular of men responded wholeheartedly, saying, "Behold, Lord, the half of my goods I give to the poor; and if I have defrauded anyone of anything, I restore it fourfold."[28] This was quite a promise, for everyone in earshot knew it wasn't a question of *whether* Zacchaeus had cheated anyone. Redeeming his pledge would have taken most, if not all, of his wealth. The importance of honesty, and also our Lord's recognition of Zacchaeus's sincerity, is demonstrated by Jesus' words: "*Today* salvation has come to this house."[29]

It was from tax collectors — men universally assumed to be greedy and dishonest — that Jesus chose one of His Apostles.[30] We have no way of knowing whether St. Matthew was personally dishonest, relatively honest, or completely honest prior to his calling — but his eager response to Christ, and his years of service as an apostle and evangelist, indicate that from the time He was called, his life was marked by integrity and righteousness.

The Church has always valued honesty, for God's grace can be fully active only within persons who humbly and truthfully admit

---

[27] See the chapter on business difficulties.

[28] Luke 19:8.

[29] Luke 19:9.

[30] Mark 2:14.

their need for it. This is why, for instance, St. Ignatius of Loyola, following his conversion, prepared very carefully before making a general confession (in which a person confesses the sins of his entire life). It took him three days to remember and write down all his sins. God rewarded this honesty by giving the founder of the Jesuits a profound understanding of the workings of the human soul, allowing Ignatius to become one of history's spiritual geniuses.

Honesty is not only a matter of proclaiming the truth, but also of treating others justly — especially when someone's life is at stake. The fourteenth-century nobleman St. Conrad of Piacenza was out hunting one day and ordered his attendants to flush out game by setting fire to some brushwood. Unfortunately, a sudden wind carried the fire into a cornfield, and from there it spread to the neighboring villages. Unable to extinguish the fire, Conrad and his attendants returned home, intending to say nothing, but a poor man gathering firewood nearby was blamed for the disaster and sentenced to death. Learning of this, Conrad was filled with remorse and publicly admitted his responsibility. He was ordered to pay restitution for all the damage, which took virtually everything he owned, plus his wife's dowry. Accepting this as a sign from God, the two of them gave away the remainder of their estate, and then each entered religious life.

Honesty demands a suitable respect for other people's property. St. Edward the Confessor, who became King of England in 1042, was told that a certain tax was still being levied on the people, even though its original purpose had long since passed. Seeing the vaults containing the money that had been raised in this way, the holy king exclaimed, "On every chest I see a black devil sitting and sticking his hooked claws into the gold. They are the rulers down here, not I. Let the money be distributed to the poor, and stop collecting the tax, and so we shall rid the realm of these devils." On another occasion St. Edward's keen sense of justice led him to order the return of money that had been collected as a gift to him from all his subjects — the poor included. He knew that divine riches cannot be mingled with earthly wealth that has been acquired in an unjust or uncharitable way.

We must take this lesson to heart. Ours is the richest society in history — and also one severely lacking in honesty and justice. Only if we as individuals and as a nation strive to be honest will we experience, in Jesus' words, the truth that sets us free.[31]

For Further Reflection

"God will not hear our prayers unless we acknowledge ourselves to be sinners. We do this when we ponder our own sins alone, and not those of our neighbor." — *St. Moses of Ethiopia*

"Truly honest persons possess a harmonious and pleasant demeanor: nothing reproachable can be found in their actions, nothing inappropriate in their words, nothing indecent in their manner. Being spontaneous and respectful, their behavior wins the admiration and goodwill of all." — *St. Anthony of Padua*

"Whoever manages his affairs with artifices and subterfuges offends the Providence of God and renders himself unworthy of His paternal care." — *St. Vincent de Paul*

Something You Might Try

♦ How do you develop the virtue of honesty if you've been lacking in it? Aristotle says, "One becomes a mason only by laying bricks and a sculptor by handling the chisel; even so one acquires a virtue only by exercising it." This means that the only way to become honest is by *being* honest. Start with yourself; admit your faults. Then be honest with God; admit your absolute need for Him. Then be honest with others; actively look for opportunities to tell the truth in situations when it goes against your own

---

[31] Cf. John 8:32.

interests or when you'd normally lie. Reward yourself each time you tell the truth, especially when telling the truth isn't easy.

♦ When it comes to business and financial transactions, St. Francis de Sales offers us this advice: "Always be impartial and just in your deeds. Put yourself in your neighbor's place, and then you will judge fairly. When you buy, act as though you were the seller, and when you sell, act as though you were the buyer, and you will buy and sell with justice." Looking out for the interest of the other person, instead of your own, may strike you as self-defeating — but in fact, it's a way of unlocking God's blessings (for the Lord is never outdone in generosity), while giving you an inner peace that no amount of money can buy.

Further Reading

Scripture: Psalm 24:3-5; John 18:37.

Classics: St. Francis de Sales, *An Introduction to the Devout Life*.

Contemporary works: James A. Magner, *Mental Health in a Mad World*.

☞

O Lord almighty,
Father of Jesus Christ, our Lord,
grant us, we pray Thee,
to be grounded and settled in Thy truth
by the coming down of the Holy Spirit in our hearts.
That which we know not, do Thou reveal;
that which is wanting in us, do Thou fill up;
that which we know, do Thou confirm,
and keep us blameless in Thy service,
through the same Jesus Christ, our Lord. Amen.

St. Clement of Rome

Distractions during Prayer

*For all men who were ignorant of God were foolish by nature;
and they were unable from the good things that are seen to know Him
who exists, nor did they recognize the Craftsman while paying heed to His
works . . . For as they live among His works they keep searching, and
they trust in what they see, because the things that are seen are beautiful.*

Wisdom 13:1, 7

St. Bernard was traveling with a poor, uneducated farmer, who noticed that the abbot kept his eyes cast downward. When the farmer asked why the saint wasn't looking at the beautiful countryside, Bernard explained that he wanted to avoid distractions while praying. In response, the farmer boasted, "I'm never distracted when I pray." Bernard objected, "I don't believe it. Now let me make a bargain with you. If you can say the Our Father without one distraction, I'll give you this mule I'm riding. But if you don't succeed, you must come with me and be a monk." The farmer agreed and began praying aloud confidently, "Our Father, who art in Heaven, hallowed be Thy name . . ." Then, after pausing for a moment, he asked St. Bernard, "Does that include the saddle and the bridle, too?"

Almost everyone experiences distractions of some sort while praying, as St. Bernard managed to demonstrate to the farmer (so

71

the man ended up joining him in the monastery). Occasionally we hear of someone so deep in prayer — perhaps in spiritual ecstasy — that nothing can take his or her attention away from God.

Much more common, however, is the experience of the seventeenth-century religious St. Margaret Mary Alacoque, who had difficulty meditating in the formal way expected of the sisters, or the eleventh-century bishop St. Wulfstan, who found himself distracted by the smell of meat while saying Mass. His remedy was one that many people would find extreme: he vowed never again to eat meat during his life.

A more attractive method of dealing with distractions — and one much easier for us to imitate — was practiced by St. Francis of Assisi. Whenever he was about to enter church for Mass or to pray, he would say, "Worldly and frivolous thoughts, stay here at the door until I return." Then he would go inside and pray with complete devotion.

Sometimes distractions are caused by an insufficient dedication to prayer. Bl. Clare of Rimini was leading a carefree life in which religion wasn't something to take too seriously. At age thirty-four, she entered church one day, only to hear a rather blunt message from Heaven: "Clare, try to say one Our Father and one Hail Mary to the glory of God, without thinking of other things." Chastened by this rebuke, she took her religious duties more seriously; she was granted a vision of our Lady, and after her husband's death, she devoted herself to a life of prayer and penance.

St. Bernard, who, as mentioned above, sought to avoid distractions of the eyes while praying, once had a vision in which he saw an angel in Heaven writing down in a book the words of the Divine Office (the official community prayer of the Church) as they were prayed by his fellow monks. Some of the words were written in gold by the angel, and Bernard was given to understand that these represented the perfect fervor with which they were said. Others were written in silver, symbolizing the pure intention of the one praying, even if he was distracted. Still other words were written in ink, denoting the laziness that accompanied them. There were some words written in water, which left virtually no trace in the book; these prayers had been offered in a spirit of luke-warmness and in the absence of all piety. Lastly, St. Bernard saw that there were some words that were not written down at all; in-stead, the words of Scripture came to him: "These people come near to me with their mouth and honor me with their lips, but their hearts are far from me."[32] For this reason, the Franciscan priest Bl. Thomas of Cori insisted that the Divine Office be re-cited slowly and reverently, for as he said, "If the heart does not pray, the tongue works in vain."

Jesus taught His disciples the importance of praying sincerely; indeed, He offered the Our Father as a model of such prayer.[33] We must emphasize quality over quantity; a few minutes of genuine prayer are far more pleasing to God, and spiritually valuable to us, than several hours of merely going through the motions of pray-ing. When someone asked Bl. Jordan of Saxony the best form of prayer, he said, "The way in which you can pray most fervently."

Fervent prayer is truly focused on God. Sometimes, however, in spite of our best intentions, distractions come, and our efforts to force our attention back to God seem only to make matters worse. A twentieth-century mystic, favored with conversations with Jesus, mentioned this difficulty to Him. Our Lord is said to have told her that distractions in prayer may be compared to a dog accompanying its master on a walk in the woods. The dog runs ahead, goes about sniffing and exploring, returns to its master for a moment, runs off again, returns briefly as if to check on its mas-ter, then runs ahead yet again. In the same way, Jesus explained, when we find our minds wandering away from our Master during

[32] Isa. 29:13.
[33] Matt. 6:9-13.

prayer, we should gently return, without guilt or fear, and as often as necessary.

Being single-minded increases the value of our prayer in God's eyes; St. Edmund tells us, "It is better to say one Our Father fervently and devoutly than a thousand with no devotion and full of distraction." In fact, St. Thomas Aquinas warns us, "Purposely to allow one's mind to wander in prayer is sinful and hinders the prayer from having fruit." If instead we try our best to remain focused in our prayer, we will not only please God, but also make great spiritual progress. According to St. Louis de Montfort, "He who fights even the smallest distractions faithfully when he says even the very smallest prayer, will also be faithful in great things."

To achieve this, we should begin by following the simple advice of St. Teresa of Avila: "Never address your words to God while you are thinking of something else." God is worthy of our full attention. It's admirable to pray as we work or while we drive or do other things — as long as we make the Lord's presence central to the experience and not an afterthought. In those times we set aside specifically for prayer, St. Peter Julian Eymard suggests, "Be natural in your meditation. Use up your own stock of piety and love before resorting to books. Remember that our good Master prefers the poverty of our heart to the most sublime thoughts borrowed from others. You can be sure that our Lord wants *our* heart and not that of someone else."

There are times when the source of our distraction is another person — someone in church whose restlessness or activity makes it hard for us to pray. St. Thérèse of Lisieux wrote of such an experience in her autobiography, *The Story of a Soul*: "For a long time I had to kneel during meditation near a Sister who could not stop fidgeting; if it was not with her Rosary, it was with goodness knows what else. Maybe no one else noticed it; I have a very sensitive ear. But you have no idea how much it annoyed me. I wanted to turn around and glare at the culprit to make her be quiet, but deep in my heart I felt that the best thing to do was to put up with it patiently for the love of God first of all, and also not to hurt her feelings. So I kept quiet, bathed in perspiration often enough, while my prayer was nothing more than the prayer of suffering! In the end I tried to find some way of bearing it peacefully and joyfully, at least in my inmost heart; then I even tried to like this wretched little noise. It was impossible not to hear it, so I turned my whole attention to listening really closely to it as if it were a magnificent concert, and spent the rest of the time offering it to Jesus. It was certainly not the prayer of quiet!"

This edifying story is one most of us can relate to, and it suggests a solution to our own difficulties: making our distractions part of our prayer. For instance, a woman who just can't help thinking of her upcoming dinner party when she's trying to pray should just go ahead and talk to the Lord about that party: which guests are coming, what she'll be serving, and so on. A man who's having difficulty praying at Mass because he's excited about attending a football game later that day can share his excitement with Jesus, expressing gratitude for the chance to go to the game, asking a blessing on all the players and fans who will be there, and so forth.

As St. Thérèse of Lisieux stated, "I have many distractions, but as soon as I am aware of them, I pray for those people, the thought of whom is diverting my attention. In this way, they reap the benefit of my distractions." This simple approach is one we can easily follow; we need only get into the habit of consciously incorporating every thought that comes to us in prayer into our conversation with God. Prayer doesn't have to be only about "holy" and "spiritual" things; Jesus wants us to share with Him our entire lives, including our joys and interests, our plans and concerns, our worries and feelings. Talking to Him in a very loving and comfortable way, just as we would with any other friend or loved one, can be a helpful means of overcoming distractions.

For Further Reflection

"To set about hunting down distractions would be to fall into their trap, when all that is necessary is to turn back to our heart: for a distraction reveals to us what we are attached to, and this humble awareness before the Lord should awaken our preferential love for Him and lead us resolutely to offer Him our heart to be purified. Therein lies the battle, the choice of which master to serve." — *Catechism of the Catholic Church*, par. 2729

"It is indeed essential for a man to take up the struggle against his thoughts if the veils woven from his thoughts and covering up his intellect are to be removed, thus enabling him to turn his gaze without difficulty toward God and to avoid following the will of his wandering thoughts." — *St. Ammonas the Hermit*

"The Devil is never busier trying to distract us than when he sees us praying and asking God for grace. And why? Because the enemy sees that at no other time do we gain so many treasures of heavenly goods as when we pray." — *St. Alphonsus Liguori (Therefore, we have reason to be encouraged by our distractions, even as we try to overcome them.)*

Something You Might Try

♦ St. Teresa of Avila suggests that, at the beginning of prayer, we close our eyes "in order to open wider the eyes of the soul," thereby lessening the chance of distractions.

♦ Some valuable advice on praying comes from St. Paul of the Cross: "When you want to pray, it doesn't matter if you can't meditate. Make little acts of love to God, but gently, without forcing yourself." St. Paul also says, "Concerning distractions and temptations that occur during holy prayer, you don't need to be the least bit disturbed. Withdraw completely into the upper part of your spirit to relate to God in spirit and truth. Laugh at the noises the enemy will make outside. He cannot enter in."

Further Reading

Scripture: Ecclesiastes 11:4-5; Matthew 6:6-8.

Classics: St. Thérèse of Lisieux, *The Story of a Soul*; St. Francis de Sales, *An Introduction to the Devout Life*.

Contemporary Works: Rudolf Allers, *Self-Improvement*.

God, help my thoughts!
They stray from me,
setting off on the wildest journeys.
When I am at prayer, they run off
like naughty children, making trouble.
When I read the Bible, they fly to a distant
place, filled with seductions.
My thoughts can cross an ocean with a single leap;
they can fly from earth to Heaven, and
back again, in a single second.
They come to me for a fleeing moment,
and then away they flee.
No chains, no locks can hold them back;
no threats of punishment can restrain them,
no hiss of a lash can frighten them.
They slip from my grasp like tails of eels;
they swoop hither and thither like swallows in flight.
Dear, chaste Christ, who can see into every
heart, and read every mind: take hold of my thoughts.
Bring my thoughts back to me, and clasp me to Yourself. Amen.

Celtic prayer (source unknown)

Distrust in God

Let us hold fast the confession of our hope without wavering,
for He who promised is faithful.

Hebrews 10:23

In His Sermon on the Mount, Jesus speaks very movingly about the need to rely on our Father's loving care: "Do not be anxious about your life, what you shall eat or what you shall drink, nor about your body, what you shall put on. Is not life more than food, and the body more than clothing? Look at the birds of the air: they neither sow nor reap nor gather into barns, and yet your heavenly Father feeds them. Are you not of more value than they? And which of you by being anxious can add one cubit to his span of life? . . . Therefore do not be anxious, saying, 'What shall we eat?' or 'What shall we drink?' or 'What shall we wear?' For the Gentiles seek all these things; and your heavenly Father knows that you need them all. But seek first His kingdom and His righteousness, and all these things shall be yours as well."[34]

God has shown Himself worthy of our trust, and being willing to take this step of relying on Him is an essential part of our growth in holiness.

[34] Matt. 6:25-27, 31-33.

Saintly Solutions

None of us has the power to save or justify himself; we are completely dependent on God's mercy and grace. We must trust that God wants to save us and that He will give us the resources we need to cope with life's challenges and to achieve our eternal destiny. The saints had a profound awareness of the Lord's presence in their lives — so profound that they didn't seek miraculous confirmation or run after wonders and signs. Once, during the reign of St. Louis IX of France, when Mass was being said in the palace chapel, a miracle occurred during the Consecration: Jesus appeared visibly at the altar, in the form of a beautiful child. Everyone there gazed on Him in wonderful awe and contemplation, recognizing this miracle as a proof of the Real Presence. Someone hurried to tell the king, who was absent, so that he might come and witness the event. But Louis declined, explaining, "I firmly believe already that Christ is truly present in the Holy Eucharist. He has said it, and that is sufficient; I do not wish to lose the merit of my faith by going to see this miracle."

God meets our spiritual needs, just as He promised. He also provides for our physical needs, as long as we place our trust in Him. St. John of the Cross, on being informed by the cook in his monastery that there was no food for the following day, answered, "Leave to God the care of providing food. Tomorrow is far enough off; He is well able to take care of us." The next morning there was still no food — until a wealthy benefactor came to the door. He explained that he had dreamed the previous night that the monks might be in need and had brought enough food and supplies to sustain them, just in case that was so.

Other saints had similar experiences. In the early nineteenth century, Bl. Anne-Marie Jahouvey established a religious congregation, over the strong objections of her father. She and the other sisters were running an orphanage, and when they ran out of money for food one day, Anne-Marie went into church to pray: "I need help. I know that I have been imprudent, and perhaps I have gone beyond Your will in many ways. But I have done it for the children. They are more Yours than they are mine. If I have made mistakes, punish me — not them. I beg You, don't forsake them. Please, please help." Anne-Marie then heard the voice of the Lord clearly: "Why have you come here to expose your doubts? Have you no faith in me? Have I ever disappointed you? Go back to the children." Anne-Marie returned to the orphanage expecting a miracle. Confidently she went to the pantry and opened the door, only to find that the shelves were still empty. Had she misunderstood? Then she heard the wheels of a cart on the cobblestones of the courtyard. There with a wagonload of food was her father, who said, "I don't know why I am doing this, but I suppose I can't let you starve." Anne-Marie realized that God had not only tested her faith, but had also confirmed His loving care for her — for indeed, moving her unwilling father to bring assistance for all the orphans and sisters was perhaps a greater miracle than if He had stocked the pantry shelves with food suddenly created out of nothing.

St. John Bosco amazed many people by managing to care for a large number of orphans and other boys apparently without sufficient resources. Each time his assistants told him that dire financial problems could no longer be put off, he assured them, "God will provide" — and in every instance, he was right.

Another famous Italian, St. Frances Cabrini, showed this same childlike trust during her long ministry in the United States. She and the sisters of her religious order encountered many difficulties in their labors on behalf of poor Italian immigrants, but they managed to create and staff many schools, hospitals, and orphanages. Whenever a problem arose, Mother Cabrini would ask, "Who is doing this? We — or the Lord?"

Trusting God means believing in His care for us even when evil seems to be gaining the upper hand — a point understood by the sixth-century abbot St. Stephen of Rieti. When a wicked man burned down the barns holding all the monastery's corn, the monks exclaimed to Stephen, "Alas for what has come upon you!" The abbot answered, "No, say rather, 'Alas for what has come upon him that did this deed,' for no harm has befallen me." As Stephen knew, God's providential care is far greater than any human treachery.

According to St. Albert the Great, "The greater and more persistent your confidence in God, the more abundantly you will receive all that you ask." This point is echoed by St. Teresa of Avila, who reassures us, "God is full of compassion and never fails those who are afflicted and despised, if they trust in Him alone."

If, indeed, we are trying to do God's work, instead of our own, we need not fear the results. The Lord is an expert at solving problems and providing for us in our need (even to the point of working miracles, if need be). The one thing He can't do, however, is force us to trust in Him. If we freely choose to do this, we're cooperating with His grace, and the results are guaranteed to be wonderful and amazing.

For Further Reflection

"Do not fear what may happen tomorrow. The same loving Father who cares for you today will care for you tomorrow and every day. Either He will shield you from suffering, or He will give you unfailing strength to bear it. Be at peace, then, and put aside all anxious thoughts and imaginings." — *St. Francis de Sales*

"A few acts of confidence and love are worth more than a thousand 'Who knows? Who knows?' Heaven is filled with converted sinners of all kinds, and there is room for more." — *St. Joseph Cafasso*

"Those whose hearts are enlarged by confidence in God run swiftly on the path of perfection. They not only run, they fly; because, having placed all their hope in the Lord, they are no longer weak as they once were. They become strong with the strength of God, which is given to all who put their trust in Him." — *St. Alphonsus Liguori*

Something You Might Try

♦ St. Rose of Lima was afraid of the dark — a trait she inherited from her mother. Her mother and father once went looking for her after dark. This had an effect on Rose, who thought, "How is this? My mother, who is as timid as I, feels safe in the company of her husband. And am I afraid, accompanied by my Spouse, who without ever leaving me, is continually at my side and in my heart?" From then on, St. Rose no longer feared anything. You can benefit from her experience by continually reminding yourself that Jesus is with you, which means that you have nothing to fear.

♦ Trust in God even when things seem bleakest. A very upset mother superior once came to St. Joseph Cottolengo, who asked, "What's the trouble, Sister?" She answered, "I have so many things to buy, Father, and this is all the money I have." St. Joseph agreed that it was a very small sum, so he took the money, tossed it out the window, and consoled the shocked nun: "That's all right; it has been planted now. Wait a few hours, and it will bear fruit." Later that day, a woman came to see the saint and donated a large sum of money — more than enough to meet the community's needs. You're not expected to throw money away (although you *are* supposed to be generous to those in need). The Lord does ask you, however, to trust in His care for you. Sometimes you have no apparent options, but — like St. Joseph Cottolengo — you can always choose to trust in God, and this allows Him to help you, often in ways you can't foresee.

Further Reading

Scripture: Psalm 25:1-3; Psalm 37:3; Luke 16:10; 1 Corinthians 13:7.

Saintly Solutions

Classics: St. Alphonsus Liguori, *The Practice of the Love of Jesus Christ*; Thomas à Kempis, *Imitation of Christ.*

Contemporary Works: Rudolf Allers, *Self-Improvement.*

*O Christ Jesus, when all is darkness
and we feel our weakness and helplessness,
give us the sense of Your presence,
Your love, and Your strength.
Help us to have perfect trust in Your
protecting love and strengthening power,
so that nothing may frighten or worry us, for,
living close to You, we shall see Your hand,
Your purpose, Your will through all things.*

St. Ignatius of Loyola

Doubts

*Blessed are those who have not seen
and yet believe.*

John 20:29

St. Thomas the Apostle may have received a bad rap: everyone remembers him for doubting the other Apostles' excited report that
they had seen the risen Lord,[35] but we usually overlook his earlier
willingness to die for Jesus[36] and his later missionary activity and
his death as a martyr. Indeed, far more important than Thomas's
initial difficulty in believing was his proclamation of faith: "My
Lord and my God!"[37] Moreover, Thomas's doubts actually fulfilled
God's plan. St. Gregory the Great writes, "Do you really believe
that it was by chance that this chosen disciple was absent, then
came and heard, heard and doubted, doubted and touched, touched
and believed? It was not by chance, but in God's Providence. In a
marvelous way, God's mercy arranged that the disbelieving disciple, in touching the wounds of his Master's body, should heal our
wounds of disbelief. The disbelief of Thomas has done more for

[35] John 20:24-25.
[36] John 11:16.
[37] John 20:28.

85

our faith than the faith of the other disciples. As he touches Christ and is won over to belief, every doubt is cast aside, and our faith is strengthened. So the disciple who doubted, then felt Christ's wounds, becomes a witness to the reality of the Resurrection."

Doubt is not a sin when it leads us to greater faith; an honest wrestling with the truth can result in a stronger, more mature commitment to Christ. Skepticism that is at least willing to be convinced allows God to do great things. We see this in the case of St. Bartholomew, also known as Nathanael. When his friend St. Philip spoke of Jesus of Nazareth as the One prophesied to come, Bartholomew wondered whether anything worthwhile could come from such an insignificant place as Nazareth. However, because he was "an Israelite indeed, in whom [was] no guile,"[38] Bartholomew was able to recognize and accept Jesus very quickly.

To recognize Jesus as Lord, however, does not immunize us from crises of faith. St. Jane Frances de Chantal suffered frequent doubts and temptations against the Faith late in life, but she remained cheerful and active; St. Thérèse of Lisieux responded to a similar situation with determination, crying out, "I will believe!" when tempted by disbelief. It's true that faith is a gift from God, but it must also be a choice on our part — and when we decide we *do* believe and act accordingly, even though it seems difficult or impossible (or even like so many empty words), we give great glory to the Lord.

Holy people are quite capable of experiencing doubts, and, because they've felt a deeper sense of God's presence in the past, the loss of His consolations can seem all the more painful. The devout Italian priest Bl. Padre Pio of Pietrelcina, who died in 1968, described his spiritual sufferings in a letter to a fellow priest: "Blasphemies cross my mind incessantly, and even more so false ideas, ideas of infidelity and unbelief. I feel my soul transfixed at every

[38] John 1:47.

instant of my life; it kills me. . . . My faith is upheld only by a constant effort of my will against every kind of human persuasion. My faith is only the fruit of the continual effort that I exact of myself. And all of this, Father, is not something that happens a few times a day, but it is continuous. . . ." Padre Pio had received many spiritual gifts, and his prayers were known to be particularly efficacious with God — yet the Lord allowed him to suffer intense doubts.

The path of holiness is often a rough one, many times lacking signs to reassure us of our direction, but God is with us in our journey, helping us every step of the way. He will work miracles on our behalf if necessary, but He often chooses instead to use other people — all the better to test our faith in Him.

It's said that, a few days after drowning in the Mediterranean Sea near the Holy Land in 1237, Bl. Jordan of Saxony appeared in a dream to a young Carmelite monk who was plagued by doubts about his vocation and reassured him: "Fear not, brother. Everyone who serves Jesus Christ to the end will be saved." Perseverance is necessary, but not always easy. St. Ambrose, bishop of Milan, had a sister who was herself committed to growing in holiness, but who suffered from doubts against the Faith. Responding to her request for advice in overcoming these temptations, he wrote, "Every morning and night say with fervor the Apostles' Creed, and when such temptations come, say it again, and you will easily overcome them." She followed this suggestion and found great assistance through it.

Faith isn't just a feeling we have; it's a decision we make. When we choose to believe in God, He will give us the means not only to persevere in our faith, but ultimately to make it deeper and stronger.

For Further Reflection

"The First Commandment requires us to nourish and protect our
    faith with prudence and vigilance, and to reject everything
    that is opposed to it. There are various ways of sinning against

the Faith: *Voluntary doubt* about the Faith disregards or refuses to hold as true what God has revealed and the Church proposes for belief. *Involuntary doubt* refers to hesitation in believing, difficulty in overcoming objections connected with the Faith, or also anxiety aroused by its obscurity. If deliberately culti-vated, doubt can lead to spiritual blindness." — *Catechism of the Catholic Church*, par. 2088

"In her voyage across the ocean of this world, the Church is like a great ship being pounded by the waves of life's different stresses. Our duty is not to abandon ship but to keep her on course." — *St. Boniface*

"Faith opens the door to understanding; unbelief closes it." — *St. Augustine*

Something You Might Try

♦ St. Alphonsus Liguori tells us, "Faith is the foundation of love, on which love is built. But love is what brings faith to perfec-tion. The more perfectly we love God, the more perfectly we be-lieve in Him." Therefore, if we have trouble making an act of faith in God, it's all the more important that we make an act of love — by going out of our way to do a good deed, by doing a favor for someone we dislike or usually take for granted, or by any act of charity that we specifically do in Christ's name.

♦ Remember that God is with you. When St. Catherine of Siena was going through a long period of spiritual dryness and temptation, she cried out, "Where have You been, Lord? I have been having terrible thoughts and feelings." She heard God an-swer her, "Catherine, I have been in your heart all this time. It was I who was giving you courage and strength to keep going each day!" God was with Catherine all the time — and, if you're truly searching for Him, He will be with you.

Further Reading

Scripture: Wisdom 16:26; James 1:5-8.

Classics: St. Alphonsus Liguori, *The Practice of the Love of Jesus Christ.*

Contemporary Works: Rudolf Allers, *Self-Improvement.*

In dangers, in doubts, in difficulties,
think of Mary, call upon Mary.
Let not her name depart from your lips,
never suffer it to leave your heart.
And that you may more surely obtain
the assistance of her prayer,
neglect not to walk in her footsteps.
With her for guide, you shall never go astray;
while invoking her, you shall never lose heart;
so long as she is in your mind,
you are safe from deception;
while she holds your hand, you cannot fall;
under her protection you have nothing to fear;
if she walks before you, you shall not grow weary;
if she shows you favor, you shall reach the goal.

St. Bernard

Drunkenness

Wine is a mocker, strong drink a brawler;
and whoever is led astray by it is not wise.

Proverbs 20:1

A man was on his deathbed. Knowing that his departure was only a few days off, his family had gathered around him, and he was reminiscing about his life. One of his grown daughters asked him, "Father, why did you never drink? Was it because you didn't like alcohol?" The man looked at her with love, smiled, and answered honestly, "No, it was because I *did* like it."

The subject of drunkenness is difficult to address, for the simple reason that many people find it hard to consider it in a balanced way. The use of wine and other alcoholic beverages can be either a blessing or a curse; there are scriptural references attesting to both realities.

For instance, we're told that cultivating God's earth brings forth "wine to gladden the heart of man"[39] and are instructed, "Go, eat your bread with enjoyment, and drink your wine with a merry heart."[40] On the other hand, the Bible warns, "Do not aim to be

[39] Ps. 104:15.
[40] Eccles. 9:7.

91

valiant over wine, for wine has destroyed many"[41] and instructs us, "Do not get drunk with wine, for that is debauchery."[42]

This ambivalent message is also reflected in the lives of some of the saints. The positive benefits of alcohol were recognized by St. Paul, who told Timothy, "Use a little wine for the sake of your stomach."[43] Likewise St. Boniface, although he himself never drank anything stronger than water, wrote to his friend Egbert, Archbishop of York, "I am sending, by the bearer of this letter, two little kegs of wine. . . . I beg you to use it for a day of rejoicing with your friends." A similar outlook was manifested by the Irish monk St. Ceowulf, who convinced his abbot to allow the monks to "take a little beer or even wine" after laboring all day in the fields.

But alcohol has frequently had a negative influence on people. Alcoholism is a serious problem, both for problem drinkers and for their loved ones, and it often calls for professional help. Sometimes it requires both a change of lifestyle (as reflected in the emphasis on total abstinence preached by Alcoholics Anonymous) and a spiritual conversion.

St. John of God serves as an example here. He was a Portuguese mercenary soldier and, as such, engaged in activities often used by soldiers to occupy their free time, including drinking and gambling. In fact, he had a reputation for being a drunkard. This, of course, changed after his conversion (although, until he was given proper spiritual guidance, his impetuous behavior in the name of religion continued to raise questions about his character and sanity).

Because John had been addicted to alcohol for years, his conversion was fairly powerful and dramatic. The case of St. Monica was considerably simpler and more straightforward. When she was a girl, it was her duty to go down to the wine cellar and draw forth

---

[41] Sir. 31:25.

[42] Eph. 5:18.

[43] 1 Tim. 5:23.

the wine needed for the household meals. She began taking sips secretly and before long was drinking cups at a time. A slave observed her and, during an argument, accused her of this secret vice. Greatly ashamed, young Monica vowed never again to give in to this temptation.

An addiction to alcohol always leaves victims, especially innocent family members. The patroness of such persons might be said to be St. Bertilla Boscardin, a religious sister who died early in the twentieth century. Her father was an alcoholic with a violent, jealous personality; as a result, Bertilla witnessed frequent arguments and even physical violence in her home while growing up. (In giving evidence for her canonization, Mr. Boscardin himself admitted this.) This suffering gave Bertilla a compassionate heart, as demonstrated during her short life by her ministry to the sick, particularly to soldiers wounded in battle during World War I. Sr. Bertilla died in 1922, and was canonized in 1961. When she was beatified in 1952, the congregation assembled for the event included some of the soldiers she had cared for and some members of her family — including her now-recovered father.

The religious foundress St. Bartholomea Capitanio was also the daughter of an alcoholic. But her gentleness and willingness to serve him — even when she was ill — touched his heart and led to his conversion before his death.

It's beyond the scope of this book to provide anything more than the few examples given above and the short reflection to follow, regarding the need to use alcohol responsibly. Drunkenness is a moral failing, regardless of whether it's a rare event or a regular occurrence. Scripture tells us that God has made man "little less than God, and [crowned] him with glory and honor,"[44] but the misuse of alcohol threatens this dignity, temporarily or permanently. Some people have a predisposition to alcoholism, and every episode of

---

[44] Ps. 8:5.

irresponsible drinking brings them closer to crossing that threshold — after which there's no turning back. Even those not afflicted with this disease can, as a result of impaired judgment due to drunkenness, inflict lasting harm on themselves and others. The Fifth Commandment, which tells us "You shall not kill,"[45] also requires us to respect our bodies and to avoid any actions that unnecessarily threaten our health — thereby forbidding the misuse of alcohol (and every other form of substance abuse).

God does not expect victims of alcoholism, whether the problem drinkers themselves or their family members, to cope with this problem on their own; it pleases Him when they seek assistance in a spirit of honesty and humility.

For Further Reflection

"The virtue of temperance disposes us to *avoid every kind of excess: the abuse of food, alcohol, tobacco, or medicine. Those incur grave guilt who, by drunkenness or a love of speed, endanger their own and others' safety on the road, at sea, or in the air.*" — *Catechism of the Catholic Church,* par. 2290

"The first draft a man drinks ought to be for thirst, the second for nourishment, the third for pleasure, and the fourth for madness." — *Anonymous (Thus, what serves a worthwhile purpose at the beginning can, if caution is not exercised, soon degenerate into something harmful.)*

A point to consider: the root word of *intoxicated* is *toxic,* which the dictionary defines as poisonous.

Something You Might Try

◆ Ven. Matthew Talbot had been addicted to alcohol as a young man, a problem made worse by an irreligious life. One of his

---

[45] Exod. 20:13.

sisters later testified, "I heard him say [after his conversion] that even when drinking he was devout in his mind to the Blessed Virgin and used to say an odd Hail Mary, and he attributed his conversion to this." Deciding to repent after what proved to be his final binge, Matthew took the pledge (a solemn promise not to drink) for three months, went to Confession, and attended Sunday Mass and received Holy Communion for the first time in years. He became a changed man, and from then on, he worked faithfully, avoided his former drinking companions, went to church regularly, and never drank again.

If you have a drinking problem, this method may not have the same immediate results for you, but there's no doubt you'll never overcome your addiction without God's help. Humbly admit your need for Him, and steadfastly use the spiritual and moral resources He offers through the Church and through the people who care about you.

◆ If you have a drinking problem, seek professional help or the assistance of a group such as Alcoholics Anonymous.

Further Reading

Scripture: Proverbs 23:20-21, 29-35; Galatians 5:19-21.

Contemporary Works: Ted Lawson, *Understanding Alcoholism;* Catholic Update #C0991, *When Someone You Love Has an Alcohol or Drug Problem;* James A. Magner, *Mental Health in a Mad World.*

⌒

Lord, help me to use alcohol only in the manner You wish,
whether that means moderate drinking or complete abstinence.
May my behavior and example never cause pain or worry
to my loved ones or scandal to those who observe me,

and may my influence never contribute to
the downfall of a fellow human being.
Help me to respect the body You have given me
and to live the life You desire for me.
Remind me always,
as often and as powerfully as necessary,
that without You I am nothing,
I have nothing, and I can do nothing.
Let me be intoxicated only with love for You,
so that my words and deeds may
sing Your praises and bring others to know You,
inspiring us all to trust in You alone
and to place our lives completely in Your hands. Amen.

Envy

But if you have bitter jealousy and selfish ambition in your hearts,
do not boast and be false to the truth. This wisdom is not such as comes
down from above, but is earthly, unspiritual, devilish. For where jealousy
and selfish ambition exist, there will be disorder and every vile practice.

James 3:14-16

God created us to live in a state of perfect order and holiness —
meaning that our desires would be fully in harmony with the truth;
we would want only those things we truly needed, and only to the
extent that they were good for us. Original Sin, however, upset
this balance, and one of its effects was to introduce a new motive
for desiring things: envy. Now, in our sinful state, we often want
something not because we actually need it ourselves, but because
we see someone else possessing it. Envy can lead to a host of other
moral transgressions — theft, calumny, jealousy, slander, and even
murder — and thus, it is considered to be one of the *Seven Deadly*
Sins.[46]

Several of the saints struggled with envy before their conversions or before they made good progress on the path of holiness.

---

[46] The seven deadly, or capital, sins are pride, envy, sloth, lust,
greed, intemperance, and anger.

We need only turn to the Gospels for several examples. Jesus visited the home of Sts. Martha and Mary, the sisters of Lazarus. Martha, ever the dutiful hostess, busied herself in the kitchen, but when Mary neglected to help her and instead sat with Jesus, Martha complained. We can hear a touch of envy in her words, "Lord, do you not care that my sister has left me to serve alone?"[47] Martha would have liked to spend her time listening to Jesus, just as Mary was doing. In fact, such a thing was not only possible, but actually the Lord's preference for her, for He responded, "You are anxious and troubled about many things; one thing is needful."[48] Jesus was telling Martha not to be envious of Mary, but to join her and do as she was doing.

Another example from Scripture involves no less a figure than St. Peter himself. Our Lord, after His Resurrection, appeared to some of His apostles at the Sea of Galilee, and He gave Peter the opportunity to erase his threefold denial by three times professing his love. Peter did so in a spirit of humility and contrition, but then seems to have fallen into the trap of envy. Jesus foretold the manner in which Peter would die; rather than reflecting on the implications of this revelation, the leader of the Apostles, noticing John, asked, "Lord, what about this man?" That this was a case of envy is suggested by the Lord's mild rebuke: "If it is my will that he remain until I come, what is that to you? Follow me!"[49] God gives each of us our own unique calling and responsibilities, and instead of comparing these with the vocations of other people, we are asked to concentrate on our own mission.

Envy is the desire to have what someone else has, instead of being content with what is our own and with making good use of what God has given us. St. Augustine reflected on this experience

[47] Luke 10:40.
[48] Luke 10:41-42.
[49] John 21:21-22.

in his *Confessions*. As a boy, he was jealous of the attention his younger brother received from his mother, St. Monica; he also found it somehow more satisfying to eat fruit stolen from his neighbor's pear tree than fruit he had legitimately picked from a tree on his own family's property. Because of our sinful nature, it is often true that the forbidden fruit does indeed taste sweeter.

Our envy can cause us to act unjustly toward others and sometimes even hinder the unfolding of God's plan. For instance, the great Apostles to the Slavs, Sts. Cyril and Methodius, encountered much opposition during their successful careers as missionaries — not from pagans or enemies of the Church, but from German clergy who were envious of their success. (Moravia, where the saints were laboring, was seeking political and religious independence from German rule, and an intermingling of politics and religion was one of the results.) It took a direct appeal to the Pope before the saints' authority was confirmed.

All things are meant to work together for God's glory, but envy — first on the part of the Devil, then by humanity — interferes in this process. According to St. Francis of Assisi, "When a man envies his brother for the good that God says or does through him, it is like committing a sin of blasphemy, because he is really envying God, who is the only source of every good."

St. John Vianney warned that "whoever is envious is proud" — for when we improperly desire something God has not made available to us, we in our pride act as if we know better than the Lord. The sins of pride and envy go hand-in-hand — but, seen positively, this means that our efforts to remain humble can help us fight against *two* capital sins at once. Humility, of course, means seeking God's glory instead of our own, and one very practical way of doing this is to rejoice in other people's good fortune — for it may be that God is rewarding them for some sacrifice they made or preparing them for a special mission (things that may not be true in our case). St. John Vianney suggests, "If we are tempted to thoughts of envy against our neighbor, far from letting him see it by our cold manner, we must go out of our way to be friendly and do him any service that lies in our power."

We must also avoid envy in our financial transactions and business affairs. St. Francis de Sales tells us, "Do not give way to the wish for that which is another's until he on his part wishes to part with it; then his desire will render you not only just, but charitable. I would not forbid you to increase your means and possessions, as long as you do it not only with justice, but with gentleness and charity."

Earthly wealth and success have their place — but this place is very limited. Jesus has prepared a home for us in His Father's kingdom[50] — a dwelling place of unimaginable richness and beauty. Yearning for the things of this world can lead us into sin; yearning for the kingdom of God will lead us into everlasting joy.

For Further Reflection

"Envy is a capital sin. It refers to the sadness at the sight of another's goods and the immoderate desire to acquire them for oneself, even unjustly. When it wishes grave harm to a neighbor it is a mortal sin: St. Augustine saw envy as 'the diabolical sin.' 'From envy are born hatred, detraction, calumny, joy caused by the misfortune of a neighbor, and displeasure caused by his prosperity.' Envy represents a form of sadness and therefore a refusal of charity; the baptized person should struggle against it by exercising good will. Envy often comes from pride; the baptized person should train himself to live in humility. . . ." — *Catechism of the Catholic Church*, par. 2539-2540

"The same hope inspired us [St. Gregory of Nazianzus and his friend St. Basil the Great]: the pursuit of learning. This is an

---

[50] John 14:3.

ambition especially subject to envy. Yet between us there was no envy. On the contrary, we made capital out of our rivalry. Our rivalry consisted, not in seeking the first place for oneself but in yielding it to the other, for we each looked on the other's success as his own." — *St. Gregory of Nazianzus*

"Jealousy and strife have overthrown great cities and uprooted mighty nations." — *St. Clement of Rome (writing about the martyrdom of the early Christians)*

Something You Might Try

◆ According to St. Bernard of Clairvaux, it's our human nature to set a higher value on the things we don't have than on those we do have — and this can eventually bring us to God, once we've realized that all this world's pleasures have not satisfied our deepest needs. Therefore, ask yourself honestly if you've received true and lasting satisfaction whenever you've finally obtained what you desired or envied. If not, this should, as St. Bernard says, convince you of the need to seek God above all else. Once you allow yourself to be consumed by this desire, you will begin making great spiritual progress.

◆ We can overcome the temptation to be envious by instead seeing it as an opportunity to praise our Lord. St. John Chrysostom suggests, "Would you like to see God glorified by you? Then rejoice in your brother's progress, and you will immediately give glory to God. Because His servant could conquer envy by rejoicing in the merits of others, God will be praised."

Further Reading

Scripture: Sirach 30:24; Mark 7:20-22; 1 Corinthians 3:3.

Classics: St. Augustine, *Confessions*; St. Bernard, *On the Love of God*; St. Francis de Sales, *An Introduction to the Devout Life*.

Saintly Solutions

Contemporary Works: Rudolf Allers, *Self-Improvement*;
James A. Magner, *Mental Health in a Mad World*.

*God of all generosity,
Source of every blessing and gift:
help me conquer the tendency
to envy the good fortune of others.
Remove this vice that is rooted deeply within me,
and replace it with a genuine satisfaction
over the success of those around me.
May I always remember that, in loving You,
I am rich beyond all measure;
may I always trust that You will provide
me with everything I need.
Please bless all those who, at any time
and in any way, have been the victims
of my envy and displeasure, and
please give me a proper spirit
of gratitude for all Your gifts.
May Your name be praised
forever and ever. Amen.*

Failure

Let no one deceive himself. If anyone among you thinks that he is
wise in this age, let him become a fool that he may become wise.
For the wisdom of this world is folly with God.

1 Corinthians 3:18-19

Mother Teresa of Calcutta often spoke these reassuring words: "God does not call us to be successful; He calls us to be faithful." What a hope-filled message this is — for quite often we fail, not only according to the standards of this world, but — more important — according to God's. Nevertheless, we can achieve sanctity by taking up our cross faithfully each day, and it is on this basis that we will be judged.

You and I, even if we fail in all things, can still become saints. We know this is true precisely because many of the saints were themselves, in one way or another and at one time or another, failures. Even someone as talented and dynamic as St. Basil the Great, for instance, could lament, "For my sins, I seem to fail in everything."

Sinfulness has hampered the efforts of some of the greatest saints. The apostle Peter, for instance, was — by any human measure — totally unsuited to become the head of Christ's Church. (To his credit, he himself recognized this, for he once said to Jesus,

"Depart from me, for I am a sinful man, O Lord."[51]) This leader, to whom the Lord entrusted such an important responsibility, was at times proud, boastful, impetuous, and cowardly, and in Jesus' hour of greatest need, he first fell asleep, then ran away in fear — even though he had earlier promised to give his life for Christ, if necessary. Soon after this he denied ever knowing the Lord. All of these things constitute failure — except when divine mercy washes away sin from repentant hearts, and divine grace supplies strength and courage to those whose spirits are willing but whose flesh is weak.

The Church has among her saints Peter, who denied knowing his Master;[52] Thomas, who doubted the Lord's Resurrection, even though the Lord had spoken of it before His death;[53] and Mark, who gave up and went home during his first experience as a missionary.[54] The experiences of these men show that no failure is lasting for those who place their hope in God.

Our sinful weakness no doubt contributes to much of our difficulty in life, but failure is a companion never far from any of us, even when we're acting entirely from holy and admirable motives. Many of the saints did their very best to spread the Gospel and uphold the truth — but failed to one degree or another. St. Ansgar labored many years as a missionary in Denmark and Sweden in the ninth century; most of his hard-won accomplishments on behalf of the Church disappeared after his lifetime, as these countries reverted to paganism.

St. Olaf, the patron saint of Norway, became king in 1016, but his efforts to Christianize his people led to a rebellion in which he was forced to flee. When he later returned and attempted to reconquer his rightful kingdom, he was killed in battle.

---

[51] Luke 5:8.
[52] Matt. 26:69-75.
[53] John 20:24-29.
[54] Acts 13:13.

St. Louis IX, although a successful king of France, did not succeed as a Crusader. In his first attempt to defeat the Moslems, he was taken in battle and held for ransom. In his second attempt some years later, he died of dysentery without having accomplished anything. During this same period St. Francis of Assisi tried to conquer the Moslems in a very different way: by traveling to the Holy Land and seeking to convert the sultan to Christianity. He, too, failed, although the Moslem leader was greatly impressed by the saint's humility and sincerity.

Many of the Church's greatest popes were canonized saints — but they, too, had their share of difficulties, problems, and mistakes. In the eleventh century, Pope St. Leo IX worked energetically on behalf of Church reform, although this involved him in political controversies and disputes — even to the point of leading an army in battle. In 1053 Leo's troops unsuccessfully opposed a Norman invasion, and the Pope himself was captured and imprisoned. The following year Leo rejected some proposals of the Patriarch of Constantinople, ultimately leading to the breaking away of the Eastern Churches from the authority of Rome — a separation that continues to this day.

Leo's assistant in many of these efforts was a young monk named Hildebrand, who in 1073 was himself elected Pope: St. Gregory VII. It was Gregory who, in an effort to regain for the Church the power to choose her own bishops (a power kings and nobles had usurped for themselves), excommunicated the powerful Emperor Henry IV of Germany. A penitent Henry appeared outside the castle of Canossa, where the Pope was in residence, and waited three days in the snow before Gregory lifted the excommunication. It seemed that papal authority had humbled earthly power, but Henry's repentance was a sham; he went to war against the papacy, driving Gregory from Rome. The city was recaptured on Gregory's behalf by a Catholic prince from Normandy, but at such a cost in destruction and loss of life that the people turned against the Pope, forcing him to flee once again. Gregory died the following year in Salerno, saying on his death-bed, "I have loved righteousness and hated iniquity; that is why I die in exile."

Jesus never promised Peter and his successors that they would be successful in all their endeavors, only that their efforts to serve Him would be rewarded. One who experienced the truth of this promise was St. Celestine V, who was one of the most unsuited popes in Church history (as he himself foresaw). In 1294 a papal conclave, failing to agree on a candidate after two years of deliberation, finally chose in desperation a holy, eighty-year-old monk named Peter of Morrone. Although he wanted nothing more than to finish out his life as a hermit, Peter reluctantly accepted for the good of the Church. However, as Pope Celestine V, he was misled and manipulated by his advisers, failed in almost everything he attempted, and finally resigned in disgrace. His successor, Pope Boniface VIII, thereupon had Celestine imprisoned, lest he be used by the new Pope's enemies. St. Celestine remarked ironically, "I wanted nothing in the world but a cell, and a cell they have given me."

Holiness is no guarantee of worldly success — even when we're working in the Lord's name. St. Bogumilus was a conscientious bishop in twelfth-century Poland, but he was unable to impose necessary reforms on his clergy. Not wanting to condone a situation he couldn't change, he sought and obtained permission to resign.

Another example of a leader who failed in spite of personal holiness is St. Ebba the Elder. This seventh-century abbess was unsuccessful in her efforts to reform the religious sisters under her authority.

Failure was also the fate of the pope Bl. Urban V. For most of the fourteenth century, the Pope resided in Avignon, France; this gave rise to a number of abuses, including French meddling in the affairs of the Church, but the popes of the day found Avignon more comfortable than Rome. At the urging of many people concerned for the well-being of the Church, Urban returned to Rome, but, encountering numerous difficulties there, he mistakenly thought it would be better if he returned to France. The people of Rome begged him to stay, and St. Bridget of Sweden warned the Pope that if he left the Eternal City he'd die soon afterward, but Urban paid them no mind. He departed from Rome in September 1370 and died three and a half months later. Had he stayed in Rome, Urban could have prevented the Great Western Schism — a scandal in which there were simultaneously two, and later three, popes, each claiming to be the only true leader of Christendom.

St. Pius V is remembered for what seems in retrospect to have been a great mistake on his part: excommunicating Queen Elizabeth I of England. Her father, Henry VIII, had formed the Anglican Church for political reasons, being angry at the Church's refusal to annul his marriage to Catherine of Aragon; Catholics fell under suspicion because of their loyalty to Rome, but were still somewhat tolerated. When Elizabeth began interfering with the rights of the Church, however, Pius — hoping to rob her of popular support and pave the way for the restoration of a Catholic monarchy — formally excommunicated her. This only had the effect of strengthening Elizabeth's hold on power and provoking her to persecute Catholics — hardly the results Pius had sought.

Another pope by that name also experienced a great failure in the political realm. St. Pius X, elected early in the twentieth century, provided the Church with strong leadership, but his efforts to prevent the outbreak of World War I — which he foresaw as a great disaster for humanity — did not succeed, and he died a heartbroken man a few weeks after hostilities began.

Sometimes failure is a sign from God. This was true for St. Alphonsus Liguori; he was a promising young lawyer, but the loss of an important court case prompted him to give up his legal career and become a priest instead.

St. Rose Philippine Duchesne and a few other nuns sought to reestablish their convent, which had been closed during the French Revolution. When they failed, Rose discerned a call to missionary work among the American Indians, although even there her dedication and hard work did not always meet with success.

St. Francis Borgia had great worldly prestige as a duke and a member of the royal court in sixteenth-century Spain, but he set it all aside to become a Jesuit priest. He soon became known for his holiness and for his ability to help sinners come to repentance — but not even a saint can overcome human free will. On one occasion, Francis heard of a young man, notorious for a sinful life, who was stricken with a fatal illness. The saint began by praying for the youth's conversion, then hurried to his side, but the youth wanted nothing to do with religion. Francis prayed again, then returned to the dying young man; he held up his crucifix and urged him to repent and to call upon God's mercy, but to no avail. The youth turned his face away and died in despair. Tragedies like this can occur, even in spite of the best efforts of saints, for nothing on this earth is guaranteed.

Why does the Lord allow failure? According to St. Paul of the Cross, "The works of God always meet with opposition so that the Divine Magnificence may shine forth. It is when things appear to be crashing to the ground that you will see them even more be raised on high." Just as "God is able to write straight with crooked lines," so His servants, with the help of His grace, are able to grow in holiness in spite of their setbacks. St. John Vianney reminds us, "The saints did not become saints without many a sacrifice and many a struggle," and St. John of the Cross offers these reassuring words: "The Lord measures our perfection neither by the multitude nor the magnitude of our deeds, but by the manner in which we perform them."

Talented and productive hands count for much less in God's eyes than a loving heart; we are therefore advised by Bl. Zeferino Agostini, "Do not be dismayed by toil or suffering, nor by the meager fruit of your labors. Remember that God rewards not according to results but [according to] efforts." By Heaven's standards, faithfulness equals success, especially when serving the Lord involves something contrary to our own preferences. As St. Vincent de Paul notes, "One act of resignation to the divine will, when it ordains what is repugnant to us, is worth more than a hundred thousand successes according to our own will and pleasure."

As Christ's servants, we must let our own desires be secondary, for as Jesus promised, those who lose everything in His name receive infinitely more back.[55] St. Augustine assures us, "Conquer yourself, and the world lies at your feet." Once we've overcome our human desire for popularity and success, the world is no longer able to ensnare us or lead us astray — and on that day we will truly become successful in God's sight.

For Further Reflection

"He does much in the sight of God who does his best, be it ever so little." — *St. Peter of Alcantara*

"See that you are not suddenly saddened by the adversities of this world, for you do not know the good they bring, being ordained in the judgments of God for the everlasting joy of the elect." — *St. John of the Cross* (*In other words, failure may even be helpful or necessary in our efforts to reach Heaven.*)

"To rely on our talents is a cause of great loss. For when [someone] places confidence in his own prudence, knowledge, and intelligence, God, to make him know and see his insufficiency, withdraws from him His help and leaves him to work by himself.

[55] Cf. Matt. 16:25.

Whence it happens that all his plans and labors produce little or no fruit. This is often why our undertakings fail." — *St. Vincent de Paul*

Something You Might Try

♦ When she was appointed novice mistress, St. Thérèse of Lisieux, profoundly aware that she was unequal to the task, "went to God in the spirit of a child that throws itself into its father's arms, and nestles its head against his shoulder." Admitting her spiritual poverty, she trustingly asked the Lord for all the help she'd need in fulfilling her duties — and her prayer was answered. We must approach God in the same manner, admitting our total dependence on Him and firmly believing in His care for us. Then we will either succeed or fail; in either case, however, He will be with us and will help us in our efforts to glorify His name.

♦ If our standards are too high, we'd do well to remind ourselves that it's impossible for us to know or do everything; keeping this in mind can help us cope with failure more effectively.

Further Reading

Scripture: Sirach 24:21; Matthew 25:20-21.

Classics: St. Thérèse of Lisieux, *The Story of a Soul.*

Contemporary Works: Rudolf Allers, *Self-Improvement;* Rev. Robert DeGrandis, *Failure in Your Life.*

*I bind unto myself today
The power of God to hold and lead,
His eye to watch, His might to stay,
His ear to hearken to my need,
The wisdom of my God to teach,*

His hand to guide, His shield to ward,
The Word of God to give me speech,
His heavenly host to be my guard.
Christ be with me, Christ within me,
Christ behind me, Christ before me,
Christ beside me, Christ to win me,
Christ to comfort and restore me,
Christ beneath me, Christ above me,
Christ in quiet, Christ in danger,
Christ in hearts of all that love me,
Christ in mouth of friend and stranger.

St. Patrick

False Accusations

*Blessed are you when men revile you and persecute you
and utter all kinds of evil against you falsely on my account.
Rejoice and be glad, for your reward is great in Heaven.*

Matthew 5:11-12

In her autobiography, *The Story of a Soul*, St. Thérèse of Lisieux wrote, addressing one of her superiors, "Here is an example which will probably make you smile. You had been ill for some days with bronchitis, and I was rather anxious. One morning I came softly to your infirmary to put away the keys of the Communion grille, for I was sacristan. I was secretly rejoicing at this chance to see you, but one of the Sisters was afraid I was going to wake you up and, in her zeal, tried to relieve me of the keys. I told her very politely that I was just as anxious as she was to make no noise, but that it was my duty to replace them. I know now that it would have been better if I had simply handed them to her, but I did not think so at the time. I tried to push my way in, in spite of her opposition. Then it happened . . . the noise we were making awakened you, and everything was blamed on me! The Sister made quite a speech, the burden of which was: 'It was Sister Thérèse of the Child Jesus who made all the noise.' I simply longed to defend myself, but happily I had a bright idea. I knew I would certainly lose my peace of mind if I tried to justify myself; I knew, too, that I was not virtuous enough to remain silent in the face of this accusation. There was only one way out — I must run away. No sooner thought than done; I fled . . . but my heart was beating so violently that I could not go very far, and I sat down on the stairs to enjoy quietly the fruits of victory. A strange kind of bravery, but it was better than exposing myself to certain defeat!"

Is there anyone among us who has not been wrongly accused of something? Certainly the saints often had this happen to them, again and again — quite often in regard to matters far more serious than the one described by St. Thérèse. For instance, St. Elizabeth of Portugal was accused of treason by her husband, King Denis, and was temporarily banished from court (but Denis afterward repented).

Pope St. Damasus I was elected Bishop of Rome in 366, but a deacon named Ursinus was elected antipope at the same time. Even though the civil government intervened on Damasus' behalf, the supporters of Ursinus took the saint to court and forced him to defend himself against charges of such unlikely crimes as adultery.

St. Methodius, who, with his brother St. Cyril, was a missionary to the Slavic people, had to suffer the active opposition of German bishops who were not eager to see a Slavic hierarchy established in Moravia. Methodius was falsely charged with heresy by the German Church leaders — apparently out of jealousy over his success — and was imprisoned by them for two years.

Sometimes the saints have responded vigorously in their own defense; the foremost example of this is St. Paul, whose letter to the Galatians is largely a defense of his ministry against his accusers and who speaks unashamedly in his letters to the Corinthians of his fidelity to the Gospel.

To speak the truth on our behalf is often necessary and defensible. Quite often, though, saints have chosen to imitate the example of Jesus, who did not respond to the charges made against

Him.[56] For example, the Italian monk St. Romuald was once wrongly accused of a scandalous crime, and his fellow monks believed the accusation; rather than defending himself, Romuald practiced mortification by humbly accepting the punishment he was given.

St. Gerard Majella, a lay brother, was once slandered by a young woman; he did not respond to the charges, so his Redemptorist community excluded him from Communion for several months until the woman retracted her statement.

Bl. Simon of Todi chose to listen in silence when grave charges were made against him by his fellow Augustinian monks; he didn't insist on an inquiry to prove his innocence for fear that the resulting acrimony might cause scandal and dissensions within the order.

Wrongful accusations have often created great suffering for their victims. St. John of the Cross made some powerful enemies during his efforts to reform the Carmelite Order. He later suffered, at the hands of his fellow religious, imprisonment, insults, slander, and rough handling; even after he was vindicated, there were those who would not let him alone. During his final illness, he was subject to various forms of pettiness, ill treatment, and neglect, which caused him great physical pain and may have hastened his death before the age of fifty.

Even worse was the fate of St. Helen of Skovde, the widow of a Swedish noble in the twelfth century. On returning from a pilgrimage to Rome, she was accused of complicity in the death of her son-in-law; by the time the true perpetrators were discovered, it was too late: Helen had been executed.

Death was also the fate of the seventh-century bishop St. Leodegarius who, having earlier been blinded and having his tongue cut out by an enemy, found himself accused by this same

---

[56] Cf. Matt. 26:63.

enemy of murder. The saint was imprisoned, tortured, and put to death two years later.

More fortunate was St. Richardis, the wife of the Holy Roman Emperor Charles the Fat. When he accused her of infidelity (with the Bishop of Vercelli, no less), Richardis denied it and insisted on proving her innocence by undergoing trial by fire (in which, supposedly, only the guilty would be harmed). Richardis passed through the flames unscathed. (It's probably not surprising that she then left Charles and retired to a convent.)

When the Dominican friar St. Peter of Verona was banished to a remote priory after being wrongly accused of receiving a woman into his cell, he knelt before the crucifix and cried out, "Lord, You know I am not guilty. Why do You permit me to be falsely accused?" Jesus answered him, "And I, Peter, what did I do to deserve my Passion and death?" Peter was consoled by this answer, and soon afterward, his innocence was proven.

A partial list of saints who have been wrongly accused includes Bl. Miguel Pro, a priest executed in 1927 by Mexican authorities on charges that he was involved in an assassination attempt against government officials, even though there was no evidence against him; St. Joan of Arc, who was burned at the stake for allegedly practicing witchcraft; St. Jan Sarkander, wrongly identified as a spy during the Thirty Years War; the Spanish priest Bl. Francis Palau Y Quer, who supposedly provoked labor strikes in early twentieth-century Spain; Pope St. Paschal I, who was wrongly believed to have instigated the murder of two of his own papal officials who opposed one of his decisions; and St. John of Matera, who was imprisoned (and later escaped with the help of an angel) after being suspected of keeping hidden treasure he found while rebuilding a ruined church.

Perhaps the most ironic story of an accusation involves the third-century martyr St. Nemesius. Arrested for theft, he managed to prove his innocence, but was then accused of being a Christian.

After confessing his Faith, Nemesius was scourged twice as much as the actual thieves and was put to death. Ironically, the saint was innocent of the first accusation and guilty of the second — and each helped him attain eternal life.

St. Raymond Nonnatus, who in the thirteenth century, offered himself as ransom to the Moselms in exchange for Christians they were holding, is considered the patron saint of those who are falsely accused, and if the experiences of the saints are any indication, there are probably many people who need his assistance. Those of us who suffer from wrongful accusations — whether prompted by malice or misunderstanding — can turn to the saints for help, knowing that they understand and sympathize with us.

We also have the consolation of knowing that this painful experience can be the source of great grace. St. Francis de Sales tells us that "To put up with infamy is the touchstone of humility and of true virtue." And St. John Vianney reassures us, "Are you falsely accused, or loaded with insults? All the better! It is a good sign; don't worry about it. You are on the road which leads to Heaven." May the Lord give each of us the courage and strength to travel this road.

For Further Reflection

"Respect for the reputation of persons forbids every attitude and word likely to cause them unjust injury. He becomes guilty . . . of *calumny* who, by remarks contrary to the truth, harms the reputation of others and gives occasion for false judgments concerning them." — *Catechism of the Catholic Church*, par. 2477

"Souls that are weak and too much attached to their own reputation make a great stir and commotion, and can have no peace if any calumny is spread against them. It is not thus with generous souls who aim at nothing except to please God. They know very well that He sees their innocence and has it at heart more than they themselves, and therefore He will not neglect to defend them as their greatest good requires." — *St. Augustine*

Speaking of the Holy Spirit, St. Irenaeus said, "Since we have our accuser, we need an Advocate as well." (*Thus, we must rely on the Holy Spirit when we're falsely accused.*)

Something You Might Try

♦ Young St. Dominic Savio was once blamed by other school-boys for their own misdeed; he remained silent in imitation of Christ. You don't necessarily have to remain silent when falsely accused, but you should remember that such experiences can be a share in the sufferings of Christ. St. Francis de Sales advises, "If you are falsely accused, excuse yourself meekly, denying your guilt, for so much you owe to truth and the edification of your neighbor. But if, after your true and honest excuse, your accusers persist, give yourself no further trouble, and do not persevere in your defense, for having paid tribute to truth, now pay tribute to humility."

♦ St. Paul of the Cross says, "When you are accused of something unjustly, it is so hard to be nice to your accusers. Yet these are the instruments God is using to enrich your soul with virtues. Seek every opportunity to be nice to these people and to do all the good to them that you can in meekness and love."

Further Reading

Scripture: Psalm 37:6; 1 Peter 2:20-21; Ephesians 4:2.

Classics: St. Francis de Sales, *An Introduction to the Devout Life*; St. Alphonsus Liguori, *The Practice of the Love of Jesus Christ*.

☞

Jesus, You were falsely accused,
so You know what I'm going through. It hurts.

*I feel violated and betrayed. I want to lash out,
or at least see my accusers covered with shame —
at the very least, forced to apologize to me.
I want everyone to know that I'm innocent,
but I'm afraid that they won't know, that they'll think
badly of me, and that I'll suffer for it.
Help me, Lord, I beg You, to bear this cross and
to forgive those who are sinning against me.
Give me the courage to go forward and the strength
to forgive those who have wrongly accused me and
those who have believed the worst about me.
If it is Your will, let me be vindicated, and —
regardless of what happens — let me be gracious
to those who have harmed me.
May I offer this sacrifice to You for Your greater glory —
a glory that no one can ever take away. Amen.*

Family Difficulties

He who loves father or mother more than me is not worthy of me;
and he who loves son or daughter more than me is not worthy of me;
and he who does not take his cross and follow me is not worthy of me.

Matthew 10:37-38

Chances are you've heard the saying "You can choose your friends, but not your family" and have responded by nodding appreciatively. Family members! It so often seems that we can't live with them and we can't live without them; they can be our greatest source of strength or our greatest problem. That's an exaggeration, of course, but probably a justifiable one. Certainly many of the saints would think so, for they've had their share of family difficulties, and so their example can be instructive.

It should be noted at the outset that there have been families of saints. For instance, St. Macrina the Younger was the daughter of St. Basil the Elder and St. Emmelia, and the sister of St. Basil the Great, St. Peter of Sebaste, and St. Gregory of Nyssa. Macrina had an important part in the education of her brothers, including, on one occasion, rebuking Basil for excessive pride.

The family of the seventh-century widow St. Waudru (known also as Waldetrudis) was very holy: her parents, Walbert and Bertilia; her sister Aldegund; and her husband, Vincent Madelgarus, and their four children, Landericus, Dentilin, Aldetrude, and Madelberte, are all considered saints.

But even families of saints aren't spared disputes and misunderstandings. It may not surprise us that the family of the fifth-century laywoman St. Melania the Younger was opposed to her religious devotions (although her patience and charity eventually won over her husband and her widowed mother); what is surprising is that she sometimes had strained relations with her grandmother, who was also a canonized saint: St. Melania the Older. The grandmother was a friend of St. Jerome and, like him, had a forceful personality, and it seems she and her holy granddaughter didn't always see eye to eye.

Family ties are no guarantee that our loved ones will treat us properly or that what they want for us is truly for our own good. Early in the third century, St. Perpetua was one of several Christians arrested by the Roman authorities. Perpetua's father, a leading pagan noble in Carthage, visited her in prison and tried to convince her to renounce her Faith. In her diary, Perpetua wrote a description of his visit: "When my father in his affection for me was trying to turn me from my purpose by arguments and thus weaken my faith, I said to him, 'Do you see this vessel — water pot or whatever it may be? Can it be called by any other name than what it is?' 'No,' he replied. 'So also I cannot call myself by any other name than what I am — a Christian.' " Perpetua's father departed sadly, having failed to accomplish what he mistakenly thought was in her best interests. The saint herself, of course, was also saddened, but she knew that her first loyalty was to Christ. St. Perpetua and her companions died bravely as martyrs during the public games held in the city's amphitheater.

The first saint to be born in the United States, St. Elizabeth Ann Seton, burned her family bridges behind her when she converted to Catholicism. She belonged to a very prominent Episcopalian family in New York and, as a young woman, married a prosperous merchant, but after eleven years of marital happiness, Mr. Seton lost his fortune as a result of a business failure and soon afterward contracted tuberculosis and died. Because her family opposed her new Faith, she and her five children found themselves in severe financial difficulty, so she accepted the invitation of a priest to establish a school for girls; eventually she and a group of like-minded women established a religious congregation, the Sisters of Charity; and Elizabeth, who became known as Mother Seton, found her identity as a member of God's family in the Church.

Many of the saints had difficulties with parents who opposed or didn't understand their religious vocations. We immediately recall St. Francis of Assisi, whose father disowned and disinherited him — not entirely without cause: Francis had taken some items from the family business and sold them to raise money for repairing a dilapidated church. Francis also helped his friend St. Clare of Assisi leave home secretly so as to enter a convent — much against her family's wishes. Clare's sister St. Agnes of Assisi later followed her, again ignoring the family's desires. Eventually the sisters' widowed mother (perhaps figuring that "if you can't beat 'em, join 'em") also entered the convent — whereupon St. Francis formed the three of them as the nucleus of the religious community known as the Poor Clares.

Both St. Albert the Great and St. Thomas Aquinas pursued their religious vocations (each of which was marked by outstanding learning and service to the Church) over the fierce opposition of their families. St. Casimir, a fifteenth-century prince of Poland, was a great disappointment to his royal father, for the king wanted him to concentrate on warlike activities and on marrying and producing royal heirs, rather than on praying and on deeds of charity.

St. Rose of Lima desired to enter a convent, but her parents insisted she marry. For ten years it was a standoff; finally her parents relented to the extent of letting her enter the Third Order of St.

Dominic as a layperson, while living a life of semi-solitude in a private room in their poor home. Rose was trying to imitate St. Catherine of Siena, a fourteenth-century virgin who was the youngest of twenty-five children. Her parents wanted her to marry someone wealthy, but she refused: her life belonged to God. Catherine's mother nagged her about making herself beautiful so as to find a husband, to which Catherine responded by cutting off her hair. Her punishment for this act of defiance was to perform the hardest household work and to serve the rest of the family — which she did so cheerfully and patiently that her father finally decreed that she be left in peace and allowed to live as a recluse in her room.

Less fortunate was St. Hermenegild, whose sixth-century royal father actually ordered him executed when he refused to renounce his Catholic Faith. In the early sixteenth century, the child martyr Bl. Christopher of Mexico was also killed by his own father after converting to Catholicism.

Some of the saints encountered opposition, or worse, from family members other than parents. Following the death of her husband, St. Jane Frances de Chantal suffered greatly at the hands of her father-in-law. The eleventh-century bishop St. Peter Damian, being orphaned at an early age, was raised by an older brother who treated him as little better than a slave. In the tenth century, St. Wenceslaus, king of Bohemia, was invited by his brother Boleslav to meet him for Mass, but Boleslav had arranged for his supporters to ambush and murder the king while on his way to church.

Mistreatment by other people — especially by our family — doesn't justify an unloving response on our part. St. Thomas More, for example, allowed his Lutheran son-in-law to live in his home, even though the younger man (a former Catholic) claimed to abhor his father-in-law. St. Francis de Sales insists, "We must not be satisfied with the aromatic fragrance of honey, that is, with agreeable and courteous dealings toward strangers, but we must have the milk of charity toward our own households, and not re-semble those who are angels abroad and devils at home."

Kindness within the home is sure to be rewarded; as St. Alphon-sus Liguori tells us, "You may be certain of this: if you practice love within your own family, God will help you outside it." The Lord gives us our families for our mutual growth in grace; when, for whatever reason, this is not possible, we ourselves are still required to advance in holiness. Patiently bearing misunderstanding and mistreatment from those in our own homes is a powerful, although admittedly difficult, means of doing this.

For Further Reflection

"Family ties are important but not absolute. Just as the child grows to maturity and human and spiritual autonomy, so his unique vocation which comes from God asserts itself more clearly and forcefully. Parents should respect this call and encourage their children to follow it. They must be convinced that the first vo-cation of the Christian is to *follow Jesus. . . .*" — *Catechism of the Catholic Church,* par. 2232

"Love your father, but not more than you love your God. Love your mother, but not more than the mother that gave you birth to eternal life. Furthermore, from this same love of your par-ents, see how much you ought to love God and the Church. For if so much love is owed to those who begot you to a life that must end with your death, how much more grateful love is owed to those who begot you for an eternal destiny!" — *St. Augustine*

"With what certainty may we hope, since our salvation depends upon the sentence of a good Brother and a kind Mother!" — *St. Anselm (Thus, even if relations are strained within our earthly families, we have the assurance of true love and acceptance from Jesus and Mary.)*

Saintly Solutions

Something You Might Try

♦ St. Stanislaus Kostka suffered mistreatment from his noble father and especially from his older brother Paul, and had to run away to pursue his vocation in the Jesuit Order. However, Stanislaus died while still a young novice — partly as a result of the physical abuse he had earlier received. His fellow Jesuits never knew of this until Paul himself admitted what had happened; Stanislaus never spoke of it. We are not required to keep quiet about physical abuse, and we *must* report it to the authorities when we see someone else being abused. For lesser offenses committed against us by family members, however, St. Stanislaus gives us a noble example to follow: to avoid making our family problems public.

♦ Bl. Bernard of Offida, a seventeenth-century Franciscan, had a special gift of mediating family quarrels and feuds; those who serve in this manner perform a very valuable function. If you have the ability and opportunity to restore frayed relationships within your own family, do so. In a family dispute, it often happens that all the parties involved are hoping to be reconciled, but no one wants to make the first move. If you — whether as a direct participant in the quarrel or as an uninvolved observer — help bridge the gap between family members, you will be bringing peace to others while at the same time glorifying God.

♦ According to St. Francis de Sales, "Among all those who are included under the title of neighbor, there are none who deserve it more, in one sense, than those of our own household. They are nearest of all to us, living under the same roof and eating the same bread. Therefore they ought to be one of the principal objects of our love, and we should practice in regard to them all the acts of a true charity, which ought to be founded not upon flesh and blood, or upon their good qualities, but altogether upon God." In other words, you must relate to those who reject you, not on the basis of your own strength or their loving reasonableness, but through divine grace. This means that if members of your family reject you, you must not reject them; instead of responding to them harshly, remain peaceful and forgiving, while keeping them always in your prayers.

Further Reading

Scripture: Matthew 12:46-50; Psalm 133:1; Mark 3:21; Matthew 10:34-36.

Classics: St. Alphonsus Liguori, *The Practice of the Love of Jesus Christ* and *The Glories of Mary*.

Contemporary Works: Catherine Martin, *Strengthening Family Life*.

Dear Holy Family — Jesus, Mary, and Joseph:
look with compassion upon me and my family, and
help us to live together in harmony and mutual respect.
Forgive us our failings and insensitivity,
our unkind remarks and lack of courtesy to one another;
enlighten us with the spirit of love and understanding,
and make our home a true refuge in a harsh and unfriendly world.
We often fail to support one another or to be present in times of need;
show us our faults, that — by following Your holy example —
we may overcome them and live as our heavenly Father desires.
Help us to live now in such a way that we may one day together
enter the kingdom of eternal glory, there to dwell forever
as children in the family of God. Amen.

Financial Difficulties

Remove far from me falsehood and lying;
give me neither poverty nor riches;
feed me with the food that is needful for me,
lest I be full, and deny Thee, and say, "Who is the Lord?"
or lest I be poor, and steal, and profane the name of my God.

Proverbs 30:8-9

If America is truly the richest and most materially prosperous society in history — as indeed it is — why is it that many of us are always in need of more money than we have? Yes, God provides for our needs, but why does it have to be so difficult sometimes? The Church needs more financial support; local communities and schools need greater revenues; most families need a larger income.

Worries about money unfortunately seem to be part of life. Where does faith enter into this reality?

Quite a few saints knew what it was like to be in financial need. Many of them lived in poverty — beginning with St. Joseph and the Virgin Mary, whose home in Nazareth was certainly a poor one. Jesus, as the Eternal Word of God through whom all things were created, chose to be born and to live in poverty, rather than in wealth, so that no one could use a lack of material resources as an excuse for not following Him. Most of those whom He called as disciples during His lifetime were poor. If we ourselves are poor, we have numerous examples to remind us that we can nonetheless become rich in grace.

When money is a problem, it makes sense for us to pray for assistance from the saints mentioned above: the Blessed Virgin Mary, St. Joseph the Worker and the Apostles. We might also remember St. Callistus, who, as a slave in an important Roman household, managed to lose some money entrusted to his care, and St. Guy of Anderlecht, who, seeking to raise additional money to give to the poor, lost his savings in a bad investment.[57] (We obviously don't want these two to intercede for similar results for us, but certainly they can look upon us with compassion in our financial needs.)

In dealing with our own financial worries, it's helpful — although probably difficult, at first — for us to adopt the same attitude as St. John Bosco, the Italian priest who devoted his life to caring for delinquent boys. Even with the assistance of wealthy patrons, John's orphanages, schools, and workshops never seemed to have quite enough money to accomplish everything that was needed. But the saint refused to worry. To every warning of impending financial disaster, John merely smiled and answered, "God will provide." Rather than winning admiration, this trusting attitude caused some people to doubt his sanity.

God does not want us to drive ourselves mad worrying about money; perhaps, if we're having difficulties, it's a message from Him: maybe we need to be more generous in sharing what we already have, or more willing to trust in Him instead of our own efforts, or more careful in our priorities in life. (After all, the higher we rank money in importance, the more of it we'll become convinced we need.) The Lord will provide, but He asks that — first and foremost — we actively trust in Him.

[57] See also the chapter on business difficulties.

For Further Reflection

"Everyone has the right of economic initiative; everyone should make legitimate use of his talents to contribute to the abundance that will benefit all and to harvest the just fruits of his labor. He should seek to observe regulations issued by legitimate authority for the sake of the common good." — *Catechism of the Catholic Church*, par. 2429

"Nothing makes us so prosperous in this world as to give alms." — *St. Francis de Sales*

"Think of the little children who with one hand hold fast to their father while with the other they gather berries. If you handle the goods of this world with one hand, you must also always hold fast with the other to your heavenly Father's hand, and turn toward him from time to time to see if you are pleasing Him. Above all, be sure that you never leave His hand and His protection, thinking that with your own two hands you can gather more or get some other advantage." — *St. Francis de Sales*

Something You Might Try

♦ St. Paul of the Cross advises, "When you need something, take heart and cry out to the Lord. But remain in peace in the will of God without the least anxiety." God wants you to turn to Him in all your needs — financial needs included. He also desires that, once you've expressed your needs to Him, you trust in His Providence and love.

♦ A message on a bumper sticker says, "If you love Jesus, tithe! Any fool can honk." Tithing — donating ten percent of your income to the Church or to a charity — is a powerful way of showing your love for God and also of unlocking His blessings, for it's said that the Lord is never outdone in generosity. If you're not tithing, it's something to pray over. If it's too financially difficult right now, or too big a leap to take, consider tithing just one month a year. Then, when you've gained experience in this form of sacrificial giving, you can expand it to two months a year, then three months a year, and so on.

Further Reading

Scripture: Sirach 11:21-22; Psalm 86:1-4; Matthew 6:19-21, 24.

Classics: St. Francis de Sales, *An Introduction to the Devout Life*.

Contemporary Works: Philip Lenahan, *Finances for Today's Catholic Family*.

Father, Creator of all,
sustain me in my need,
and help me to meet my obligations.
Sometimes, Lord, I worry about money;
it's hard to keep up, let alone get ahead.
There are so many needs and so many possibilities;
I feel I'll never be able to meet them all.
Let this be a reminder to me, Lord,
that I cannot succeed on my own;
I need You. Yes, Lord, I'm relying on You,
for I've not been able to succeed on my own.
Help me to be generous to others,
even as I ask You to continue to be generous to me.
Give me what I need,
and help me to be grateful for what I receive.
Even if I must be poor by this world's standards,
may I grow ever richer in Your sight. Amen.

Giving Up

Count it all joy, my brethren, when you meet various trials,
for you know that the testing of your faith produces steadfastness.
And let steadfastness have its full effect, that you may be
perfect and complete, lacking in nothing.

James 1:2-4

A young man visited a hermit with a reputation for great holiness, seeking to learn from him, and this holy desert father taught him many methods of prayer. One day the disciple asked, "What can I do to attain God?" The master responded, "What can you do to make the sun rise?" As the implications of this response sunk in, the disciple became angry and demanded, "Then why are you giving me all these different ways of praying?" With great wisdom and patience, the desert hermit explained, "To make sure you're awake when the sun rises."

We don't earn our salvation, nor do we discover God on our own, but we're called to be awake when He appears in our lives. This means, more than anything else, that we must persevere in our efforts to live out our Faith and to do God's will. It's relatively easy to make one great sacrifice, if we know it will be the last time anything is asked of us; a more difficult challenge for most of us is that of making many smaller sacrifices, day after day, without apparent end. Quite often, however, this is the nature of the cross we bear: continuing to pray and to go to Mass even as most of our family members have stopped doing so; keeping on with our Bible study and other educational efforts even though we're tired or discouraged; maintaining our commitment to doing what's morally right even though few others seem to care; and persevering in our charitable activities and our willingness to do favors, even though we're rarely thanked or acknowledged. It would be so easy to give up, but that's not Christ's way. He calls on us to stay awake and be ready and promises His blessings to those who remain faithful to Him.[58]

Some of the saints are models of perseverance; others struggled to remain faithful to their call. We can't help but admire the example of St. Paul, who gladly paid a heavy price for his efforts to continue serving Christ Jesus, as we see in the Acts of the Apostles and in some of his New Testament letters.

Another magnificent example of dedication and commitment is given to us by St. Athanasius, the great fourth-century bishop whose unyielding opposition to the heresy of Arianism (which denied the divinity of Christ) was essential in preserving the true teaching of the Church. Many bishops, priests, and laypersons wavered, but not Athanasius. He was exiled five times for steadfastly defending Church dogma and was forced to spend seventeen of his forty-six years as bishop away from his diocese of Alexandria.

Missionaries frequently have a difficult time: far from home, they live among people of a different culture and often encounter hostility and suspicion, which sometimes culminates in physical danger and even death. Such was the case of St. Noel Chabanel, one of the martyrs of North America. Some of his fellow French Jesuits seemed to have little trouble coping with the problems involved in preaching the Gospel to the North American Indians, but this was not so for Fr. Noel. He had great difficulty learning the

[58] Mark 13:33.

Huron language, he found some of their customs repulsive, he could not stomach their food, and he experienced intense homesickness and depression. What did he do? The saint made a solemn vow to stay at his post for as long as God chose. Fr. Chabanel fulfilled this promise, remaining with the Hurons until finally he was martyred by them.

One of St. Noel Chabanel's contemporaries, St. Louise de Marillac, didn't face the same dangers as he did, but she had her own obstacles to overcome in her efforts, with St. Vincent de Paul, to establish a religious order for women: the Daughters of Charity. Her health was poor, and circumstances were often against her, but the combination of her persistence and divine grace helped her achieve her goal.

Because they keep their focus on the life to come, the saints are usually able to overcome temporary difficulties that would discourage other people. It's much easier to endure suffering when we know there's a purpose to it. This was the case for Pope St. Martin I, who died in exile after opposing a heresy favored by the emperor. In a letter Martin wrote, "For forty-seven days I have not been given water to wash in. I am frozen through and wasting away with dysentery. The food I get makes me vomit. But God sees all things, and I trust in Him."

Not all the saints had an easy time trusting in God; some of them were known to turn back from their original efforts at ministry — perhaps out of fear or a change of heart, perhaps out of a desire to search for God in a different manner.

Second thoughts affected St. Gregory of Nazianzus, a great theologian whose personal shyness inclined him toward solitude. In the year 380, his eloquent efforts to strengthen the Church in the imperial city of Constantinople led to his being acclaimed as bishop there (a very important and prestigious post); after only a few weeks, however, Gregory resigned, so as to spend the rest of his life in prayer and meditation.

Fear temporarily hindered the mission of St. Augustine of Canterbury. Pope St. Gregory the Great chose him to take some missionaries to England, but on reaching the English Channel, the group was frightened by stories of harsh storms and fierce natives; they waited there while Augustine returned to Rome to ask the Pope whether this missionary journey was truly necessary. Gregory reassured the frightened Augustine and sent him back on his way; as it turned out, he and his companions were well received, and their efforts in England bore much fruit.

Even when we're not journeying far from home or placing our lives at risk, the difficulties involved in serving God can be tiresome and discouraging, and the temptation to give up is never far away — especially when it seems as if our efforts aren't appreciated or respected. At the beginning of the nineteenth century, St. Clement Hofbauer established an orphanage, and he frequently begged in order to support it. He once entered a tavern and asked for alms, but a man playing cards spat in his face. Rather than walking away, Clement calmly said, "That was a gift to me personally; now please let me have something for my poor children." Impressed by the saint's humility and persistence, the man not only apologized and made a small donation, but from then on became one of the priest's regular penitents and a firm supporter of his ministry. As long as we don't give up on persons or circumstances too quickly, divine grace can work miracles; and a willingness to continue on in faith can be a powerful expression of our love for God.

According to St. Augustine, "Our task [as Christians] is to make daily progress toward God. Our pilgrimage on earth is a school in which God is the only teacher, and it demands good students, not ones who play truant." We will graduate with honors from the school of life if we remain faithful to Jesus, not only in our words, but also in our deeds. St. Ignatius of Antioch states, "A tree is shown by its fruits, and in the same way, those who profess to belong to Christ will be seen by what they do. For what is needed is not mere present profession, but perseverance to the end in the power of faith."

If we are to succeed, we must rely totally on God's grace. St. Paul of the Cross tells us that we must also devote ourselves totally to the will of God, whether we find it enjoyable or painful. The more we surrender to God, the more we will be filled with His grace. St. Vincent de Paul assures us, "If today we have had power to overcome one difficulty, tomorrow and the day after we shall be able to surmount others that are much greater and more distressing."

Jesus tells us not to worry about tomorrow, for today's challenges are sufficient in themselves.[59] We're meant to live in a trusting spirit one day at a time, for as St. Augustine says, "Hold out, be steadfast, endure, bear the delay, and you have carried the cross." As we see in the lives of the saints, to persevere in our efforts to follow Jesus isn't always easy, but with God's grace, it's possible, and it's worth the cost.

For Further Reflection

"We must endure and persevere if we are to attain the truth and freedom we have been allowed to hope for. Faith and hope are the very meaning of our being Christians, but if faith and hope are to bear fruit, patience is necessary. . . ." — St. Cyprian

"He who does not acquire the love of God will scarcely persevere in the grace of God, for it is very difficult to renounce sin merely through fear of chastisement." — St. Alphonsus Liguori (In other words, fear is not a good long-term motivation for doing good; only a genuine love for God and our neighbor will help us continue doing what's right even when we'd prefer to give up.)

[59] Matt. 6:34.

"Faith believes, hope prays, and charity begs in order to give to others. Humility of heart forms the prayer, confidence speaks it, and perseverance triumphs over God Himself." — *St. Peter Julian Eymard*

Something You Might Try

♦ St. Augustine says that if we're too happy or comfortable with life, we won't remember that we're on a journey to Heaven; we must be dissatisfied with ourselves — especially with our sinful nature — so that we'll fight against sin and use God's grace to make ourselves better. Therefore, remind yourself from time to time about the imperfections of this life and the joys of the life to come. Make a list of "Things I Look Forward to in Heaven," adding at least one item every day for a week; then review it every now and then. This can motivate you to continue to grow in grace and to persevere when life becomes difficult.

♦ Learn from the example of St. Thérèse of Lisieux. Before she entered the Carmelites, she decided to pray for the conversion of sinners, and specifically for one hardened, unrepentant murderer who was sentenced to death. She offered many prayers and sacrifices for him and had the joy of learning that this criminal, just before his execution, kissed a crucifix with reverence and begged God's forgiveness. Thérèse was ecstatic: her first of many sinners was saved. To make your own goal possible, start with one particular person or objective, and take it from there, one step at a time.

Further Reading

Scripture: Jeremiah 29:13; Luke 8:15; Luke 9:62; James 5:10-11; 2 Peter 1:5-11.

Classics: St. Augustine, *Sermon 169, Commentary on Psalm 59;* St. Teresa of Avila, *Autobiography.*

I pray You,
O most gentle Jesus,
having redeemed me by Baptism
from Original Sin,
so now by Your Precious Blood,
which is offered and received throughout the world,
deliver me from all evils, past, present, and to come.
By Your most cruel death, give me a lively faith,
a firm hope, and perfect charity,
so that I may love You
with all my heart and all my soul and all my strength.
Make me firm and steadfast in good works,
and grant me perseverance in Your service,
so that I may be able to please You always.

St. Clare of Assisi

Gloominess

You have sorrow now, but I will see you again
and your hearts will rejoice,
and no one will take your joy from you.

John 16:22

A famous statement is attributed to St. Teresa of Avila: "From silly devotions and sour-faced saints, good Lord, deliver us!" Not only was this remark very much in character for her, but it also expresses two important ideas about what religion is (or more accurately, *isn't*) supposed to be. Genuine religion shouldn't involve "silly devotions" — that is, pointless rituals that are little more than superstition and do nothing to aid our spiritual growth or bring us closer to God (a point Jesus makes very strongly in Matthew 15:1-20). Nor should religion create only a sense of gloom and dismay.

There are times when we should be solemn and somber — after all, salvation *is* a very serious business — but that doesn't mean that holiness has nothing to do with laughter and the enjoyment of God's gifts. Faith isn't supposed to suck the joy out of life, but is supposed to deepen and enrich it. Heaven will be filled with laughter and delight. There are times on earth when we're honestly not capable of such joyful experiences (after all, persons grieving the loss of a loved one or going through a family crisis have every reason to be sad), but as a general rule, our outlook toward life should be an expression of hope and of our longing for the joys that await us. The saints understood this, and many of them are excellent role models for us as we try to delight in God's love on our journey through this vale of tears.

St. Teresa of Avila was known for her lively and affectionate personality, her sharp (although not unkind) wit, and her ever-present sense of humor. She treasured her friends and once said, "I have no defense against affection; I could be bribed with a sardine." Teresa enjoyed life, food included. Someone once sent her a partridge for her meal, which she ate with relish. A visitor was scandalized that a saint was taking delight in her food and wondered aloud what people would think. "Let them think what they please," Teresa answered. "There is a time for partridge and a time for penance."

Shortly before she entered the Carmelite convent as a young woman, Teresa attended a party, where a young man admired her beautiful feet. "Take a good look, Sir," she told him. "You won't be getting another chance." As she steadily progressed in spiritual growth and holiness, Teresa related to the Lord on increasingly familiar terms. There's an often-told story of how she once fell into a mud puddle and complained about it to God. The Lord is supposed to have spoken aloud to her, saying, "Teresa, this is how I treat my friends." The saint immediately rejoined, "Then it's no wonder You have so few of them."

Other saints were also known for their humor and good spirits, including St. Philip Neri, a sixteenth-century Italian priest who firmly believed that faith and virtue can be combined with humor and a wholesome enjoyment of life. The religious order he established in Rome, the Congregation of the Oratory, united service of God's people with a cheerful, engaging outlook on life, thereby raising the suspicions of those who were used to experiencing religion in a more somber way. Philip enjoyed practical jokes, especially when people began taking his reputation for holiness too seriously (for instance, shaving off half his beard and pretending to be drunk), and it's said the two books he most valued were the New Testament and a volume of riddles and jokes.

St. Francis of Assisi, while not necessarily known for being a humorous man, was nonetheless a very joy-filled person, and his gentleness, love of nature, and positive outlook on life (often in spite of great physical and emotional suffering) have made him attractive to many people of every religion and every era of history.

Joy and humor played an important part in the lives of many of the Church's holiest men and women. Bl. Miguel Pro was a high-spirited and mischievous child, so it's no surprise he enjoyed donning disguises and outwitting the police during his ministry to the persecuted Catholics of Mexico. St. John Bosco was known for his sense of humor, as was St. Thomas More. Thomas's sense of humor remained with him to the very end. As he climbed up to the platform where he was to be beheaded, he asked the executioner for assistance, saying, "I pray you, see me up safe, and for my coming down, let me shift for myself."

It's said that St. John of Vercelli found it impossible to frown, and St. Athanasius, the biographer of the desert Father St. Anthony of Egypt, wrote, "Strangers knew [Anthony] from among his disciples by the joy on his face."

Cheerfulness isn't just an attitude or personality trait; it can be, and quite often should be, part of our response to God's gift of life — even when life isn't easy. According to Bl. Julian of Norwich, "The greatest honor you can give to Almighty God is to live gladly, joyfully because of the knowledge of His love." The fourth-century abbot St. Apollo — who was known for his cheerful expression — insisted that his monks remain joyful when doing penance, for he believed that joy is the fruit of charity and is necessary to maintain our spiritual fervor. The eighteenth-century priest Bl. Sebastian Valfre was always so happy that everyone assumed he hadn't a care in the world — even when he experienced a prolonged and terrible desolation and was constantly tempted by fears that he had lost his faith.

A joyful countenance can help us persevere in challenging times; it can also help us remember that the Gospel is truly *good* news. A charming story is told about Bl. Jordan of Saxony, who succeeded St. Dominic as the second Master General of the Dominican Order in the thirteenth century. Once during night prayer, a novice experienced a giggling fit. It quickly proved contagious, and soon all the novices were giggling. A scandalized brother tried to threaten them into silence, but Jordan rebuked him, saying, "Who made you novice master?" and then told the young men, "Laugh on! You may well laugh, for you have escaped from the Devil, who formerly held you in bondage. Laugh away, dear sons!"

Too often people have the mistaken idea that we must choose between holiness and happiness, but as St. Thomas Aquinas said, "Happiness is the natural life of man." It's said that when young Dominic Savio decided to become a saint, he began by no longer playing games with the other boys and by wearing a solemn expression. St. John Bosco asked him what was wrong, and when the youth explained, John praised his intention, but advised him to remain cheerful and active, for serving God is supposed to make us joyful and spiritually attractive to others. John used to tell everyone, "Enjoy yourself as much as you like, if only you keep from sin."

It's sin, of course, that ultimately robs life of its beauty and joy. St. Francis de Sales claimed that the Devil *likes* to see us sad and melancholy. Satan is going to suffer for all eternity, and in his anger and despair, he wants us to share his misery. Therefore, choosing to be happy can represent a rejection of the Devil and be an act of faith in God.

This raises an important point: just as love is an act of the will, and not primarily a feeling, so, too, to some extent, is joy. We can *choose* to be happy, even if we don't feel happy, for if we follow through on a decision to be optimistic and grateful, and refuse to give into negative thinking, our feelings will begin to change.

We hope and expect, through God's mercy, to spend eternity rejoicing in Heaven, and this belief should fill us with joy here on earth. The young Jesuit St. Aloysius Gonzaga was once playing happily with his companions when someone asked him what he would do if an angel told him he would die and appear before God's throne in fifteen minutes. Aloysius answered that he would continue playing, because, he said, "I am certain that these games are pleasing God." Just as our wholesome enjoyment of life is meant to please God, so is our wholehearted experience of religion meant to please us.

The holy abbot St. Columban once asked the young monk St. Deicolus, "Why are you always smiling?" Deicolus answered, "Because no one can take God from me." The wisdom and truth contained in this remark explain why, for a committed Christian, life is meant to be an experience of joy, not of gloom.

For Further Reflection

"A spiritual joy is the greatest sign of the divine grace dwelling in a soul." — *St. Bonaventure*

"The Holy Spirit, speaking by all the saints, and our blessed Lord Himself, assures us that a devout life is a lovely, a pleasant, and a happy life." — *St. Francis de Sales*

"Joy chases away fatigue, because out of fatigue comes discouragement, [and] there is nothing worse! . . . It could help a person's spirit to remain joyful before God." — *St. Seraphim of Sarov*

Something You Might Try

◆ St. Paul of the Cross advises us, "Keep the balsam jar of your sufferings tightly sealed by silence and acceptance, so that it does not evaporate outside by seeking comforts. This would be harmful. The more abandoned to God by silent suffering you are, the sooner the trial sent by God will end." Therefore, we shouldn't share our problems and complaints freely with others (unless we're seeking advice or unburdening our hearts to one or two trusted companions). Our difficulties will be much less likely to help us grow in holiness if we're always complaining about them. St. Philip Neri insisted, "A cheerful soul becomes holy more quickly."

♦ According to St. Alphonsus Liguori, "Whenever we feel trapped in a bad mood, we should try to dispel it immediately and not linger over it, distracting ourselves by reading a book, by singing a snatch of a hymn, or by discussing some pleasant topic with a friend."

Further Reading

Scripture: Psalm 16:11; Psalm 126:1-2; Romans 15:13; 1 Peter 4:13.

Classics: St. Ignatius of Loyola, *Spiritual Exercises*; St. Francis de Sales, *An Introduction to the Devout Life*; St. Alphonsus Liguori, *The Practice of the Love of Jesus Christ*.

Contemporary works: James A. Magner, *Mental Health in a Mad World*.

⌒

Lord Jesus,
I am not an eagle.
All I have are the eyes
and the heart of one.
In spite of my littleness,
I dare to gaze at the sun of love
and long to fly toward it.

Gloominess

I want to imitate the eagles,
but all I can do is flap my small wings.
What shall I do?
With cheerful confidence I shall stay
gazing at the sun until I die.
Nothing will frighten me,
neither wind nor rain.
O my beloved sun,
I delight in feeling small and helpless
in Your presence;
and my heart is at peace.

St. Thérèse of Lisieux

Gluttony

Healthy sleep depends on moderate eating;
he rises early, and feels fit. The distress of sleeplessness
and of nausea and colic are with the glutton.

Sirach 31:20

Once there was a monastery that had a very strict rule: the monks were never to complain about the food, except out of concern for the well-being of the other brethren. One day a monk named Brother Thomas was shocked to find a mouse in his soup. He couldn't complain about it, so what was he to do? Then an inspiration came to him. He called the monk serving as waiter that day, pointed to the monk on his right, and whispered, "Brother Michael doesn't have a mouse in *his* soup."

We often joke about food, but eating is a serious business. So is overeating, or gluttony — one of the *Seven Deadly Sins*. The Lord provides for our physical needs, but we must not selfishly take advantage of this. When God sent manna to the Israelites in the desert, He instructed them to gather only what they needed each day; those who disobeyed by deliberately collecting more found that the extra portion became wormy and rotten.[60] The experience of

[60] Exod. 16:16-20.

eating is one of life's legitimate pleasures, but we should not overdo it. Not only might our overconsumption endanger our health, but it might deprive other people of the resources they need.

None of the saints can be called gluttons, but several of them were overweight. The great Dominican scholar St. Thomas Aquinas grew very fat over the years — so much so, that a crescent had to be carved out of his work table and dining table so as to make room for his belly. The same thing was true of St. Francis Borgia in the sixteenth century; it was said that, during his years as a member of the Spanish royal court, his belt was big enough to fit around three average-size people. After Francis joined the Jesuits, however, fasting and hard work caused him to lose a considerable amount of weight.

Almost every saint fasted regularly, including St. Francis of Assisi and his friend St. Clare; St. John Vianney, who often subsisted on boiled potatoes; St. Aloysius Gonzaga, who, on entering the Jesuit novitiate, actually had to eat more regularly than he was accustomed to; St. Brendan of Ireland, who lived on a vegetarian diet and never took his first meal of the day until three o'clock in the afternoon; and St. Severinus of Noricum, a monk who made a point of never eating until after sunset. An even greater sacrifice was made by the fourth-century martyr St. Lucian of Antioch. He was imprisoned for being a Christian and given no food for two weeks; then he was provided with meat that had been offered to pagan idols, but he refused to eat, valuing his commitment to Christ far more than food or life itself.

As the saints remind us, eating must take its proper place in our list of priorities. One practical implication of this is having a concern for those less fortunate than we. As a Benedictine monk in the eleventh century, St. Peter Damian had a custom of inviting one or two poor persons to share each of his meals. Many of the saints did the same thing, and the twelfth-century priest St. Gilbert of Sempringham always had on his table what he called "the plate of the Lord Jesus," onto which the best of the food being served was placed and then sent to the poor.

In addition to showing concern for the hungry, a spiritual means of guarding against gluttony is that of placing first things first: fulfilling our duties in a conscientious and timely way. This principle is illustrated by a story from the life of the fifth-century Irish abbess St. Brigid. Visitors were always welcome at her abbey, but sometimes they had to earn their keep. On one occasion, a group of priests arrived to give a retreat to the nuns, but they asked for a meal first, as they were very hungry. Not one to mince words, St. Brigid replied, "We are hungry, too, for the word you bring us. Preach first, and then you shall be fed."

Sometimes the desires of our bodies have to be subordinated to the needs of our souls; according to St. John of the Cross, "If you do not learn to deny yourself, you can make no progress in perfection." St. John Bosco noted, "The best dish at a meal is that of good cheer," and a cheerful disposition is easier to achieve when we have a loving relationship with the Lord. The highest form of satisfaction comes from serving God. Jesus once said to His Apostles, "I have food to eat of which you do not know. . . . My food is to do the will of Him who sent me."[61] May we all be nourished in the same manner.

For Further Reflection

"Irrational feeding darkens the soul and makes it unfit for spiritual experiences. — *St. Thomas Aquinas (By the same token, fasting often has the effect of enlightening the soul and making us more grateful and more spiritually alive.)*

"Take even bread with moderation, lest an overloaded stomach make you weary of prayer." — *St. Bernard of Clairvaux*

[61] John 4:32, 34.

"Abstinence is the mother of health. A few ounces of privation is an excellent remedy for any ailment." — *Bl. Antony Grassi*

Something You Might Try

♦ The twentieth-century physician St. Joseph Moscatti, in response to a nun who complained of her rigid diet, said, "God makes us suffer here in order to reward us in the heavenly kingdom; by resigning ourselves to dietary restrictions, and suffering, we shall have greater merit in the eyes of the Almighty." Remember this each time the quality or quantity of your food isn't to your taste; your sacrifices now can help prepare you for an eternal banquet in Heaven.

♦ Try to achieve a balance in eating. St. Augustine admitted, "I struggle each day against concupiscence in eating and drinking. It is not something that I can resolve to cut off once and for all and touch no more, as I could with concubinage. The bridle put upon the throat must be held with moderate looseness and moderate firmness." That's a challenge many of us face: finding the right balance between eating and drinking too much and too little. It might be helpful to have a set time for meals, with a certain amount of food available, and limit eating between meals (perhaps by making sure that nothing but healthy food is available for such snacks). Above and beyond this, fasting is a valuable means of disciplining the body. Depending on your circumstances and your metabolism, fasting might mean eating only one meal on a given day or eating only three very small and simple meals; it might involve abstaining from meat that day, giving up dessert, or simply not eating between meals. Experiment with this until you discover what works best for you in terms of being both sacrificial and practical.

Further Reading

Scripture: Deuteronomy 8:3; Sirach 31:13, 37:29; Isaiah 55:1-2; Matthew 6:11, 25.

Classics: St. Augustine, *Confessions*.

Contemporary works: James A. Magner, *Mental Health in a Mad World*.

*Lord and Giver of every good gift,
help me truly to appreciate all that You have
granted me, including the food I eat each day.
Let me not become greedy or gluttonous,
nor displease You by overindulging myself.
May the daily bread You give me be a source of energy,
health, and strength, so that I may fulfill my duties and
do my part in working for the coming of Your kingdom.
Give me a generous spirit in responding to the needs of
the poor, and fulfill the hopes of all who trust in You.
Father, You give us the bread we need each day;
may we render unto You the glory and praise
that are Yours for all eternity. Amen.*

Gossip

One who rejoices in wickedness will be condemned, and for one
who hates gossip evil is lessened. Never repeat a conversation, and you
will lose nothing at all. With friend or foe do not report it. . . .
Have you heard a word? Let it die with you.

Sirach 19:5-8, 10

A little girl was once asked what message had been given at Mass
that day, and she responded eagerly, "Father said that we're supposed to go and spread the gossip!" This, unfortunately, seems to
be the idea many of us have — for instead of proclaiming the Gospel, we often find ourselves talking about other people in an uncharitable or judgmental way. Needless to say, this is contrary to
God's will.

One who struggled with this because of his responsibilities
was St. Gregory the Great, who would have preferred to remain in
a monastery, but was elected Pope in 590. In a homily, Gregory
once admitted, "In my position, I must often communicate with
worldly men. At times I let my tongue run, for if I am always severe
in my judgments, the worldly will avoid me, and I can never attack
them as I would. As a result, I often listen patiently to chatter.
And because I am took weak, I find myself drawn little by little
into idle conversation, and I begin to talk freely about matters that

once I would have avoided. What once I found tedious I now enjoy."

Almost seven hundred years later, Bl. Peter of Siena, considering talkativeness to be one of his worst faults, was determined to acquire the habit of silence, but it took him fourteen years to achieve this goal. The fourth-century monk St. Sisoes admitted, "I am now thirty years praying daily that my Lord Jesus may preserve me from saying an idle word, and yet I am always relapsing." Guarding against unnecessary and harmful chatter is a never-ending duty.

Many of us have probably found idle chatter to be a seeming refuge from our own worries and responsibilities. There's something deep within us that thinks, "Well, I have my faults, but at least I'm not as bad as *he* is," or "Thank goodness I don't have *her* problems." But gossip can be damaging, and so we would do well to follow the advice of the Irish abbot St. Columban, who wrote, "The most valuable objects are usually the most fragile; costly things require the most careful handling. Particularly fragile is that which is lost by wanton talk and destroyed with the slightest injury of a brother. Men like nothing better than discussing and minding the business of others, passing superfluous comments at random, and criticizing people behind their backs. So those who cannot say, 'The Lord has given me a discerning tongue, that I may with a word support him who is weary' should keep silent, or if they do say anything, it should promote peace."

Using words to promote peace was something the saints always tried to accomplish, for they knew how much harm unthinking words could cause. As a young monk, for instance, St. Patrick confided to one of his comrades his shame over a sin he had committed, and this monk later revealed the secret to someone else, causing the saint great pain and embarrassment.

Gossip, even when not ill-intentioned, can harm someone's reputation and convince others that the gossiper is unworthy of trust; therefore, we do well to control our tongues. A simple rule to follow is this: when in doubt, don't say it. St. Arsenius once remarked, "I have often been sorry for having spoken, but never for having held my tongue."

Many of us could benefit from making an effort to listen more and to speak less — and in all our conversations, to practice charity. The prayers of the saints can help us, in particular those of the thirteenth-century priest St. Peregrine Laziosi, who spent more than thirty years practicing silence and solitude whenever possible, and the fifteenth-century widow Bl. Helen of Udine, who, after becoming a tertiary of the Hermits of St. Augustine, took a vow of perpetual silence and spoke only on Christmas night each year. We, of course, are in no position to imitate these particular saints, but their prayers, and those of the entire heavenly court, can certainly help us overcome a tendency toward gossip, if we desire to do so.

For Further Reflection

"Never utter in your neighbors' absence what you would not say in their presence." — *St. Mary Magdalene de Pazzi*

"Would we wish that our own hidden sins should be divulged? We ought, then, to be silent regarding those of others." — *St. John Baptist de La Salle*

"St. Ignatius often said, 'Ignatius, conquer yourself. Ignatius, conquer yourself.' What great advice this is! Learn how to be silent, and when you speak, let your words be gentle, loving, and prudent. How it pleases God when we can refrain from careless, sharp, and hurtful words." — *St. Paul of the Cross*

Something You Might Try

♦ According to St. Ignatius of Loyola, there are two instances when it's permissible to talk about someone else's sin: when it's public or commonly known, and can serve as a cautionary example to keep others from sinning; and when a hidden sin is revealed to a third party with the reasonable hope that this person will be able to help the sinner. Whenever you're tempted to talk about someone else's faults, ask yourself whether either of these conditions applies; if not, remain silent. You might also imitate the custom of St. Aloysius Gonzaga; whenever he was about to speak with someone, he silently prepared himself by praying, "Set a guard over my mouth, O Lord, keep watch over the door of my lips!"[62]

◆ Try to prevent gossip. Research has shown that, contrary to popular belief, gossip doesn't start with a negative or unfavorable comment about someone; rather, it begins when that initial comment is seconded or agreed to. If no such acceptance is expressed, the conversation goes in a different direction. Thus, we can help prevent gossip from occurring by declining to follow up on someone's opening remark and instead changing the subject. For instance, when someone says to us, "Did you hear what happened to So-and-so?" respond, "Oh, that's too bad. Have you prayed for him?" or, "I'm very sorry to hear that. What do you think we could do to help her?" It is good for us to form the habit of replacing unhelpful words (gossip) with those that can truly help people (prayer). As St. John Vianney said, "If something uncharitable is said in your presence, either speak in favor of the absent [person], or withdraw, or, if possible, stop the conversation."

Further Reading

Scripture: Ecclesiastes 3:1, 7; Sirach 19:10-11; Matthew 12:34-37; James 3:2-5.

Classics: St. Ignatius of Loyola, *Spiritual Exercise*; St. Francis de Sales, *An Introduction to the Devout Life*.

[62] Ps. 141:3.

Contemporary Works: Rudolf Allers, *Self-Improvement*; James A. Magner, *Mental Health in a Mad World*.

I am well aware,
Almighty God and Father,
that in my life I owe You
a most particular duty.
It is to make my every thought
and word speak of You.
In fact, You have conferred on me
this gift of speech,
and it can yield no greater return
than to be at Your service.

St. Hilary

Greed

Take heed, and beware of all covetousness;
for a man's life does not consist in
the abundance of his possessions.

Luke 12:15

Jesus once said, "It is easier for a camel to go through the eye of a needle than for a rich man to enter the kingdom of God"[63] and advised His followers, "Make friends for yourselves by means of unrighteous mammon, so that when it fails, they may receive you into the eternal habitations."[64] The Gospels — Luke's in particular — emphasize the need for Christians to avoid becoming caught up in the desire for wealth, but to be generous in sharing their goods with others.

Thus, it's not surprising the New Testament praises those early followers of Christ who left everything behind to follow Him, the Apostles in particular. St. Barnabas, in fact, sold his farm and donated the proceeds to the early Church.[65] There were also many women who followed Jesus and helped support Him and His

---

[63] Luke 18:25.
[64] Luke 16:9.
[65] Acts 4:36-37.

followers financially, including St. Mary Magdalene, Joanna, and Susanna.[66]

Quite a few of the saints took seriously our Lord's command, addressed to the rich young man, "Go, sell what you have, and give to the poor, and you will have treasure in Heaven; and come, follow me."[67] These were the words that changed the life of St. Anthony. As a young man of twenty, he had inherited his parents' estate, but on hearing this Gospel passage read aloud in church, he arranged for the care of his younger sister, sold everything else, gave away the proceeds, and went off to the desert to live as a hermit for the next eighty years.

There are famous stories about some of the saints and their generosity. Everyone knows the legend of St. Nicholas, of course; to help a poor man provide dowries for his three daughters, who would otherwise have gone into a life of prostitution to support themselves, the holy bishop of Myra is said to have secretly tossed a bag of gold into the man's house on three occasions.

Also well-known is the story of St. Martin of Tours, who saw a beggar shivering in the snow. Martin cut his military cloak in two and gave half to the freezing man. That night he had a dream in which Christ appeared to him, wearing the partial cloak he had given away, and praised him for his generosity.

Yet another famous story involves the deacon and martyr St. Lawrence, who, during a persecution of the Church in Rome, was ordered to gather the Church's wealth and surrender it to the authorities. Lawrence instead gave everything away, and then presented the poor, the widows, the orphans, and the lame to the Roman prefect, saying, "Here is the Church's treasure."

St. Lawrence saw the truth clearly: people are more important than material things. Many of us, however, struggle to obtain this

[66] Cf. Luke 8:2-3.
[67] Mark 10:21.

perspective; we find ourselves easily influenced by the desire for wealth and the earthly advantages it brings — even to the point of neglecting or undervaluing the people around us. Intellectually we *know* that money will never satisfy our deepest needs, but how do we let this knowledge shape our desires in a spiritually healthy way?

Perhaps an image suggested by St. Bernard of Clairvaux might be helpful. He writes, "Suppose you saw a starving man inhaling great deep breaths, filling his cheeks with wind to stay his hunger; would you not call him mad? And it is just as mad to think that blowing yourself out with earthly goods can satisfy your hunger." We need to remind ourselves, as often as necessary, that it's foolish and useless to devote our lives to something that will only leave us feeling empty and spiritually malnourished. Trying to develop this type of higher perspective can keep us from making many avoidable mistakes. As St. Alphonsus Liguori noted, "Those who desire nothing from this world are masters of the whole world." Moreover, St. Gregory the Great advises us, "Be not anxious about what you have, but about what you are." A greedy spirit is spiritually deadening, whereas a generous spirit allows us to be filled with God's grace.

Not all the saints understood this truth at first; some of them, instead of being naturally generous, had to overcome a problem with greed. Indeed, several used illegal or immoral means to obtain money before becoming true followers of Christ. St. Moses of Ethiopia, who was born into slavery in the fourth century and worked in the home of an Egyptian official, was disciplined because of his vicious nature and a habit of stealing. Moses thereupon escaped and became the leader of a band of robbers who terrorized the area, but after taking refuge from the authorities among some hermits in the Egyptian desert, he was converted. Having discovered the spiritual nature of true wealth, he became a monk and later was martyred as a bishop.

Another criminal who became a saint was Peter Armengol in thirteenth-century Spain. Because of a difficult home life, he ran away and joined a group of bandits; however, when his companions were about to rob a group of travelers, Peter recognized his own father among them and begged his forgiveness. Peter entered the Order of Mercedarians, who sought to redeem Christian captives from the Moslems. On one occasion, he gave himself as a hostage to free eighteen young boys, and although he survived torture and an attempted hanging, he later died as a result of these injuries.

Still another thief-turned-saint was Joan Delanoue, although in her greed she attempted to acquire money somewhat more legally. Late in the seventeenth century, Joan inherited her parents' religious-goods store, and, being preoccupied with making money, she overcharged customers and even kept her store open on Sundays. After her conversion, however, Joan became more concerned with spending money on the poor than with acquiring it for itself, thus replacing her earlier miserliness with great generosity.[68]

The classic story of a repentant thief, of course, is that of St. Dismas, the "Good Thief" who was crucified for stealing worldly goods and who obtained heavenly wealth simply by asking.[69] May we in the same manner conquer our greed so as to become truly rich.

For Further Reflection

"Whatever you possess must not possess you; whatever you own must be under the power of your soul; for if your soul is overpowered by the love of this world's goods, it will be totally at the mercy of its possessions. In other words, we make use of

[68] See also the chapter on business failures.
[69] Cf. Luke 23:39-43.

temporal things, but our hearts are set on what is eternal. Temporal goods help us on our way, but our desire must be for those eternal realities which are our goal." — *St. Gregory the Great*

"There is a vast difference between having poison and being poisoned. Doctors have all kinds of poisons for their use, but they are not poisoned. In like manner, you may possess riches without being poisoned by them. . . ." — *St. Francis de Sales*

"Earthly riches are like the reed. Its roots are sunk in the swamp, and its exterior is fair to behold; but inside it is hollow. If a man leans on such a reed, it will snap off and pierce his soul, and his soul will be carried off to Hell." — *St. Anthony of Padua*

Something You Might Try

♦ Remember that nothing you have or possess is truly yours, but is given by God to benefit you and others. In her autobiography, St. Thérèse of Lisieux wrote about feeling offended when someone to whom she had made an insightful comment repeated it to others without giving her the credit; after all, she said, "There are certain movements of the mind and heart, deep-reaching thoughts, that go to form a treasury of your very own; nobody else, you feel, has a right to tamper with it." However, on further reflection, Thérèse realized, "An idea occurs to me, and I say something which is well received by the other sisters — why shouldn't they adopt it as their own? I find it quite natural. You see, this idea doesn't belong to me; it belongs to the Holy Spirit. . . . To suppose that this 'thought' belongs to me would be to make the same mistake as the donkey carrying the relics, which imagined that all the reverence shown to the saints was meant for its own benefit!"

♦ A good way to counteract greed is to practice some form of generosity, and we all have opportunities to do so. According to

St. Leo the Great, "There is no more profitable practice as a companion to holy and spiritual fasting than that of almsgiving. This embraces under the single name of mercy many excellent works of devotion, so that the good intentions of all the faithful may be of equal value, even where their means are not. . . . The works of mercy are innumerable. Their very variety brings this advantage to those who are true Christians, that in the matter of almsgiving, not only the rich and affluent but also those of average means and the poor are able to play their part. Those who are unequal in their capacity to give can be equal in the love within their hearts."

Further Reading

Scripture: Proverbs 19:22; 1 Timothy 6:9-10; Hebrews 13:5.

Classics: St. Thérèse of Lisieux, *The Story of a Soul*; St. Francis de Sales, *An Introduction to the Devout Life*; St. Alphonsus Liguori, *The Practice of the Love of Jesus Christ*.

Contemporary works: James A. Magner, *Mental Health in a Mad World*.

Lord, teach me to be generous.
Teach me to serve You as You deserve;
to give and not to count the cost;
to fight and not to heed the wounds;
to toil and not to seek for rest;
to labor and not to ask for reward,
save that of knowing that I do Your will.

St. Ignatius of Loyola

Grief

For the Lamb in the midst of the throne will be their Shepherd,
and He will guide them to springs of living water;
and God will wipe away every tear from their eyes.

Revelation 7:17

If you're grieving the loss of a loved one and you know that no one can take that person's place, there are few words that can truly console you. Nevertheless, through God's grace, the support of those who love you, and the passage of time, you will get through this period of sorrow. Happiness will someday return to your life; in the meantime, it may be of some consolation to know that many of the saints grieved like you. These saints, who knew God's love in a wondrous way and who believed in eternal life with all their hearts, nevertheless had to struggle with their own human feelings of grief.

Consider our Lady. Mary suffered widowhood; we don't know exactly when St. Joseph died, but, because of the perfect love they shared and because she knew the gates of Heaven weren't yet open, it must have been a heart-wrenching experience for her. Some time after this, her Son left home to begin His public ministry.

An early event in Christ's public life shows Mary's perfect acceptance of God's plan. At the wedding feast of Cana, Mary noticed that the wine was almost gone and brought this to the attention of Jesus, implying that He could solve this problem. Our Lord responded, "O woman, what have you to do with me? My hour has not yet come."[70] The unspoken message was "Mother, if I perform this first miracle, our privacy and our time together is over. Word will spread, and I will no longer belong entirely to you, but to the world. Is this what you want? Are you ready to make this sacrifice?" Mary understood what her Son was saying and gave her response to the servants: "Do whatever He tells you."[71] She indicated her willingness to make this sacrifice — a sacrifice that ended, as she knew it would, with the Cross. In the words of the thirteenth-century hymn *Stabat Mater*, "Through her heart, His sorrow sharing, all His bitter anguish bearing, now the sword at length had passed" — the sword of sorrow, which, thirty-three years earlier, Simeon had foretold would pierce our Lady's heart.[72]

Although no grief could compare with Mary's, many other saints drank deeply from the cup of sorrow. For instance, the first American-born saint, Elizabeth Ann Seton, was very happily married for eleven years, but then her husband's business failed, and he contracted tuberculosis and soon died; moreover, because Elizabeth converted to Catholicism (she had been raised an Episcopalian), her family and many of her friends rejected her. The saint was able to persevere by relying on the Lord's strength and by trusting in Scripture's promise: "God is faithful, and He will not let you be tempted beyond your strength."[73]

Another saint who experienced intense grief as a young widow of twenty was St. Elizabeth of Hungary, a princess whose husband

---

[70] John 2:4.

[71] John 2:5.

[72] Luke 2:35.

[73] 1 Cor. 10:13.

died while taking part in a Crusade; it's said that on being informed of her husband's death, the saint cried, "The world is dead to me, and all that was pleasant in it," and then ran through the castle shrieking hysterically. Like her American counterpart, Elizabeth Ann Seton, the Hungarian princess found no support from her relatives; her husband's family resented her spending money on the poor, and — according to legend — her brother-in-law forced her and her children to leave the castle in the dead of winter. She, too, found the strength to bear her cross in the love of Christ, although it was very difficult at first.

Terrible grief was also the experience of St. Paula in the fourth century, widowed with five children at age thirty-two. In fact, it's recorded that her grief was almost excessive; she started to come out of it only when St. Marcella — herself a widow — finally convinced her that the Lord was calling her to spend the remainder of her life serving Him. Both Paula and Marcella became important friends and supporters of the great scholar St. Jerome, who later on helped Paula cope with the sudden death of her oldest daughter, St. Blesilla. Jerome wrote a letter to console her, but he also gently reproved Paula for mourning excessively over one whose death was actually an entry into heavenly life.

Other saints who suffered intense sorrow include St. Frances of Rome, who lost her husband after forty years of married life (during which it's said they never quarreled); St. Margaret of Scotland, who was on her own deathbed when both her royal husband and oldest son were both treacherously killed by enemies, thereupon hastening her own death; St. Paulinus of Nola, who, with his wife, grieved over the death of their infant son (who had been the answer to their prayers after many childless years of marriage) and then responded to this tragedy by dedicating their lives to God; St. Stephen of Hungary, whose son St. Emeric — whom Stephen had carefully prepared to succeed him as king — was killed in a hunting accident; St. Gerlac of Valkenburg, who renounced the world and lived as a hermit after the tragic death of his young wife; St. Opportuna, who died of grief soon after the murder of her brother, a bishop; St. Bridget, whose own death was hastened by grief over her son, who died after a dissolute life; St. Jane Frances de Chantal, who lost several of her children, her husband, and her great friend St. Francis de Sales; and St. Clotilda, wife of the Frankish king Clovis, whose mourning over the death of her husband was intensified when her three sons fought over their royal inheritance — a conflict so intense that one of them murdered two of Clotilda's grandchildren.

Sometimes the death of a loved one — painful as it is — marks the beginning of a new stage of life in which our vocation is significantly changed. For example, in the sixth century, St. Hormisdas was happily married, but after the death of his wife, he became a priest and was elected Pope in 514. (His son St. Silverius later became Pope himself.)

Grief can also be an impetus to a change of heart or a moral conversion. St. Bavo had been a wealthy but immoral landowner in the seventh century, but after his wife's death, he repented of his sins and spent his life doing penance. (He once encountered a man whom he had sold into slavery years before; in reparation, Bavo had the man lead him in chains to the town prison.)

Coping with grief often requires us to look for new ways to be of service to God and neighbor. In the sixth century, St. Monegundis experienced overwhelming grief when her two daughters died. Because the grief was prolonged, the saint — in a moment of insight — feared she was becoming self-centered and in danger of neglecting her duties to God. Prayer suggested a remedy: with her husband's permission, she devoted herself entirely to the Lord by shutting herself up in a simple cell and there living a life of penance and solitude.

Bl. Teresa Grillo Michel used a different approach in the twentieth century. She married at age twenty-two, but fourteen years later, her husband died of sunstroke. Teresa went through a long period of profound grief; spiritual reading and the love and support of her family helped her recover. She began reaching out to others in need and eventually established a new religious order in Italy: the Congregation of the Little Sisters of Divine Providence.

The saints discovered a certain solace through service — that is, in responding to the needs of others, they found it easier to bear their own sorrows. It's unwise (and often impossible) to begin something like this too soon after the death of a loved one, particularly a spouse; grief must be acknowledged, and this takes time (for many people, a year or more). It's also unwise for people to make major decisions while mourning. After they have worked through their grief, however, it's often helpful for them to become involved in some form of service. This pleases God and allows Him to bless and sustain them in additional ways.

A healthy response to grief requires a willingness to trust in God and to move forward, one day at a time. Because God is the author of life, He not only is able to reunite us with our deceased loved ones in the joy of His kingdom, but also to help us find purpose and value in life — even in the midst of intense grief.

Death can cause great pain and sorrow, not necessarily for the one dying, but for the loved ones left behind. Nevertheless, our Christian Faith teaches us that our grief and separation from the ones we love need only be temporary. This was the theme of a letter written by St. Aloysius Gonzaga to his mother shortly before he died from the plague at the age of twenty-three: "Our parting will not be for long; we shall see each other again in Heaven; we shall be united with our Savior; there we shall praise Him with heart and soul, sing of His mercies forever, and enjoy eternal happiness. When He takes away what He once lent us, His purpose is to store our treasure elsewhere more safely and bestow on us those very blessings that we ourselves would most choose to have."

This is indeed part of the Good News: death and sorrow do indeed exist, but for those who have faith in Jesus, they shall be replaced by everlasting life and joy.

For Further Reflection

"Let your understanding strengthen your patience. In serenity look forward to the joy that follows sadness." — *St. Peter Damian*

"Upon the death of family members, instead of wasting time in pointless tears, let us use it to pray for their souls and offer up to Jesus Christ the pain we feel at having lost them." — *St. Alphonsus Liguori*

[To a woman whose son had died]: "When you commend your child to the Divine Majesty, simply say to Him, 'Lord, I commend to You the offspring of my womb, yes, but even more truly the child sprung from the depths of Your mercy; born of my blood, true, but reborn from Yours.' And leave it at that." — *St. Francis de Sales*

Something You Might Try

♦ Bl. Arnould Jules Reche was once asked, "How can we reduce our sorrows?" He responded, "Well, above all, don't think too much about them. Forget those from yesterday: they no longer exist. Don't think of tomorrow's: God will take care of them. Today's sorrows are enough!" It's sometimes hard to maintain this attitude, but it's worth the effort. If we never let go of past grief, it can become overwhelming. If necessary, we should ask the Lord to set us free from past sorrows and trust that He will help us bear our present burdens.

♦ Don't try to bear all your grief alone; accept offers of help from loved ones and, when you're ready, invitations from friends and acquaintances. Don't be afraid to seek help when sorrow and loneliness become too much to bear. God wants and expects us to be present to one another at such times. Almost every community has some sort of support group for the grieving; your parish (or local funeral home) can provide you with such information, along with helpful pamphlets and other materials on grieving. To grieve is necessary; to bear such a burden alone when help is available usually isn't healthy or wise.

◆ The Virgin Mary became a widow when St. Joseph died, so she has a special concern for those who lose their spouses. Many widows and widowers have found consolation and strength by asking for her intercession and seeking her motherly care. In addition to having Masses celebrated at your parish for your spouse, ask which devotions to our Lady your parish offers, and do your best to participate in them.

◆ Learn to thank God even in your grief. On her deathbed, St. Bartholomea Capitanio, although only in her twenties, consoled her mother by saying, "You know that everyone has to die. If I were to live forty more years, I would still have to die. This is the moment when God in His mercy wills to receive me into Paradise. Do not be saddened by my death, but instead thank God!" It's possible to thank God as you grieve, and your prayers for your deceased loved ones can be a source of consolation. If it helps, talk to your deceased loved ones (something many people do in cemeteries), or write them a letter, or imagine them perfectly glorious and happy in God's presence. Finally, remember this: your separation is temporary, but, through Christ, the love that you shared will last forever.

Further Reading

Scripture: Psalm 126:5-6; Lamentations 3:17-25; John 16:20; Deuteronomy 24:17, 19; Sirach 35:14; Zechariah 7:10; Mark 12:41-44.

Saintly Solutions

Classics: St. Augustine, *Confessions*; St. Francis de Sales, *An Introduction to the Devout Life*.

Contemporary Works: Medard Laz, *Coping When Your Spouse Dies*; Cathleen Curry, *When Your Spouse Dies*; Msgr. Thomas Hartman, *The Matter of Life and Death: Surviving Loss and Finding Hope*; Helen Reichert Lambin, *The Death of a Husband*; Robert L. Vogt, *The Death of a Wife*; Elaine Stilwell, *Stepping Stones for the Bereaved*; Elsie Hainz McGrath, *Prayers in the Cemetery*; Beverly S. Gordon, *Toward Peace: Prayers for the Widowed*.

⁓

Lord Jesus Christ, You suffered the loss
of Your beloved foster-father, St. Joseph;
You wept at the death of Your friend Lazarus; and
from Your Cross You beheld the grief of Your Mother, Mary.
Look upon me in my grief, and touch my wounded heart.
Welcome all my deceased loved ones into Your kingdom,
and help me to surrender them to Your merciful love.
Grant me peace in the midst of distress, courage in the
midst of loss, and hope in the midst of sorrow. Fill me with
the strength I need just to make it through another day.
Help me to remember that You will never abandon me,
that You will never forget me, and that You will see me
through this time of suffering and trial.
I offer You my tears, and I give You my
wounded heart; receive them gently. Amen.

Guilt

I said, "I will confess my transgressions to the Lord";
then Thou didst forgive the guilt of my sin.

Psalm 32:5

No matter how terrible the worst of your sins, no matter how much you regret your actions, no matter how sorry you are over what you've done, it's highly unlikely that your sense of guilt can begin to compare with that of the medieval saint known to us as St. Julian the Hospitable.

According to legend, Julian was a young nobleman who left home in search of his fortune. In reward for his faithful and courageous service to a royal prince, he was given in marriage a wealthy young widow and allowed to take possession of her lands and castle. One night Julian returned home and, in the darkness, saw the forms of two people in his bed. Thinking the worst — that he had caught his wife in an act of infidelity — he drew his sword and killed them both. Then, to his absolute horror, Julian discovered he had actually slain his own mother and father. They had come in search of their long-lost son, and Julian's wife had allowed them to rest in her husband's bed until he returned.

Julian fell into despair over what he had done, and he solemnly vowed never to rest until he was certain God had forgiven his terrible and impetuous act. Julian and his wife thereupon left their home and journeyed to the bank of a great river, where they built a refuge for the poor and for travelers. From then on, they cared for the sick, the needy, and the homeless, offering shelter to all who passed by. After many years, the holy couple one day tended to a leper, who, before going on his way, turned to the saint and said, "Julian, our Lord has sent me to you to send you word that He has accepted your penance." Soon afterward, St. Julian and his wife both died in a state of great grace and peace.

God forgives our sins and frees us from our guilt. When we deliberately and knowingly perform terrible deeds, or even merely act rashly, as did St. Julian, our consciences torment us. This is as it should be, for it is guilt over our sins that prompts us to seek reconciliation with God.

We might say that guilt performs the same service for our spirits that pain performs for our bodies. Physical pain causes us to cease doing something that could cause us lasting harm, such as compelling us to removing our hand from a hot burner on a stove, instead of keeping it there. Pain also warns us of a dangerous health condition, as chest pains indicate the onset of a heart attack, allowing us to seek immediate medical treatment. Pain is often the body's way of shouting that things are not as they should be and of compelling us to take care of the situation. The same role is played by guilt in regard to our souls. A guilty conscience warns us that we've done something morally wrong — something that is harming us or preventing our personal and spiritual growth — and, unless we ignore or suppress it, it prompts us to admit our fault and to ask God's forgiveness. This is an example of healthy guilt — that is, the guilt we need to have, working in the manner it's supposed to.

There's also such a thing as unhealthy guilt, in which our conscience convicts us of sin (real or imagined), but doesn't lead us to seek reconciliation with God or, if we honestly asked for God's forgiveness, doesn't allow us to believe that we're truly forgiven.

Once guilt has caused us, humbly and sincerely, to seek God's forgiveness, *it has served its purpose and is no longer needed or appropriate*. Just as we rightly take steps to free ourselves from physical pain once we've received and acted on our body's message to us, so we should be able to be free of spiritual pain (guilt) once we've responded to it as God desires. For Catholics, this response can include receiving the sacrament of Reconciliation, in addition to asking the Lord's forgiveness in our private prayers.

Scrupulosity is a type of unhealthy guilt — an ongoing and irrational fear that, in spite of careful attempts to follow the moral law and the teachings of the Church, we haven't truly been able to satisfy God or to receive complete forgiveness of our sins.

Some saints suffered from scrupulosity, beset by severe doubts about God's mercy or their own faithfulness in answering His call, or both. The twelfth-century orphan St. Drogo, for example, learned at age ten that his mother had died giving birth to him. The boy was seized with guilt and imagined himself to be a murderer. Although this belief was completely irrational, Drogo often wept in remorse and begged both God and his deceased mother for forgiveness. Only gradually did he learn to trust in God's mercy.

One of the Church's greatest moral theologians, St. Alphonsus Liguori, continually emphasized the need to trust in God's mercy. Accordingly, he strongly believed that sinners should be treated with patience and moderation, rather than being threatened or condemned. (This pastoral approach is, of course, particularly valuable when dealing with the scrupulous, for they already believe in Divine Justice; it's a practical, experiential belief in Divine Mercy that's often lacking.) Ironically, St. Alphonsus himself experienced a severe attack of scrupulosity during the last eighteen months of his life, but with the help of God's grace, he was able to die peacefully.

A deathbed struggle with scruples sometimes represents Satan's final assault against one whose life has been spent in the service of

God. In 806, just before his death, St. Tarasius, the Patriarch of Constantinople, is said to have fallen into a trance in which he was apparently defending himself against unseen accusers. The experience was causing him great agitation, until at last a profound peace overcame him, allowing him to die with a beautiful sense of serenity and joy.

Bl. Sebastian Valfre suffered from terrible spiritual desolation and was tempted to believe that God had forsaken him. He even feared that he had lost his faith and was destined for Hell. Nevertheless, he remained outwardly cheerful, and he, too, was eventually given the grace of a happy death.

Cheerfulness is a wise response to an attack of scruples, for it not only helps us keep things in a healthier perspective, but can also represent — in the face of our fears and worries — an act of trust in God. St. Philip Neri, a priest known for his joyful spirit, used to tell his excessively worried penitents, "Leave something for the angels." This good advice, from which we, too, can benefit, means that we may assign some of our worries, fears, and problems to our guardian angels; we don't have to control or take responsibility for everything. St. Paul of the Cross advises, "Do not seek to become perfect by your own strength. When you are humble enough, God will give you all."

Humility is essential when you're struggling with scrupulosity, for as St. Alphonsus Liguori warns us, a disturbed conscience interferes with sound judgment, and in our pride we can easily be led astray by our own mistaken beliefs regarding what God wants of us. Instead, Alphonsus says, "There is only one course of action: go ahead in blind obedience."

The saints were not, as a rule, plagued by unhealthy guilt or scrupulosity; they understood that, although we are sinners, Christ came to save sinners. Many of them, however, developed such a horror of sin that they performed acts of penance on behalf of themselves and others, or considered themselves profoundly unworthy of religious actions and honors that other people take for granted. St. Francis of Assisi, for instance, chose to remain a religious brother; he would not consent to be ordained a priest, for — even as one of the holiest persons in history — he considered himself terribly unworthy of such an honor.

In the fourth century, a converted prostitute named St. Thais withdrew to the desert to spend her life doing penance; even though she knew she had been completely forgiven by God, she never dared pronounce His name, thinking that her lips and tongue were unworthy to do so. Instead, she frequently prayed, "O Thou, who has created me, have mercy on me!"

Satan, of course, wants to make us feel profoundly unworthy of God — so unworthy that, unlike St. Thais and every other saint, we never dare to approach Him and ask for forgiveness. There's a legend that St. Antoninus, the holy Bishop of Florence, once saw the Devil hovering over a man whose confession he was about to hear. Antoninus demanded, "What are you doing there?" to which the evil spirit surprisingly answered, "I'm making restitution." When Antoninus expressed disbelief that the Devil could in any way make restitution, the demon insisted, "Yes, when I wanted to lead this man into sin, I took his shame away from him; now that it is a question of Confession, I'm restoring it to him!"

Shame and pride are merely two sides of the same coin. Jesus calls us to put aside our pride and, in all honesty and humility, return to Him. The saints have always been able to do this, and this must also be our goal. As St. John Vianney noted, "God makes greater speed to pardon a penitent sinner than a mother to snatch her child out of the fire." A similarly reassuring message is given to us by St. Thérèse of Lisieux: "If my conscience were burdened with all the sins it is possible to commit, I would still go and throw myself into our Lord's arms, my heart all broken up with contrition. I know what tenderness He has for any prodigal child of His who comes back to Him."

Growing in holiness and being spiritually ready for divine judgment require us not only to admit our sins, but — even more important — to trust in God's willingness to forgive us. St. John Chrysostom warns us, "To grieve to excess over the failings for which we must render an account is neither safe nor necessary. It is more likely to be damaging or even destructive." Rather than wallowing in our guilt, we must turn to the Lord in confidence. According to St. Francis de Sales, "The past must be abandoned to God's mercy, the present to our fidelity, the future to Divine Providence."

The thirteenth-century friar St. Nicholas of Tolentino demonstrated such trust, for on his deathbed he echoed the words of St. Paul: "I have nothing on my conscience, but that does not mean I stand acquitted."[74] God alone is our judge, but if our well-formed consciences do not accuse us, and if we've honestly tried to love God and our neighbor, we need not approach the Lord with guilt and fear. Our Father loves us and invites that same response on our part. As Scripture tells us, "Perfect love casts out fear."[75]

For Further Reflection

"The contrition called 'imperfect' (or 'attrition') is also a gift of God, a prompting of the Holy Spirit. It is born of the consideration of sin's ugliness or the fear of eternal damnation and the other penalties threatening the sinner (contrition of fear). Such a stirring of conscience can initiate an interior process which, under the prompting of grace, will be brought to completion by sacramental absolution. By itself, however, imperfect contrition cannot obtain the forgiveness of grave sins, but it disposes one to obtain forgiveness in the sacrament of Penance." — *Catechism of the Catholic Church*, par. 1453

[74] Cf. 1 Cor. 4:4.
[75] 1 John 4:18.

"Do not continue to dwell on your past sins. If the thoughts come, humble yourself gently before God, strike your breast, and put away these thoughts as temptations. The disturbances that arise, the fears at the moment of death, the doubts you have are all from the Devil. Be of good heart. God has forgiven you." — *St. Paul of the Cross*

"If you offend or hurt Christ by sinning grievously, as soon as you offer Him a flower of regret or a rose of sincere confession, He immediately forgives your offenses, forgives you your sins, and hurries to embrace and kiss you." — *St. Anthony of Padua*

"It is morally impossible that a will whose good intentions have been tried and tested for a long time should all of a sudden change and consent to a mortal sin without clearly realizing it. Mortal sin is so hideous a monster that it could not enter a soul that has long abhorred it, without the soul's full awareness." — *St. Alphonsus Liguori (Therefore, if you're not sure whether you've committed a serious or mortal sin, be assured that you haven't.)*

Something You Might Try

♦ Learn from St. Ignatius of Loyola an effective way to deal with guilt. In his "Method of Making the General Examination of Conscience," he suggests these specific steps:

- Give thanks to God for favors received.
- Ask for grace to know your sins and to rid yourself of them.
- Demand an account of your soul from the time you awoke. Go over one hour after another, one period after another. Examine your thoughts first, then your words, and finally, your deeds.
- Ask pardon of God for your faults.
- Resolve to amend with the grace of God.
- Close with an Our Father.

◆ St. Philip Benizi was once physically attacked by a mob led by an angry young man, but that same evening the remorseful youth came and begged his forgiveness. In response to the young man's request for guidance, St. Philip told him, "Return home and rid yourself of your addictions and selfishness. Practice honesty and purity and humility. Listen to the voice of your conscience, and do what God will lead you to. It won't be easy, but pray. The Lord is with you." After we've confessed our sins, our sincere efforts to follow this advice will help us overcome any lingering feelings of guilt. After all, this worked for St. Philip's attacker: he's now known as St. Peregrine Laziosi.

◆ St. Teresa of Avila reminds you that the Devil will try to upset you by suggesting a thousand false fears or by accusing you of being unworthy of the blessings that you've received. He wants to distract you and even trick you into ignoring or discarding the graces that God has given you. St. Teresa advises you simply to remain cheerful and do your best to ignore the Devil's nagging. If need be, even laugh at the absurdity of the situation: Satan, the epitome of sin itself, accuses *you* of unworthiness! Furthermore, as the saying goes, "When the Devil reminds you of your past, remind him of his future!"

Further Reading

Scripture: Proverbs 28:1; Psalm 51:1-9; Isaiah 1:18; Psalm 34:6; Romans 5:8-9; Romans 8:31-33; Tobit 13:6; Wisdom 12:18-19; Nehemiah 9:17; Psalm 130:3-4; John 3:17; Romans 12:1-2.

Classics: St. Bonaventure, *Mirror of the Blessed Virgin Mary and the Psalter of Our Lady*; St. Catherine of Siena, *Dialogue*; St. Francis de Sales, *An Introduction to the Devout Life*; St. Ignatius of Loyola, *Spiritual Exercises*; St. Teresa of Avila, *The Way of Perfection*; St. Alphonsus Liguori, *The Practice of the Love of Jesus Christ*.

Contemporary Works: Eamon Tobin, *How to Forgive Yourself and Others*; Jack Wintz, *Guilt — A Tool for Christian Growth*; James A. Magner, *Mental Health in a Mad World*; Russell Abata, *Why Am I Scrupulous?*

O Lord,
the house of my soul is narrow;
enlarge it, that You may enter in.
It is ruinous, O repair it!
It displeases Your sight;
I confess it, I know.
But who shall cleanse it,
to whom shall I cry but to You?
Cleanse me from my secret faults, O Lord,
and spare Your servant from strange sins. Amen.

St. Augustine

Illness

When the sun was setting, all those who had any that
were sick with various diseases brought them to Him;
and He laid His hands on every one of them and healed them.

Luke 4:40

Ministering to the sick and the suffering is an important part of
the Church's worldwide ministry. Many saints demonstrated true
Christian love by caring for the sick; these saints include Bl. Andre Bessette, the Canadian religious brother whose prayers and
visits to the ill were reputed to work miracles; St. John of God,
who, after his conversion from a sinful lifestyle, established a hospital and is now considered the patron saint of nurses and of the
sick; St. Luke, referred to in Scripture as the "beloved physician";[76]
St. Charles Borromeo, who, as Archbishop of Milan, personally
tended to the ill and dying during a plague; St. Frances Cabrini,
who founded sixty-seven institutions in the United States to care
for the poor, the sick, and the uneducated; and the eleventh-
century abbot St. Dominic of Silos, with whom many miracles are
associated and of whom it was said that there were no diseases
known to man not cured by his prayers.

[76] Col. 4:14.

Illness is a part of life. This realization came to St. Katherine Drexel, a wealthy American who, as a result of nursing her stepmother through a long illness, saw that riches and status do not exempt anyone from suffering and death. Coping with sickness and physical ailments is a way in which we can follow Christ's command to take up our cross each day.[77]

Sometimes illness can be a sign from God. The Italian monk St. Romuald had a very important mission: to help reform monastic life in the eleventh century. But he greatly desired to be a martyr, and after many years, obtained the Pope's permission to go as a missionary to Hungary. When he set out, though, he became seriously ill — only to recover when he halted his journey. This happened several times, so he finally accepted this as a sign from God that he was to remain in Italy and continue as he had been doing.

Some people require even stronger messages. The nineteenth-century priest St. Gabriel Possenti lived a carefree life as a youth, until he contracted a serious illness; he promised to enter religious life if he recovered. He did recover, but did nothing to follow up on his promise. A year later he was again at death's door and renewed his promise; this time, after recovering, he kept his word by entering the Passionists.

Illness helped the great scholar St. Bonaventure discover his vocation. As a youth, he was cured of a serious illness through the prayers of St. Francis of Assisi and afterward decided to join the Franciscan Order.

Many of the saints knew first-hand what it was to suffer, and so they are very sympathetic in interceding for us and obtaining help for us in bearing our physical burdens. St. John Baptist de La Salle had asthma and rheumatism. St. Leopold Mandic suffered terrible arthritis. St. Peregrine Laziosi had cancer of the foot, but, after praying all night before his foot was to be amputated, was found to

---

[77] Matt. 16:24.

be miraculously cured. St. Thérèse of Lisieux was afflicted with tuberculosis. St. Ignatius of Loyola's leg was broken by a cannon-ball, set improperly, and then had to be rebroken; after undergoing several operations, he was stretched on a rack as part of his physi-cal therapy and also suffered a gangrenous infection. St. Francis of Assisi was half-blind and seriously ill for the last two years of his life. St. Seraphina was unable to move after suffering paralysis as a girl and after her mother died, had no one to care for her because of the repulsive sores covering her body. St. Theophanes suffered from a kidney stone. Bl. Junipero Serra suffered a life-threatening illness after his leg was infected by an insect bite. St. Gaspar Bertoni endured *three hundred* operations on his infected right leg and called his hospital bed "the school of God." St. Camillus de Lellis, known for caring for the sick, endured a disease in his leg for forty-six years, a ruptured muscle for thirty-eight years, frequent sores on his feet, and a distaste for food and an inability to retain it.

As a rule, the saints bore their sufferings with patience and an awareness of God's care for them; several of them prayed for, and sometimes received, miraculous cures. Often, however, they had the experience of St. Paul, who wrote, "To keep me from being too elated by the abundance of revelations, a thorn was given me in the flesh, a messenger of Satan, to harass me, to keep me from be-ing too elated. Three times I besought the Lord about this, that it should leave me; but He said to me, 'My grace is sufficient for you, for my power is made perfect in weakness.' "[78] God knows better than we do whether we can give Him greater service when we're well or when we're ill. According to St. Augustine, it's good to pray for health, but if this prayer isn't granted, we must firmly be-lieve that our illness or affliction will somehow benefit us in the long run. As St. John Vianney stated, "At the hour of death, you will see that you have saved more souls by your illness than by all

[78] 2 Cor. 12:7-9.

the good works you might have accomplished in health." It may also be helpful to look upon illness as a mark of favor; as St. Thérèse of Lisieux stated, "The greatest honor God can do a soul is not to give it much, but to ask much of it."

As Christians, we want to serve God, but many times we wish to do so on *our* terms, not on His. Such a desire can actually become a form of stubbornness or pride. St. Francis de Sales notes that for an ill person to desire to minister, serve others, and perform the duties of someone healthy is not only a fruitless wish; it may also cause the person to ignore what God is actually asking — namely, that he or she be obedient, patient, and resigned to His will. In other words, we can either "waste" our illness by rebelling against it, or we can use it to grow spiritually by surrendering ourselves into the Lord's hands. According to St. Vincent de Paul, "We must remember that all incapacity and distress is sent to us by God. Life and death, health and sickness, are all ordered by Him; and in whatever form they come, it is always to help us and for our good." This holy French priest also says, "If we could but know what a precious treasure lies concealed in infirmities, we would receive them with as much joy as we would the greatest benefits, and we would bear them without any complaint or any sign of annoyance." Similarly, St. John of Avila says, "You may well be content to serve our Lord in illness, for when He calls people to suffer instead of working for Him, He is calling them to a higher state."

A proper attitude in our suffering can give great glory to God, and humor can play a part in the patient acceptance of our illnesses. In the seventeenth century, a dying St. John Berchmans was being attended to by a doctor who prescribed an unusual treatment: bathing the patient's forehead with vinegar wine. The saint is said to have remarked, "It's a good thing I haven't long to live! I can't afford such an expensive disease."

More important than humor, of course, is an awareness that we can offer up our sufferings as a sacrifice for ourselves and others, and as a prayer of praise to God; this can give meaning to what we endure, and perhaps even be part of our calling from God. St. Bernadette, to whom the Virgin Mary had appeared at Lourdes, suffered from asthma and other painful ailments in the convent; she once told a visitor, "I am getting on with my job." The surprised visitor, seeing Bernadette confined to bed, asked, "What job?" to which the saint responded, "Being ill."

When we're sick and unable to perform our regular duties, our job is to pray — not necessarily in a formal way, which might be beyond our strength — but in the manner that St. Charles of Sezze describes: "The prayer of the sick person is his patience and his acceptance of the sickness for the love of Jesus Christ. This has great worth when it is motivated by the imitation of how much He suffered for us, and by penance for our sins."

This type of holy resignation to God's will was manifested by St. Lydwina, who was paralyzed at age sixteen as a result of an ice-skating accident. For the next thirty-eight years she was an invalid, confined to a bed of rough boards, covered with ulcers, and in constant pain. Lydwina never complained, but instead used to say, "God's eye is on me; He sees and knows all. That is sufficient." It is indeed enough for us that the Lord never forgets us; both in sickness and in health, He holds us in the palm of His hand.

For Further Reflection

"Illness and suffering have always been among the gravest problems confronted in human life. In illness, man experiences his powerlessness, his limitations, and his finitude. Every illness can make us glimpse death. Illness can lead to anguish, self-absorption, sometimes even despair and revolt against God. It can also make a person more mature, helping him discern in his life what is not essential so that he can turn toward that which is. Very often illness provokes a search for God and a return to Him." — *Catechism of the Catholic Church*, par. 1500-1501

"If God causes you to suffer much, it is a sign that He has great designs for you, and that He certainly intends to make you a saint. And if you wish to become a great saint, entreat Him to give you much opportunity for suffering; for there is no wood better to kindle the fire of holy love than the wood of the Cross, which Christ used for His own sacrifice of boundless charity." — *St. Ignatius of Loyola*

"What beautiful virtues can be practiced in sickness! Above all, love of humiliation, helplessness, gratitude, and gentleness of heart toward those who take care of you, blind obedience to the doctor and the nurses. Keep your countenance cheerful and remain in bed as on the Cross of the Savior. Love to suffer those pains and fevers as the Lord sends them." — *St. Paul of the Cross*

Something You Might Try

◆ St. Paul of the Cross advises, "Be obedient to your doctor. Then, even if you don't get better right away, you have at least fulfilled your own responsibilities before God. Eat and sleep enough to regain your strength, and even while you are sick you will be glorifying God and giving Him pleasure." The saint also suggests, "Concerning bodily ailments, be obedient to your doctor. Tell him what is wrong with you, briefly, modestly, and clearly. When you have said what is necessary, be quiet and let him do the rest. Don't refuse medicine. Take it in the loving chalice of Jesus with a gentle countenance and with gratitude to those who take care of you."

◆ "When you are sick," St. Francis de Sales tells you, "offer to Christ our Lord all your pains, your suffering, and your languor, and beseech Him to unite them to those He bore for you."

Further Reading

Scripture: Proverbs 3:7-8; Proverbs 17:22; Sirach 30:15-16; James 5:14-16.

Classics: St. Francis de Sales, *An Introduction to the Devout Life;* St. Alphonsus Liguori, *Conformity to the Will of God.*

Contemporary Works: Richard P. Johnson, *Body/Mind/Spirit — Tapping the Healing Power Within You;* Joni Woelfel, *Tall in Spirit: Meditations for the Chronically Ill.*

⌒

Litany for Health

Even if you're praying this litany alone, the response "pray for us," rather than "pray for me," is recommended, for when we pray for others who are suffering as we are, instead of only for ourselves, our prayers are more likely to be heard.

If, because of your illness, the list of invocations (ending with "pray for us") in this litany is too long to use, pray only part of it, ending with the last invocation ("All holy men and women . . .").

From all evil and distress, *deliver us, O Lord.*
From all suffering and illness, *deliver us, O Lord.*
From all fear and anxiety, *deliver us, O Lord.*
From all restlessness and worry, *deliver us, O Lord.*
From all grief and misfortune, *deliver us, O Lord.*
From all our doubts and our lack of belief, *deliver us, O Lord.*
From our failures to trust in You, *deliver us, O Lord.*
From our faults and sins, *deliver us, O Lord.*
From our need to have everything our
own way, *deliver us, O Lord.*
From everything that keeps us from coming
closer to You, *deliver us, O Lord.*

Holy Mary, Mother of God, *pray for us.*
St. Joseph, *pray for us.*
St. John the Baptist, *pray for us.*
St. Peter, *pray for us.*
St. Paul, *pray for us.*

St. Mary Magdalene, *pray for us.*
St. Martha, *pray for us.*
St. John of God, *pray for us.*
St. Camillus de Lellis, *pray for us.*
St. Peregrine Laziosi, *pray for us.*
St. Scholastica, *pray for us.*
St. Giles, *pray for us.*
St. Francis de Sales, *pray for us.*
St. Matrona, *pray for us.*
St. Dymphna, *pray for us.*
St. Vitus, *pray for us.*
St. Lucy, *pray for us.*
St. Teresa of Avila, *pray for us.*
St. Fiacre, *pray for us.*
St. Roch, *pray for us.*
St. Albert the Great, *pray for us.*
St. Agatha, *pray for us.*
St. Elizabeth of Hungary, *pray for us.*
St. Luke, *pray for us.*
Sts. Cosmas and Damian, *pray for us.*
St. James, *pray for us.*
St. Marculf, *pray for us.*
St. Blase, *pray for us.*
St. Apollonia, *pray for us.*
Bl. Andre Bessette, *pray for us.*
St. Raphael, *pray for us.*
St. Rose of Lima, *pray for us.*
St. Aloysius Gonzaga, *pray for us.*
St. Fidelis, *pray for us.*
St. Peter Claver, *pray for us.*
St. Martin de Porres, *pray for us.*
St. Charles Borromeo, *pray for us.*
St. Didacus, *pray for us.*

St. Frances Cabrini, *pray for us.*
St. Bertilla Boscardin, *pray for us.*
St. Catherine of Siena, *pray for us.*
St. Henry Morse, *pray for us.*
St. Brigid, *pray for us.*
St. Dominic of Silos, *pray for us.*
St. Jane Frances de Chantal, *pray for us.*
St. Andrew Bobola, *pray for us.*
St. Philip Neri, *pray for us.*
St. Cajetan, *pray for us.*
St. Jerome Emiliani, *pray for us.*
St. John Leonardi, *pray for us.*
St. Peter Canisius, *pray for us.*
St. Francis of Assisi, *pray for us.*
St. William Firmatus, *pray for us.*
St. Katherine Drexel, *pray for us.*
St. Romuald, *pray for us.*
St. Gabriel Possenti, *pray for us.*
St. Bonaventure, *pray for us.*
St. Angadrisma, *pray for us.*
St. John Baptist de La Salle, *pray for us.*
St. Leopold Mandic, *pray for us.*
St. Mary Magdalene de Pazzi, *pray for us.*
St. Thérèse of Lisieux, *pray for us.*
St. Ignatius of Loyola, *pray for us.*
St. John Bosco, *pray for us.*
St. Theophanes, *pray for us.*
Bl. Junipero Serra, *pray for us.*
St. John Berchmans, *pray for us.*
St. Bernadette, *pray for us.*
St. Lydwina, *pray for us.*
All holy men and women of God, *pray for us.*
Our Father . . . Hail Mary . . . Glory be to the Father . . .

Impatience

Be patient with . . . all. See that none of you repays evil for evil,
but always seek to do good to one another and to all.

1 Thessalonians 5:14-15

Almost all of us need to grow in patience . . . but most of us are in
no particular hurry to do so. One of the drawbacks of living in an
"instant society" — as ours has been called — is a tendency to
believe that we should receive what we need or want right *now*
and that having to wait for something is an unreasonable burden
or expectation.

Our impatience tends to carry over into our relationships with
others; we often expect them to conform to our standards, to our
biases, and to our schedules; and when they don't, many of us
aren't at all shy about letting them know how we feel. There are
even times when impatience can show up in our relationship
with God: "When will this Mass be over?" "How long does God
expect me to put up with this?" "Why isn't the Lord answering my
prayer?"

It's true that, seen from a larger perspective, our lives on earth
seem to pass quickly and that time is too precious for us to waste,
but this doesn't mean we're entitled to have all our demands met
immediately, regardless of the cost. We're created to live eternally,

and, as the saints realized, humbly practicing the virtue of patience is an important way of preparing ourselves for Heaven.

There are two main ways in which we are called to practice this virtue: by being patient ourselves and by putting up with people who seem to lack patience. St. Sylvester, the thirty-third Pope, gives us an example of the latter. Christianity had been an illegal religion in the Roman Empire, and those who practiced it were subject to imprisonment, torture, and death during times of persecution. But this changed in the year 313. The Roman Emperor Constantine became convinced that he had been victorious over his rivals during the famous Battle of Milvian Bridge because of the intervention of Christ. In response to a dream in which he saw a cross and heard the words "In this sign you shall conquer," he had the cross emblazoned on his soldiers' insignias, and they went on to victory. In gratitude, Constantine issued the decisive Edict of Milan, which legalized the practice of Christianity.

St. Sylvester was elected Pope the following year — a time of great promise and adjustment for the Church. Not only did he have to find his way in an unprecedented situation; he also had to deal patiently with Constantine, who had one of the most dominating personalities in that (or any other) era. The emperor was convinced God had given him the responsibility not only of political leadership, but also of influencing and directing the Church. Like a large, friendly dog that doesn't know its own strength and is used to getting its way, Constantine wanted to be involved in everything. He had genuine religious motives, sincerely believing in Christianity (although he waited until just before his death to be baptized), but he also thought in political terms: if the Church was a unifying element, that would aid the overall strength of the empire. Thus, the emperor tended to meddle in religious affairs that, strictly speaking, weren't any of his business. St. Sylvester had to bear all of this patiently, finding the difficult balance between keeping the emperor happy and preserving the Church's independence (the same dilemma many popes have faced). By and large, he succeeded; St. Augustine might well have been thinking of this holy Pope when he stated about a hundred years later, "Patience is the companion of wisdom."

The twelfth-century bishop St. Albert of Montecorvino was, in his old age, given a priest named Crescentius to assist him as vicar. However, Crescentius was unscrupulous and ambitious and actually hoped Albert would die so that he might succeed him. Crescentius and his associates, rather than helping the bishop, played cruel practical jokes on him and dropped unsubtle hints about their desire for his death and the need for new leadership in the diocese. Instead of complaining that his assistants were making his job harder, Albert understood a truth later put into words by his vicar's namesake Bl. Crescentia of Kaufbeuren: "The practices most pleasing to God are those which He Himself imposes — to bear meekly and patiently the adversities which He sends or which our neighbors inflict on us."

Another saint who demonstrated the virtue of patience was the abbot St. Aelred. Once, when a noble criticized him in the presence of the king, Aelred listened meekly and then thanked the man for pointing out his faults. The noble was so touched by Aelred's humility and patience that he begged his forgiveness. Being patient can have a very positive effect on other people.

Usually the impatient people we need to placate or satisfy aren't powerful authority figures, but the members of our own families. In the eleventh century, when his parents died, St. Peter Damian was left in the care of an older brother who was not only impatient, but deliberately unkind and neglectful. Peter learned to cope with this situation until another brother took over his care and arranged for his education. Peter's difficult childhood experiences made him particularly sensitive to the needs and feelings of others; he was not only generous to the poor, but also very patient with those who disagreed with him. In fact, because everyone found it so easy to get along with Peter, the Pope frequently used him as a mediator in various disputes involving the Church and local officials and in questions of jurisdiction involving different monasteries.

We are called to deal patiently with other people, but that's not always easily done. As a young monk in the sixth century, St. Dositheus was assigned to care for the sick members of the community. The self-centeredness to which illness sometimes gives rise can make people unreasonable in their demands; when this happened in the monastery, Dositheus would lose his patience and speak harshly to his charges. Then, filled with remorse, he'd run to his cell and, throwing himself on the floor, weep bitter tears, and beg God's mercy. His genuine contrition allowed divine grace to work within him, and with God's help, Dositheus eventually became so kind, patient, and cheerful that those who were sick loved having him present.

St. Cyprian, the great third-century Bishop of Carthage, wrote a famous sermon on the importance of patience, but he himself often had trouble practicing this virtue. Cyprian had a strong personality and fiercely defended Church teachings; he could be both gentle and forgiving, but also strict and uncompromising, and this made him a "lightning rod" in times of religious controversy (such as how strictly the Church should treat lapsed Christians) and a target in times of persecution by the state. St. Cyprian was executed by the authorities in 258; well over a hundred years later, another famous bishop from North Africa, St. Augustine, wrote that Cyprian atoned for his frequent anger and impatience by means of his glorious martyrdom.

Heroic measures are sometimes called for in our effort to rein in our impatience. The first step is to recognize that, although we can't usually control what happens to us, we can always decide how we'll respond. That's why St. Philip Neri remarked, "Sufferings are a kind of paradise to him who suffers them with patience, while they are a hell to him who has no patience." When we choose to accept life's irritations as part of God's plan for us, they are transformed from temptations or possible occasions of sin into a valuable means of grace and spiritual growth.

In terms of our relationships with other people, St. Bonaventure warns, "Beware of becoming vexed or impatient at the faults of others; for it would be folly, when you see a man falling into a ditch, to throw yourself into another for no purpose." In other words, we shouldn't allow someone else's faults to cause us to sin through impatience. The people who most get on our nerves are the ones to whom we most need to show acceptance and understanding. They may not "deserve" such consideration, but we must try to extend it to them if we wish to please God.

St. Francis de Sales advises us, "Resist your impatience faithfully, practicing, not only with reason, but even against reason, holy courtesy and sweetness to all, but especially to those who weary you most."

How can we overcome our natural inclinations in this regard? Simply by reminding ourselves that we're being patient not primarily for the sake of the person who is irritating us, but as an expression of our love for Jesus. Following Him often means putting up with people, events, and situations we'd prefer to avoid entirely. This effort is very valuable, for, as St. Katherine Drexel noted, "The patient endurance of the Cross — whatever nature it may be — is the highest work we have to do."

According to St. Alphonsus Liguori, "The happiest man in the world is he who abandons himself to the will of God and receives all things, whether prosperous or adverse, as from His hands." Thus, it can be said that — whether we realize it or not — when we choose either a patient or impatient response to the world around us, we're deciding whether we'll be happy or unhappy. There are some persons, such as St. Margaret Mary Alacoque and St. Bernadette, who are by their nature very gentle and patient; for many of us, however, gentleness and patience are virtues we need to develop as we go through life. Let us remind ourselves of what the saints knew very well from their own experience: God is infinitely patient with each one of us, so it's not too much for Him to ask that we try to show a little patience toward others.

For Further Reflection

"If you seek patience, you will find no better example than the Cross. Great patience occurs in two ways: either when one patiently suffers much, or when one suffers things that one is able to avoid and yet does not avoid. Christ endured much on the Cross, and did so patiently. . . ." — *St. Thomas Aquinas*

"He who bears his sufferings with patience for God's sake, will soon arrive at high perfection. He will be master of the world and will already have one foot in the other world." — *Bl. Giles of Assisi*

"When you are overtaken by some misfortune, seek the remedies that God affords you — for not to do so would be to tempt His Divine Providence — but having done so, await the result He may appoint with perfect resignation. If He sees fit to permit the remedies to overcome the evil, thank Him humbly; but if, on the other hand, He permits the evil to overcome the remedies, patiently bless His holy name and submit." — *St. Francis de Sales*

Something You Might Try

♦ Assess and strengthen your patience. According to St. Francis of Assisi, "We can never tell how patient or humble a person is when everything is going well with him. But when those who should cooperate with him do the exact opposite, then we can tell. A man has as much patience and humility as he has then, and no more." Thus, the people or situations that cause you to become impatient are actually opportunities to prove to God and to yourself how patient and humble you are. If you frequently fall short, you have a clear indication that you need to grow in patience. Make a resolution to try a little harder to resist each temptation to impatience, and ask the Lord (and your favorite saints) to help you carry it out.

◆ Many of us particularly dislike being interrupted when we're praying, but as St. Francis de Sales notes, a true spirit of prayer recognizes that we can serve God at that moment either by meditating or by responding to the immediate needs of another person. We should set aside time for prayer, but if that time is interrupted, we should let our patient response be another way of expressing our love for God.

Further Reading

Scripture: Proverbs 14:29; Sirach 7:10-11; 2 Peter 2:9; Colossians 3:12.

Classics: St. Francis de Sales, *An Introduction to the Devout Life*; St. Catherine of Siena, *Dialogue*.

Contemporary Works: Rudolf Allers, *Self-Improvement*.

Traditional Novena to the Holy Spirit
(to be prayed daily for nine days)

O Holy Spirit,
You are the Third Person of the Blessed Trinity!
You are the Spirit of truth, love, and holiness,
proceeding from the Father and the Son,
and equal to Them in all things!
I adore You and love You with all my heart.
Teach me to know and to seek God,

by whom and for whom I was created.
Fill my heart with a holy fear and a great love of Him.
Give me compunction and patience,
and do not let me fall into sin.
Increase faith, hope, and charity in me, and
bring forth in me all the virtues proper to my state in life.
Help me to grow in the four cardinal virtues,
Your seven gifts, and Your twelve fruits.
Make me a faithful follower of Jesus,
an obedient child of the Church,
and a help to my neighbor.
Give me the grace to keep the commandments
and to receive the sacraments worthily.
Raise me to holiness in the state of life
to which You have called me, and
lead me through a happy death to everlasting life.
I ask this through Jesus Christ, our Lord. Amen.

Grant me also, O Holy Spirit,
Giver of all good gifts,
the special favor for which I ask
(an increase in patience, or any other request),
if it be for Your honor and glory and my well-being.
Glory be to the Father . . .

Irreligious Children

I have been young, and now am old; yet I have not seen
the righteous forsaken or his children begging bread. He is ever
giving liberally and lending, and his children become a blessing.
Depart from evil, and do good; so shall you abide forever.
For the Lord loves justice; He will not forsake His saints.

Psalm 37:25-28

In the Rite of Baptism, parents are told, "You are accepting the responsibility of training [your children] in the practice of the Faith. It will be your duty to bring them up to keep God's commandments as Christ taught us, by loving God and our neighbor." This is a very important responsibility; indeed, the most important duty parents have is to prepare their children for eternity. Food, shelter, clothing, and a good education are all necessary and valuable, but the need for these things will one day come to an end. Only faith, and the love that makes faith real, will last forever.

There are, of course, many parents who understand this truth, but who judge themselves to be failures nonetheless (or who at least wonder whether God sees them that way). Many Catholics are confused and upset because their grown children, in spite of receiving a Catholic education and a good example from their parents, have left the Church or remain only as nominal members, but no longer practice the Faith. Inadequate catechesis, youthful rebellion, the allurements of this world, the bad influence of peers and role models, selfishness, and laziness all play their part. Sometimes parents themselves fail by not living out their Faith in a genuine, committed way; but even living out their Faith sincerely is no guarantee that their children will remain true to the Faith.

Although adults who come from religious homes are more likely to be religious themselves, there are many cases where this simply hasn't happened. Parents are supposed to provide discipline, but this can often be resented and rejected as tyranny; parents are supposed to offer advice and correction, but this is often viewed or experienced as nagging. In a society that undermines authority, enshrines relativism, and stresses "doing your own thing," the mission of parents seems almost impossible. God asks them to persevere even so, trusting in Him while doing their best to cooperate with His grace.

If you worry or mourn over a grown child who has let go of or rejected the Faith, it may console you to know that even some of the saints had this struggle and disappointment. They, more than anyone, knew the importance of teaching their children to love God and neighbor. Some of them succeeded; others failed.

The most famous story, of course, is that of St. Monica, whose brilliant but wayward son Augustine caused her much grief and suffering. As a pagan philosopher and teacher, Augustine believed his search for truth allowed him to live as he pleased; he rejected Monica's Christian Faith, fathered a child out of wedlock, and gently ignored her attempts to correct and enlighten him. Monica managed to convert her pagan husband, Patricius; after his death, she tried still harder to discipline Augustine (even to the extent of locking him out of her home), but to no avail.

The young man finally tired of his mother's constant prayers on his behalf, resenting them as an interference in his life. He told Monica he was going down to the docks to see off a departing friend, but he boarded the ship himself and sailed off to Italy. His heartbroken but determined mother followed. Monica eventually caught up with Augustine in Milan. There the bishop, St. Ambrose, encouraged her to persevere, promising that the beneficiary of so many prayers surely would not be lost. Within a few months, Monica's most fervent desire was granted: Augustine became a Christian and was baptized. Soon after this, St. Monica died, worn out but very much at peace. Monica is quite rightly considered a patroness of mothers — especially of those who worry over their children.

Not all saintly parents had the satisfaction of seeing their misguided children return to the Church. In the fourteenth century St. Bridget of Sweden was happily married to a Swedish nobleman, and together they had eight children. Two of the children were particularly noteworthy, although in opposite ways: a daughter, Katherine of Vadstena, who was eventually canonized a saint, and a son, Charles, who broke his mother's heart by his notorious life of sin. Bridget was partially successful in helping to improve the moral standards of the Swedish royal court, but she failed in her efforts to influence her son. The news of Charles's death after a dissolute life grieved St. Bridget very deeply and hastened her own death.

St. Elizabeth Ann Seton had a similar experience. One of her two sons lived an immoral life, in spite of her ceaseless prayers and sacrifices on his behalf.

The sixth-century queen St. Clotilda, widow of the Frankish king Clovis, suffered greatly as a result of her sons' quarreling over the royal throne; one of them was killed in battle, and another tried to secure the throne for himself by murdering his nephews (Clotilda's grandsons).

Something similar occurred several centuries later in the life of St. Matilda. The widow of King Henry I of Germany, she was the mother of St. Bruno (who caused her little trouble) and of

Emperor Otto I and Prince "Henry the Quarrelsome" (both of whom caused her considerable grief). Matilda, perhaps unwisely, favored Henry, which caused Otto to treat her poorly. Henry, instead of being grateful for her support, also treated her badly. The one thing the two brothers agreed on was that Matilda was much too generous to the poor and to the Church. She ignored their complaints, treated them with patience, and eventually died with the affection and respect of the common people.

Children can cause their parents grief by ignoring God's call, but sometimes these roles are reversed. In the eleventh century, the future St. Anselm, discerning a religious vocation, wanted to enter a monastery at the age of fifteen; his father strictly forbade this. Anselm rebelled by going to the opposite extreme: he abandoned religion altogether and lived in a carefree, irresponsible manner. Thus, an unsupportive parent was partly to blame for a youth's rebelliousness. Fortunately, Anselm later repented and thereafter answered his calling.

It's God's will that parents raise their children in righteousness and help prepare them for their spiritual pilgrimage. This means that parents must have a living faith, and as St. Francis Xavier observed, "No man ever really finds out what he believes until he begins to instruct his children." Our children are precious to us, for they have been entrusted to us by God. We want the very best for them, and so it's only natural for us to be distressed if they ignore or reject their moral and religious upbringing. In such a case, the Lord wants us to remain loving and accepting toward them, but also unceasing in our prayers and unyielding in our Faith.

While praying for her son's conversion, St. Monica had a consoling dream in which an angel reassured her, "Your son is with you." When she later told Augustine about the dream, he snidely remarked that they might easily be together — if only Monica would reject her Christian Faith. Monica immediately responded, "He did not say that I was with you; he said you were with me."

This response made a deep impression on Augustine. Similarly, we must not try to achieve a superficial family unity by giving in on moral issues or by denying our Faith, for this sort of bad example makes it even less likely that our loved ones will come to accept the truth. Rather, we must remain with the Lord on His terms, hoping and praying that our children will one day join us.

Parents and children are meant to be a source of mutual grace and encouragement, helping one another to come closer to God. Unfortunately, this doesn't always happen. Your children may have caused you grief by their unrestrained lives or by their leaving the Church. But the example of St. Monica speaks of the need to persevere in hope and in prayer. God can work miracles of grace at an instant's notice and in the most unexpected ways, and He rejoices in those loving parents who seek to cooperate with Him on their children's behalf.

For Further Reflection

"Through the grace of the sacrament of marriage, parents receive the responsibility and privilege of *evangelizing their children*. Parents should initiate their children at an early age into the mysteries of the Faith of which they are the 'first heralds' for their children. They should associate them from their tenderest years with the life of the Church. A wholesome family life can foster interior dispositions that are a genuine preparation for a living faith and remain a support for it throughout one's life." — *Catechism of the Catholic Church*, par. 2225

"It is only natural to want to plan your children's future for them and to presume that you know best what they should do. But this is not the right approach. It will only make your children angry. You have to leave them in complete freedom and trust that they will listen to God in responding to whatever vocation He gives them." — *St. Paul of the Cross*

"Before the birth of St. Augustine, his mother, St. Monica, dedicated him to Christianity and to the glory of God, as he himself tells us, a good lesson to Christian women on how they should dedicate to the Divine Majesty the fruit of their womb, for God, who freely accepts the willing obligations of a humble heart, usually causes such dedications to fructify, as in the case of Samuel, St. Thomas Aquinas, St. Andrew of Fiesole, and many others." — *St. Francis de Sales*

Something You Might Try

♦ St. Louise de Marillac wrote to St. Vincent de Paul regarding her disappointment in her son. St. Vincent responded, "The faults of children are not always imputed to their parents, especially when they have had them instructed and given good example, as, thank God, you have done. Moreover, our Lord, in His wondrous Providence, allows children to break the hearts of devout fathers and mothers. Abraham's was broken by Ishmael, Isaac's by Esau, Jacob's by most of his children, David's by Absalom, Solomon's by Rehoboam, and the Son of God's by Judas." Thus, the decisions your children have made don't make you a failure as a parent in God's eyes. You're entitled to feel sorrow, but not necessarily guilt. Do not cease praying for your children; God's grace can touch a hardened heart — as happened when St. Louise's son allowed himself to be influenced by the teaching and example of St. Vincent.

♦ Commend your children to the Immaculate Heart of Mary. An Italian priest, Fr. Stefano Gobbi, has allegedly been receiving inner locutions from our Lady since 1973. Because many people had expressed grief over grown children who had left the Faith, Fr. Gobbi asked Mary about this problem. She is said to have stated that when parents pray the Rosary for their children, at the end of each decade they should hold the Rosary aloft and say to her,

"With these beads I bind my children to your Immaculate Heart."
And then, Mary promised, "I will tend to their souls."

Further Reading

Scripture: Sirach 3:3-4,12-16; Proverbs 23:22; Luke 7:12-15.

Contemporary Works: William J. Doherty, *Take Back Your Kids;*
Dolores Curran, *Tired of Arguing With Your Kids?;* Rev. John
Hampsch, *Prayer with Rolled-Up Sleeves: Rescuing Your Loved
Ones,* and *When Loved Ones Turn from God;* Rev. Thomas
Krieg, *Keeping Your College Kids Catholic;* Lorene Hanley
Duquin, *When a Loved One Leaves the Church.*

⌒

Father in Heaven,
You know what it is to grieve over sinful,
unappreciative children, and so I turn to You in my sorrow.
My child(ren) seem(s) to have left the Faith.
I wonder if I have failed; more important,
I fear for those whom I love.
Be ever with my family, dear God, to encourage, console,
support, enlighten, and bless each member.
Bring back those who have strayed, touch those whose hearts
have hardened, and forgive those who have offended You
by selfishness, laziness, or indifference.
You sent Your Son, Jesus, to die for us;
I pray that this wondrous sacrifice not be in vain.
Give my child(ren) the grace of repentance.
Help me to persevere and to suffer all things,
and to offer all things, for Your glory.
Dearest Mary, Mother of God,
please pray for my family.
Our Father . . . Hail Mary . . . Glory be to the Father . . .

Irritations

Forbear one another and, if one has a complaint
against another, forgive each other;
as the Lord has forgiven you, so you also must forgive.

Cf. Colossians 3:13

What things irritate you? Perhaps a dog barking in the middle of the night, a rude salesclerk, an inconsiderate driver, a childproof cap on an aspirin bottle that resists your efforts to open it, family members who never turn off the lights, lectors at Mass who mumble instead of speaking clearly, people who don't send thank-you cards to acknowledge your gifts, incorrect weather forecasts, choosing the check-out lane that ends up moving more slowly than all the others, the late delivery of your morning newspaper, a furnace that breaks down on the coldest night of the year, sitting for an unreasonably long time in the doctor's waiting room, airline personnel who won't give you an honest answer about when the plane will be taking off, or finding your favorite television show has been preempted by something you consider a waste of time. These irritations, and many others you can name, can make life a little more difficult and a little less enjoyable, right?

Now, consider this question: What can you offer to God as a sacrifice or prayer? How about the very same items on the list above? That's right. Irritations are a chance for us to practice patience and grow in grace; and when you think about it, that's really the smartest and most efficient way to handle them. If we can't do anything about an irritating situation (and that's often the case), we can at least make sure we derive some spiritual benefit from it — by turning it into a prayer.

No one would reasonably claim that coping with life's minor problems and annoyances can begin to compare with enduring persecution, imprisonment, torture, and even death for the sake of Christ, as many saints have experienced throughout the ages and which Christians around the world continue to face today. Most of our crosses are relatively minor, so let us turn to the example of the saint who, more than any other, is known for growing in holiness by offering God all the small experiences of life: St. Thérèse of Lisieux, who is famous for her "little way." Thérèse chose to become a saint without fuss or fanfare, by doing everything, however small or routine, with as much love as possible. This includes, of course, patiently bearing life's irritations and annoyances.

In her autobiography, *The Story of a Soul*, St. Thérèse writes, "There was . . . a certain nun who managed to irritate me in everything she did. The Devil had a part in it, for it was certainly he who made me see all her bad points. Not wishing to give way to natural antipathy, I reminded myself that sentiments of charity were not enough; they must find expression, and I set myself to treat her as if I loved her best of all. I prayed for her whenever we met and offered all her virtues and merits to God. I was sure that Jesus would be delighted at this, for artists always like to have their work praised, and it pleases the Divine Artist of souls when, not stopping at the exterior, we penetrate the inner sanctuary where He dwells, to admire its beauty. I prayed earnestly for this Sister who had caused me so much struggle, but this was not enough for me. I tried to do everything I possibly could for her, and when tempted to answer her sharply, I hastened to give her a friendly smile and talk about something else; for, as it says in the *Imitation [of Christ]*, 'It is better to leave everyone to their own way of thinking than to begin an argument.' Sometimes, when the Devil made a particularly violent attack, if I could slip away without letting her suspect my inward struggle, I would run away from the battle like a deserter; and what was the result? She said to me one day, her face radiant, 'What do you find so attractive in me? Whenever we meet you give me such a gracious smile.' What attracted me? It was Jesus hidden in the depths of her soul, Jesus, who makes attractive even what is most bitter. I have just mentioned my last resort in escaping defeat in the battle of life . . . to act like a deserter. It is not very honorable, but it has always proved successful, and I often used it during my novitiate."

St. Thérèse gives us still more beautiful, down-to-earth advice: "Another time, washing handkerchiefs in the laundry opposite a Sister who kept on splashing me with dirty water, I was tempted to step back and wipe my face to show her that I would be obliged if she would be more careful. But why be foolish enough to refuse treasures offered so generously? I took care to hide my exasperation. I tried hard to enjoy being splashed with dirty water, and by the end of the half hour, I had acquired a real taste for this novel form of aspersion. How fortunate to find this spot where such treasures could be given away! I would come back as often as I could."

Many times we find we're most irritated by other people, and in such a state, it's very easy to start cataloging their faults (perhaps even inventing a few) and to begin passing judgment. As St. Thérèse reminds us, we need to keep in mind the bigger picture by looking at irritating persons as charitably as possible: "Should the Devil draw my attention to the faults of any one of them [the other Sisters] when I am seeking to increase this love in my heart, I call to mind at once her virtues and her good intentions. I tell myself that though I may have seen her fall once, there are probably a great many occasions on which she has won victories which, in her humility, she has kept to herself. What may appear to me to be a fault may even be an act of virtue because of her intention; and as I have experienced this for myself, I have little difficulty in persuading myself that this is indeed the case."

The saints can show us how to respond patiently to life's annoyances. Bl. Henry of Treviso was renowned for never letting anything upset him — so much so that people went out of their way to try to get a rise out of him through ridicule or petty pranks. Henry didn't resent them, but simply prayed for his tormenters.

This sort of patience often comes from a larger perspective, as illustrated in a story about St. John of Kanty. He was once invited to dinner at a nobleman's home, but when he arrived, he was denied entry because of the shabbiness of his cassock. Instead of being offended, John went home, changed into something more presentable, and returned. During the meal, a servant spilled food on John's lap, but the saint said, "No matter; my clothes deserve some dinner, because to them I owe the pleasure of my being here at all."

St. Colette once noted, "If there be a true way that leads to the everlasting Kingdom, it is most certainly that of suffering, patiently endured." Thus, we can choose to let the irritations of life bring us closer to the Lord.

But how do we live out this choice?

A key element in this process is to begin with the right perspective. St. Francis de Sales points out that the rod of Moses' brother Aaron, when lying on the ground, was a frightful serpent, but when held in Aaron's hand, it was a rod of power.[79] "It is thus," says the saint, "with tribulations. Consider them in themselves, and they are horrors; consider them in the will of God, and they are joys and delights." Therefore, every time we're annoyed by someone or something, we should ask the Lord, "Father, how are You

[79] Exod. 7:8-12.

present in this situation?" Becoming aware of the Lord's presence makes it easier to respond to all things with patience and love; indeed, as St. Thérèse discovered in her experience of being splashed by her laundry-mate, we can even come to love the things that irritate us. St. John Vianney wrote, "I have had crosses in plenty — more than I could carry, almost. I set myself to ask for the love of crosses — then I was happy."

Love can also help us persevere in trying to influence others who irritate us. For instance, St. Ignatius of Antioch once referred to a squad of soldiers escorting him to Rome (where he was to be martyred for his Faith) as "ten leopards" whose behavior "gets worse the better they are treated." When our efforts to be nice to someone don't seem to be paying off, we may be tempted to give up, but by continuing to act in charity, we pay a great tribute to God, who "makes his sun rise on the evil and on the good";[80] moreover, it's possible that our efforts will finally bear fruit.

Like St. Thérèse, all the saints came to realize that God can be found not only in the beauties and joys of life, but also in its problems, irritations, and interruptions. We needn't make grandiose promises to God or look for opportunities to do something heroic or memorable, nor should we make plans for trading in our cross for a larger one. God knows best what we need. He opens up before us the unique, perfectly tailored path that can lead us to holiness, and our simple efforts to respond to life's irritations with patience and acceptance are an important way of undertaking this journey, one step at a time.

For Further Reflection

St. Aloysius Gonzaga once made an interesting observation: putting up with the cold of winter and with summer's heat is, of all mortifications or sacrifices, especially pleasing to God — first,

[80] Matt. 5:45.

because cold and heat come from the hand of God Himself, and second, because this sacrifice is more hidden (in comparison, for instance, to fasting) and thus less likely to be motivated by pride. Thus, Mark Twain's wry comment that everybody talks about the weather but no one does anything about it no longer has to be true — we can offer it up as a sacrifice very acceptable to the Lord!

"Suffer and offer up those trifling injuries, those petty inconveniences, that daily befall you. This toothache, this headache, this cold, this contempt, or that scorn. All these small sacrifices, being accepted and embraced with love, are highly pleasing to the Divine Goodness, who for a single cup of cold water has promised a sea of perfect bliss for His faithful." — *St. Francis de Sales*

"We gain more in a single day by trials that come to us from God and our neighbor than we would in ten years of penance and other exercises that we take up ourselves." — *St. Teresa of Avila*

Something You Might Try

◆ St. John Bosco offered some practical advice to the young Dominic Savio in his efforts to become a saint: fulfill the duties of your state (in Dominic's case, as a schoolboy); treat companions kindly, especially those with disagreeable personalities; forgive persons who are vulgar or rude; avoid wasting food; fulfill all your duties, even those that are boring or unpleasant; don't complain about the weather; remain bright and cheerful under all circumstances; and be ever alert for ways to show your love for Jesus. St. Dominic Savio followed this advice, and so can you. Start by deciding to get along with the people who irritate you, and in practical terms this is very simple: merely apply the same excuses you use for our own bad behavior to those persons whose behavior annoys you.

♦ All of us quickly learn not to look directly at the sun; if we have to look in that direction, we shield our eyes or glance indirectly. St. Paul of the Cross suggests that we approach irritations and problems in the same way: not looking at them directly in the face, but instead looking at the face of our Lord and trying to see everything in light of what He suffered for us out of love. Getting into this habit will help you keep your difficulties in perspective. St. Paul of the Cross also says, "When you find yourself upset and disturbed over some situation you have to face, put yourself completely in God's hands. Accept His good pleasure in advance. If you can, seek advice and wait for the situation to mature. Trust in the Passion of Jesus, who will not allow anything to harm you."

Further Reading

Scripture: Mark 11:25; Romans 5:3-5; 2 Timothy 1:8; Ephesians 4:24.

Classics: St. Thérèse of Lisieux, *The Story of a Soul*; Thomas à Kempis, *Imitation of Christ*; St. Francis de Sales, *Introduction to the Devout Life*.

Contemporary works: James A. Magner, *Mental Health in a Mad World*.

Give me, good Lord, a humble, lowly, quiet, peaceable, patient, charitable, kind, filial, and tender mind, every shade, in fact, of charity, with all my words, and all my works, and all my thoughts, to have a taste of Thy holy blessed Spirit.

St. Thomas More

Judgmentalness

Judge not, and you will not be judged;
condemn not, and you will not be condemned;
forgive, and you will be forgiven.

Luke 6:37

The closer we come to God, the more we become aware of our sins; that's why St. Paul could, without being overly dramatic or practicing false humility, refer to himself as the worst of sinners.[81] The more we're aware of our own sins, the less inclined we should be to judge others. The old saying "There's no saint like a reformed sinner" should become true in this sense: recognizing how much we've been forgiven, we should be very slow to judge and condemn other people.

One who understood this well was St. Moses of Ethiopia, a monk and eventual martyr in fourth-century Egypt. Moses was once asked to join a meeting in which one of the other monks was to be condemned and punished for a sin against the community. The monks waited for Moses, but he failed to appear. One of the priests found him and told him, "Come, the community is waiting for you." Very reluctantly, Moses came, but only after

[81] 1 Tim. 1:15.

filling a cracked jug with water. When he carried the jug, slowly but steadily leaking its contents, into the meeting room, he was asked, "Father, what does this mean?" Moses answered, "It is my sins flowing out behind me, but I do not notice them. Thus I come to judge the sins of another." The saint's simple but profound words caused his brothers to rethink what they were about to do; as a result, they forgave their fellow monk, rather than condemning him.

St. Moses was undoubtedly remembering the many sins he had committed before his conversion, including stealing from his master, fighting with his fellow servants, and leading a group of robbers who terrorized the land.[82] He realized that he was in no position to pass judgment on anyone else. This is the charitable attitude that all Christians are called to practice.

The Church has traditionally spoken of the need to hate sin while loving the sinner, but this balance is often hard to achieve in practice. We must uphold morality, and oppose evil and injustice, even as we genuinely seek the conversion of evildoers. This is one of the main reasons for not presuming to judge sinners: if they feel rejected or condemned by us, they're much less likely to repent. Instead, we must attempt to influence them by our good example and prayers.

Another reason for avoiding a judgmental spirit is simply that we're often incapable of judging correctly; as St. John Climacus tells us, "Do not condemn, even with your eyes, for they are often deceived." One saint who had to learn this lesson was the eighteenth-century virgin Veronica Giuliani. As a girl, she was very devout, but she had the bad habit of resenting others when they didn't join in her religious devotions. St. Veronica repented of this fault after a vision in which she saw her own heart appearing to be made of iron.

---

[82] See also the chapter on greed.

St. John Climacus also advises us of the most important reason of all for not condemning others: "To pass judgment on another is to usurp shamelessly a prerogative of God, and to condemn is to ruin one's soul." God alone has the ability and the authority to look into the human soul and to render judgment on the state of an individual's conscience. Were we to attempt this, we would be guilty of the sin of pride, and would possibly harm the other person and certainly harm ourselves.

We must not only avoid condemning others for their sins — or for what we perceive to be their sins — but we must also be careful to avoid comparing ourselves favorably with them. St. John of the Cross tells us, "Do not think that, because the virtues you have in mind do not shine in your neighbor, he will not be precious in God's sight for something of which you are not thinking." Human beings are unique, and divine grace is so perfectly attuned to each one's individual needs and capacities, that we can't possibly know or understand the exact nature of our neighbor's spiritual condition. As St. Thérèse of Lisieux noted, "There will be a lot of surprises at the Last Judgment when we shall be able to see what really happened inside people's souls. . . ." Needless to say, we must do our part, through prayers and sacrifices, to ensure that these are "happy" surprises.

St. Luke's Gospel, even more than the others, stresses Jesus' willingness to forgive sinners, particularly in the beautiful stories of the Good Samaritan and the Prodigal Son.[83] Luke himself, by his writing, manifests a gentle, nonjudgmental nature.

Two saints especially known for their emphasis on God's mercy are St. Alphonsus Liguori and St. Paul of the Cross. Alphonsus, the founder of the Redemptorist Order and a great moral theologian, believed that sinners should not be threatened or condemned by the Church, but treated with patience and moderation. Paul,

---

[83] Luke 10:29-37; 15:11-32.

the founder of the Passionist Order, was a powerful preacher,[84] but was known for dealing gently with penitents in the confessional.

The example and practice of these saints encourage us to trust in God's mercy as we seek the forgiveness of our sins, and they challenge and remind us that we are not to judge others. Being judgmental is a form of pride, and it is only in the humble heart that God's grace can be most effective.

For Further Reflection

"Surely if God's goodness is so great that in one instant we can obtain pardon and grace, how can we tell that he who was a sinner yesterday is the same today? Yesterday must not judge today, nor today yesterday; it is the last day that will give the final verdict." — *St. Francis de Sales*

"Even though the poor are often rough and unrefined, we must not judge them from external appearances nor from the mental gifts they seem to have received. On the contrary, if you consider the poor in the light of Faith, you will observe that they are taking the place of the Son of God, who chose to be poor." — *St. Vincent de Paul*

"We should all stop scowling at the sins of other people. Rather, we should consider that we may be worse spiritually than they are and should say, 'Lord, if You had not helped me, I should have done worse.'" — *St. Alphonsus Liguori*

Something You Might Try

♦ St. Francis de Sales advises, "Be equal and just in your actions. Place yourself always in the position of your neighbor, and

---

[84] A soldier once told him, "Father, I have been in great battles without even flinching at the cannon's roar, but when I listen to you I tremble from head to foot."

place him in yours, and thus you will judge well. . . . Examine your heart often, whether it has such regard for your neighbor as you would wish his to have for you if you were in his place; for here is the secret of true reason." Thus, every time you're about to judge someone, take a moment to switch places mentally with him. Thinking about how you'd feel in the other person's position will help ensure that your judgments will be honest and charitable.

◆ An effective way to avoid judging others harshly is simply to apply your own excuses for your faults and bad behavior to people you're tempted to judge. After all, if these excuses are good enough to get yourself off the hook, they should also work for others.

Further Reading

Scripture: 1 Corinthians 4:5; James 4:11-12.

Classics: St. Teresa of Avila, *The Way of Perfection*; St. Francis de Sales, *An Introduction to the Devout Life*.

⌒

Lord, You are the only true Judge;
You alone can see into the human heart.
Free me from my tendency to judge others;
help me overcome the habit of criticizing,
of looking for other people's faults, and of
automatically assuming the worst about them.
I am a sinner; remind me of this truth
as often as necessary, Lord,
that I may grow in humility and grace
and truly become pleasing in Your sight.
Please bless all those whom I have judged in the past,
and all those who may have suffered
because of my judgments. Amen.

Loneliness

The hour is coming, indeed it has come, when you will be scattered,
every man to his home, and will leave me alone;
yet I am not alone, for the Father is with me.

John 16:32

We know that solitude, whatever its cause, can allow us to become more aware of the Lord's presence, but almost all of us worry to some degree about loneliness. We've all experienced it and would readily agree that — even though there are times when we need and want to be alone — it's part of our human nature to be sociable and to spend time with others.

Solitude is often seen as a problem to be solved, an emptiness to be filled, or a fate to be avoided. Indeed, sometimes it is all of these things. But solitude can also be the garden, weeded, cultivated, and tilled, from which the Lord brings forth a rich spiritual harvest. If we're feeling lonely, maybe that's a sign that we need to be with someone — or maybe it's an opportunity to remind ourselves that Jesus is with us.

Many of the saints greatly desired solitude, and we can easily admire (although probably not imitate) their fidelity in living as hermits, monks, or cloistered religious (that is, religious brothers and sisters who have little or no contact with the outside world).

But except for those called to be hermits, a solitary life is not an attractive one; even saints can experience loneliness. St. Thomas More spent fifteen months in solitary confinement after being arrested for treason by King Henry VIII. This must have been a terrible ordeal for someone as outgoing and family-oriented as he was, but it did not cause him to renounce his Faith.

The great scholar St. Thomas Aquinas, who spent many hours alone studying and writing, once remarked, "No possession is joyous without a companion," and further stated, "Notwithstanding the beasts and the plants [in gardens], one can be lonely there."

St. Fabiola was a friend of St. Jerome, and it's said she was so sociable by nature that she couldn't bear to be alone for any length of time. Indeed, St. Jerome remarked, "Her idea of the stable [that is, a retreat site] is that it should be an annex to the inn." Another saint who enjoyed company was Pius X, elected Pope early in the twentieth century. It had long been the custom that popes ate their meals alone, without dinner companions. Pius immediately ended this tradition and made a point of eating with anyone who was available: friends, relatives, priests, messengers, aides, and even the workmen from the papal gardens.

Even a great figure such as St. Patrick experienced a degree of loneliness; he was by nature very sensitive and affectionate and often remarked on how difficult it had been for him to leave his family in Britain once he had been reunited with them.

The Lord God said, in a somewhat different context, "It is not good that the man should be alone."[85] It is indeed our human nature to share life with other people. Sometimes we don't have enough solitude and privacy; other times we feel quite alone and forgotten. In either case, however, we must remember that the Lord is with us always, and if we offer our burdens to Him, we will one day rejoice with all the angels and saints in His kingdom.

[85] Gen. 2:18.

For Further Reflection

"Where I am, there You are, too, and where You are, I am. For we are a single body, and the body cannot be separated from the head nor the head from the body. Distance separates us, but love unites us, and death itself cannot divide us." — *St. John Chrysostom*

"It is in solitude that God speaks to us." — *St. John Vianney*

"The Lord said to St. Teresa one day, 'I would speak to many souls, but the world makes so much noise in their ears that they cannot hear my voice. Oh, if only they would stand a little apart from the world!'" — *St. Alphonsus Liguori (A certain amount of silence and solitude is necessary for our spiritual well-being.)*

Something You Might Try

♦ Consider the story of an intelligent but lonely high school teacher who was convinced that no one appreciated her or treated her fairly. Her aggressive attitude and quickness to take offense kept her from making friends (a further proof in her mind that life was unfair). Someone finally pointed out to her that her own attitudes were creating her sense of isolation, especially her conviction that she wasn't getting her due. Struck by this truth, she adopted a new approach: at every setback or disappointment, she told herself, "You don't deserve better treatment; that's quite all right for you." In a very short time, her new attitude toward life made her approachable and accepting of others, and she soon developed satisfying friendships. If you're experiencing loneliness, consider (perhaps with the assistance of someone you trust) whether your attitudes may be contributing to the situation. If so, take a positive step toward changing these attitudes.

♦ The easiest way to overcome loneliness is to change the focus from yourself to someone else. Join a group; volunteer your time; ask others to talk about themselves (their hopes, interests, opinions, activities, etc.); do something for another person; or contact or visit someone who's ill, lonely, or homebound.

Further Reading

Scripture: Psalm 22:20-21; Mark 1:35; Matthew 26:36-38.

Classics: St. Francis de Sales, *An Introduction to the Devout Life*.

⌒

Lord,
the trouble about life just now
is that I seem to have all the things that don't matter
and to have lost all the things that do matter.
I have life;
I have enough money to live on;
I have plenty to occupy me.
But I am alone,
and sometimes I feel that
nothing can make up for that.
Lord,
compel me to see the meaning of my Faith.
Make me to realize that I have a hope
as well as a memory,
and the unseen cloud of witnesses is around me;
that You meant it when You said that
You would be always with me;
and make me realize that as long as You leave me here,
there is something that I am meant to do;
and in doing it,
help me to find the comfort and the courage
that I need to go on.

Anonymous

Lust

Let neither gluttony nor lust overcome me,
and do not surrender me to a shameless soul.

Sirach 23:6

In the fourth century, a very beautiful young woman named Thais lived an immoral life as a prostitute. The holy bishop St. Paphnatius decided to try to convert her, so he went to her in disguise, pretending to be a client. She showed him a room, but he asked for one more isolated, so that there would be no interruptions. Thais led him to a different room, but he was still dissatisfied, so she reassured him, "No one can possibly see or hear us." Paphnatius asked, "And what of God? Is there no place where we can escape His all-seeing eye?" Shocked by these words, Thais admitted with fear, "Alas, no" and tearfully cast herself at the feet of Paphnatius, whom she now understood to be sent by the Lord. The bishop then spoke to her very powerfully about God's presence, and after Thais had confessed her sins, she went off to the desert, where she spent the remainder of her life in penance (and thus, is known now as St. Thais).

The Virgin Mary is said to have revealed to the three visionaries of Fatima that more persons are condemned to Hell for sins against the Sixth Commandment (which enjoins purity) than for any other; and the immorality of this past century makes it very easy to believe these words.

The *Catechism of the Catholic Church* defines lust as "disordered desire for or inordinate enjoyment of sexual pleasure. Sexual pleasure is morally misordered when sought for itself, isolated from its procreative and unitive purposes."[86] As one of the *Seven Deadly Sins*, lust is gravely dangerous from a moral perspective, and for many people, the attempt to overcome it is a lifelong struggle. Some of the saints were paragons of the virtue of purity, including St. Agnes, whose name means "pure," and St. Lucy, who, like Agnes, was a virgin and martyr. St. Charles Lwanga and his companions, who were pages in the court of the African King Mwanga of Uganda in the nineteenth century, were put to death when they resisted his homosexual advances. In the twentieth century, we have the witness of St. Maria Goretti, who died at age twelve as a result of resisting the sexual advances of a neighbor; St. Maximilian Kolbe, who as a youth committed himself to a life of purity; Bl. Antonia Mesina, who was murdered at age sixteen for refusing a young man's advances; Bl. Caroline Kozka, who was killed, also at sixteen, by a Russian soldier in World War I for resisting rape; Bl. Teresa Bracco, who was murdered, at twenty, by a German soldier in World War II for the same reason; and Bl. Maria Clementine Annuarite Nengapete, a religious sister in Upper Zaire whose efforts to safeguard her virtue caused an enraged officer to kill her.

Many saints, however, struggled with temptations against purity. Their example of fortitude, and their eventual victory, can encourage and inspire us.

Two saints most famous for their sinful past are St. Mary Magdalene and St. Augustine. Augustine became sexually active as a teenager, much to the horror of his mother, St. Monica, and, as a

---

[86] Par. 2351.

young man, he bore a son by his mistress. (Commenting on this situation later in life, Augustine said, "Lust served became a custom, and custom not resisted became a necessity.") Monica's ceaseless prayers eventually contributed to her son's conversion, but only after many struggles; in his search for truth, Augustine gradually came to realize the authenticity of the Gospel. But its strict moral demands created an inner conflict: he wanted to do what was right, but was afraid to pay the cost. This was the context for his famous "prayer," in which he asked, "Make me chaste, O God — but not yet."

At the peak of his spiritual crisis, Augustine read these words of St. Paul: "The night is far gone, the day is at hand. Let us then cast off the works of darkness and put on the armor of light; let us conduct ourselves becomingly as in the day, not in reveling and drunkenness, not in debauchery and licentiousness. . . . But put on the Lord Jesus Christ, and make no provision for the flesh, to gratify its desires."[87] This message finally gave Augustine a sense of peace and enlightenment, leading to his complete conversion to Christianity. There were still temptations to overcome in the future, but the saint was now armed with God's grace and thus able to triumph.

St. Mary Magdalene, according to tradition, may have been a prostitute before her conversion, but her shameful past did not prevent her from becoming one of our Lord's most faithful followers. Other saints turned from similar immoral lifestyles, such as St. Pelagia the Penitent, an erotic belly-dancer who was converted upon hearing a bishop remark that she took more care over her appearance than some bishops did over their flocks.

The conversion of St. Mary of Egypt was prompted by an uncomfortable and embarrassing experience in the Holy Land. A group of pilgrims was headed there, and she joined them — not

[87] Rom. 13:12-14.

for religious purposes, but to find opportunities to practice her trade as a prostitute. When the others entered one of the sacred religious sites, Mary tried to do so as well — but an invisible force kept her out of the church. Failing several times to enter, she realized that God was expressing His displeasure over her sinful life. Mary repented, prayed for permission to enter the church, and was able to do so; she then vowed to spend the remainder of her life doing penance, which she did in the desert beyond the Jordan River for almost fifty years.

A somewhat similar story is told about St. Margaret of Cortona, a beautiful young woman who lived in the thirteenth century. A wealthy young man enticed her into eloping with him, promising to marry her — although he never did. Instead, for nine years Margaret lived as his mistress and bore him a son. Then her lover was murdered; when Margaret saw his bloodied body, she repented of her sinful life with him. Her father would not accept her or her son, so Margaret sought shelter with the Franciscans, who became her spiritual family. She spent the remainder of her life doing penance and serving the sick and the poor. But even then, it took her three more years to overcome her struggles against the flesh.

Sexual temptations plagued a number of saints, including St. Francis of Assisi, who sought to overcome them by throwing himself into ditches filled with ice and snow and who once rolled among the thorns of a briar patch. Also afflicted were St. Jerome and St. Columban. St. Raymond Lull admitted that, as a youth, he was "shameless in pursuit of any new face that attracted me."

St. Catherine of Siena experienced some severe temptations that lasted for a long time. When our Lord afterward appeared to her, she asked Him where He was during these assaults and was surprised to hear Him say that He was within her heart. How, Catherine asked, could He dwell in one so impure as she? Jesus responded, "Tell me, did these filthy thoughts within your heart give you pleasure or sadness, bitterness or delight?" When she answered, "The most extreme bitterness and sadness," Jesus continued, "Who was it, then, that caused this great bitterness and sadness in your heart but I, who remained concealed in the interior of your soul? Believe me, my daughter, had it not been for my presence, those thoughts which surrounded your will would doubtless have conquered and entered in, and, having been received with pleasure by your free will, would have brought death to your soul. But being present within you, I infused this displeasure into your heart, and it enabled you to reject the temptation as much as you could."

In the fourth century, a monk plagued by sexual temptations came to St. Macarius the Elder for advice. Macarius told him never to eat before sunset, to pray and meditate during his work, and to labor diligently all day. The monk followed this counsel, and the lustful temptations left him and never returned.

Another early Church figure had a much more painful and costly struggle with lust. A beautiful woman named Zoe tried to seduce St. Martinian the Hermit, and at first the saint consented in his heart; then he repented and took a radical step to banish the temptation. Thrusting his feet in a fire, Martinian cried out in pain and then exclaimed, "If I cannot bear this weak fire, how can I endure the fire of Hell?" This horrifying demonstration brought Zoe herself to repentance, and when Martinian was finally able to walk again, he moved to a deserted island so as to be free of all such occasions of sin.

A similarly radical determination to resist temptation was shown by the twelfth-century abbot St. William of Vercelli. Some members of the royal court resented his good influence on King Roger II of Naples, so they tried to put William in a compromising situation. A woman of loose morals entered his room and asked to lie with him. William responded by walking to the fireplace, where he parted the burning coals with his bare hand; then, lying down among them, he invited the woman to lie with him there. She was horrified at first and then amazed when William stood up completely unharmed. This led her to renounce her former lifestyle and enter a convent.

Not only must we use God's grace to guard against temptations from within; we must also beware of persons around us who would lead us into sin. The family of St. Thomas Aquinas, instead of supporting his vocation to the Dominican Order, attempted to use lust to subvert it. At his mother's command, Thomas was kidnaped and imprisoned by one of his brothers, and a naked prostitute was sent into the room to tempt him. Thomas safeguarded his purity by chasing her out of the room with an iron poker.

A very different situation was encountered by Bl. Laura Vicuna, who was born in Chile in 1891. Her father abandoned his wife and two daughters, so her mother became the mistress of a well-to-do landowner. At the age of ten, Laura was propositioned by the man; she ran outside and not only begged God to save her and her sister, but also offered her life if that would lead to her mother's conversion. Several years later, Laura became very ill and was beaten unconscious by the landowner; after regaining consciousness for a short time, she told her mother that she had offered her life to God on her behalf. Before Laura died, her mother begged her forgiveness and promised to repent, and that evening she returned to the sacraments.

According to St. John Climacus, "Purity means that we put on the likeness of God, as far as is humanly possible." Living as obedient and loving children is very pleasing to our heavenly Father, and as St. Nicholas of Flue noted, "Purity of heart is to God like a perfume sweet and agreeable."

How, then, are we to cultivate, preserve, or reacquire the virtue of purity?

First, we must specifically and regularly pray for this grace; without God's help, we'll almost certainly fall, for it's almost impossible to avoid sexual temptations in our highly immoral society. As St. Teresa of Avila noted, it isn't possible for a person who prays regularly to remain in serious sin; because the two are incompatible, one or the other will have to be given up. Thus, if we remain faithful to prayer, God's grace will one day be victorious in us, even if we have many setbacks along the way.

Second, we must form the habit of immediately resisting lustful thoughts and temptations. St. Francis de Sales advises us, "Be extremely prompt in turning away from all that leads and lures to impurity, for this evil works insensibly and, by small beginnings, progresses to great mischief. It is always easier to avoid than to cure this."

Third, we must not become complacent or proud. St. Philip Neri warned, "Humility is the safeguard of chastity. In the matter of purity, there is no greater danger than not fearing danger. When a person puts himself in an occasion [of sin], saying, 'I shall not fall' — it is an almost infallible sign that he will fall, and with great injury to his soul." In other words, we must rely on God's strength, not on our own.

The need to seek the Lord's help applies not only to those persons with vocations to the single or religious life, but also to married couples. The Church teaches that the proper use of sex within marriage is one of God's greatest blessings, but the misuse of this gift can lead to spiritual self-destruction.

Sometimes great sacrifices are necessary to overcome lustful temptations — whether these temptations afflict us or our loved ones. This isn't a struggle that can be won on our own; God's grace is necessary. At the same time, it isn't a victory that will be achieved only by requesting God's help; we must use the grace He provides.

The misuse of sex is a serious sin, but Jesus came to forgive sins; He will wash us clean and keep us pure if this is truly what we desire.

For Further Reflection

"Purity of heart will enable us to see God: it enables us even now to see things according to God." — *Catechism of the Catholic Church*, par. 2531

"To preserve purity, three things are necessary; the practice of the presence of God, prayer, and the sacraments; and again, the reading of holy books — this nourishes the soul." — *St. John Vianney*

"When such temptation comes, the person who does not have recourse to God is lost. Chastity is a virtue that we do not have strength to practice unless God gives it to us, and God does not give this strength except to someone who asks for it. But whoever prays for it will certainly obtain it." — *St. Alphonsus Liguori*

Something You Might Try

♦ A prostitute once solicited St. Ephrem; he agreed to go with her — *if* the site of their sin was the town square. When the woman objected on account of the shame involved, Ephrem answered, "Then you fear shame before the eyes of men, and you do not fear it before the angels of God?" Whenever you're tempted, remember that all your sins, whether committed alone or with others, are beheld by the entirely heavenly court.

♦ St. Philip Neri advised a young man struggling with sin, "Say the 'Hail, Holy Queen' seven times every day, and kiss the floor saying, 'Tomorrow I might be dead!' " This advice might seem quaint to us, but it worked; the young man began overcoming his faults and growing in holiness. When tempted by lust, remind yourself that death may come at any moment and that nothing impure can enter God's kingdom.[88]

---

[88] Cf. Eph. 5:5.

Further Reading

Scripture: Sirach 9:8; Matthew 5:27-28; 1 Corinthians 6:18-20; Ephesians 5:5.

Classics: St. Augustine, *Confessions*; St. Francis de Sales, *An Introduction to the Devout Life*.

Contemporary Works: Rev. H. Vernon Sattler, *Challenging Children to Chastity*; James A. Magner, *Mental Health in a Mad World*.

Almighty God,
in whom we live and have our being,
You have made us for Yourself,
so that our hearts are restless
until they find rest in You;
Grant us purity of heart and strength of purpose,
that no selfish passion may hinder us
from knowing Your will,
no weakness from doing it;
But that in Your light we may see light,
and in Your service find perfect freedom;
Through Jesus Christ our Lord. Amen.

St. Augustine

Marital Problems

What . . . God has joined together,
let not man put asunder.

Mark 10:9

Is it true that marriages are made in Heaven? Yes — at least that's how it's supposed to be. It's part of God's plan that a man and a woman be united through the sacrament of Matrimony and spend their lives together, remaining faithful to each other, and helping each other and their children grow in grace and achieve their destiny of eternal happiness with God — all the while expressing mutual love and support. Many times it happens this way, and God is glorified and all those who know the married couple are blessed. Quite often, however, the Lord's plan is not fulfilled, because of human weakness, personality conflicts, sinfulness on the part of one or both spouses, family problems or other difficult circumstances, or various other strains or pressures on the relationship.

Many marriages end in divorce; many others continue, but with little love and with serious problems of one type or another. When both parties have given up on the marriage or are just going through the motions, little can be done. What of those cases, however, where at least one spouse truly seeks to make the relationship work? Is there any hope?

Jesus once said, "All things are possible with God."[89] The Lord must respect our free will, but a hardened human heart can be softened — often through the heroic, patient efforts of a spouse.

One of the most famous examples of this is that of St. Monica. She had to put up with her licentious pagan husband, Patricius, his ever-critical mother, and three headstrong children, including the wayward St. Augustine. Monica bore all things with amazing patience, striving to reach her family by uncomplaining love and kindness. She never reproached her husband, but praised him to her acquaintances, prayed for him unceasingly, and gradually won his respect — so much so that eventually Patricius changed his character and took instructions in Christianity. Monica brought about in this manner the conversion of her mother-in-law as well (it took quite a bit longer to achieve this with Augustine).

St. Rita of Cascia had a similar experience. The husband her parents had chosen for her was brutal and violent, frequently insulted her, and was completely unfaithful in marriage. But Rita's eighteen years of prayers and patience led to his conversion.

As a young wife, St. Catherine of Genoa moped over her husband's infidelity and vainly sought diversion in worldly amusements. Finally, she turned to God and offered her difficulties as a prayer on her husband's behalf. Her prayer was answered when he reformed before his death.

St. Elizabeth of Portugal was married at age twelve to King Denis, an able ruler but a notoriously unfaithful husband. Denis's infidelity lasted forty-one years, and at one point he even suspected his wife of treason and temporarily banished her from court. Elizabeth forgave him and continually prayed for his conversion — which finally happened on his deathbed.

In the eighteenth century Bl. Marguerite d'Youville, the first Canadian to be beatified, lost four of her six children when they

[89] Mark 10:27.

were young, and her husband, François, offered little consolation in her grief; he was an indifferent spouse and a bit of a scoundrel, spending his time smuggling liquor. When François became ill, Marguerite tenderly cared for him, winning his gratitude, and when he died two years later, she shouldered the responsibility of paying off his debts. Rather than complaining, the holy housewife remarked — perhaps a bit wistfully — "All the wealth in the world cannot be compared with the happiness of living together happily united."

Another long-suffering wife was Bl. Elizabeth Canori Mora, who was wed to a young lawyer of Rome. He proved to be immature and unfaithful, and Elizabeth was reduced to poverty, although she correctly predicted that he would eventually repent and reform himself.

In the thirteenth century, Bl. Zdislava was forced by her family to marry a wealthy nobleman, by whom she had four children. Her husband was sometimes brutal to her, but by her gentleness and patience, Zdislava eventually gained his permission to engage in works of charity. (On one occasion he was going to eject from his home a fever-stricken beggar who was there at his wife's invitation, but when he went to do so, he found the bed occupied by a figure of Christ crucified instead.) Shortly after Zdislava died, she appeared to her husband in glory, an event which greatly aided his conversion.

Not all saints succeeded in influencing their spouses, however. St. Paul the Simple, on discovering at age sixty that his wife was unfaithful to him, left her and went off into the desert to become a follower of St. Anthony of Egypt.

In the eighth century, St. Gummarus, a vassal of King Pepin, had a cruel and worldly wife whose vanity, stubbornness, and extravagance made his life miserable. Once, while he was away serving the king, she managed to alienate most of his household by refusing to give the grain harvesters their customary ration of beer (something guaranteed to make any woman unpopular). Gummarus tried very hard to convert her, and for a time it seemed he was successful, but then his wife relapsed and became even worse than before. After yet another unsuccessful attempt to change someone unwilling to change, the saint finally gave up and went off to spend the remainder of his life in a monastery.

It usually doesn't take newly married couples very long to discover why the expression "and they lived happily ever after" is often reserved for fairytales. Reality brings us face-to-face with human weaknesses, including sloppiness, annoying habits, stubbornness, and other irritations; moreover, couples can have legitimate but different interests, goals, and opinions. Unforeseen problems can quickly arise, and conflicts and misunderstandings are almost inevitable. In light of this situation, St. Francis de Sales quite rightly emphasizes the need for divine grace from the very outset of marriage: "Would that our Blessed Savior were always invited to all marriage-feasts, as to that of Cana. Then the wine of consolation and benediction would never be lacking."[90]

When married couples give God a central role in their lives, His love is able to make up for whatever may be lacking in their relationship. In the sacrament of Matrimony, God joins together a man and woman, and when they live their lives in a way that affirms and strengthens that union, they're richly blessed for cooperating with God's plan. As a practical manifestation of this, St. Francis de Sales suggests how couples might observe their wedding anniversaries: "It would be a valuable custom if, instead of worldly feasting and gaiety, husbands and wives were to dedicate that day to Confession and Communion, and more than ordinarily fervent prayer; commending their married life to God, and renewing their resolutions of sanctifying it by mutual faithfulness and love — thus, through Christ, taking breath, as it were, in the midst of the

[90] Cf. John 2:1-10.

cares attending their vocation." Romance and intimacy have a very definite and important place within marriage, but if a couple is to achieve lasting happiness, the spiritual and religious aspects of their relationship must never be forgotten.

Marriage should lead to happiness in this world; however, this goal must always be secondary to bringing about happiness in the life to come. If a marriage isn't pleasant or life-giving, it can still be spiritually valuable — for by a married person's faithfully offering everything he or she experiences, no matter how unpleasant, as a sacrifice to God and as a prayer for his or her spouse, that person may yet bring about the spouse's conversion and make possible his or her eternal salvation. There's nothing God asks of us that's nearly as important as this.

For Further Reflection

"Sacred Scripture begins with the creation of man and woman in the image and likeness of God and concludes with a vision of 'the wedding-feast marriage of the Lamb.' Scripture speaks throughout of marriage and its 'mystery,' its institution and the meaning God has given it, its origin and its end, its various realizations throughout the history of salvation, the difficulties arising from sin and its renewal 'in the Lord' in the New Covenant of Christ and the Church." — *Catechism of the Catholic Church*, par. 1602 (*Thus, husbands and wives should be aware of the dignity of their calling and make use of the Church's sacraments so as to live up to it.*)

"I will suggest some penances that will fit your married state: humility of heart, acceptance of adversity, gentleness and love for others, acceptance of the will of God, recollection of heart, the remembrance of the Most Holy Passion of Jesus Christ, making frequent use of the Eucharist, and above all, the education of your children." — *St. Paul of the Cross*

"It is a vain imagination that love is exalted by jealousy. It may testify that love is great, but not that it is good, pure, and perfect, since the perfection of love presupposes confidence in the virtue of what we love, whereas jealousy presupposes lack of confidence." — *St. Francis de Sales*

Something You Might Try

♦ Overcome difficulty with gentle patience. St. Elizabeth of Portugal bore the heavy cross of an unfaithful husband for many years. When she was criticized for treating her husband's faults too leniently, she responded, "If the king sins, am I to lose patience and thus add my transgressions to his? I love better to confide my sorrows to God and His holy saints and to strive to win back my husband by gentleness." Such an approach is truly a heroic one — and perhaps, in many cases, the only one with a chance of working.

♦ *Retrouvaille* is a Christian peer ministry for troubled marriages, in which couples explore and discuss their problems in a non-threatening way during weekend retreats, guided by facilitators. Many couples have found that these retreats strengthened their marriages. For information, contact your local parish or the Family Life Office of your diocese.

♦ Remember that marriage isn't always easy. St. Francis de Sales says, "The state of marriage is one that requires more virtue and constancy than any other. It is a perpetual exercise of mortification. . . . You must, then, dispose yourself to it with a particular care, that from this thyme plant, in spite of the bitter nature of its juice, you may be able to draw and make the honey of a holy life." Thus, try to bear with patience and to overcome your marital difficulties, so that you may grow in holiness, set a good example for your spouse, and, by offering those difficulties to God, help bring about your spouse's conversion.

Further Reading

Scripture: Ephesians 5:21; Hebrews 13:4.

Classics: St. Francis de Sales, *An Introduction to the Devout Life*.

Contemporary Works: Donna Marie Cedar-Southworth, *The Catholic Marriage Wisdom Book*; William Rabior and Susan Rabior, *Nine Ways to Nurture Your Marriage*; Gerald Foley, *Courage to Love . . . When Your Marriage Hurts*; Barbara Leahy Shlemon, *Healing the Wounds of Divorce*.

Father in Heaven,
You created marriage because it was
not good for man and woman to be alone.
I must confess, Lord,
that sometimes I've doubted this;
sometimes I've felt I'd be better off alone.
My marriage is difficult;
I know I share some of the blame,
but it seems as if my spouse, N.,
isn't willing to work with me
or to discuss our problems.
Touch N.'s heart, O Lord,
and rekindle the love
that used to exist between us.
Protect our children,
so that they may not be harmed
by the difficulties we're experiencing.
Help me to forgive N. for all that I've suffered
and to be honest in admitting the ways
I've failed in my marital duties.

*Strengthen and bless all those
who are suffering in their own marriages,
and bless also those couples
preparing to be married;
may this experience become
and remain for all of us
a pathway of grace and hope.
I turn to You in my need, O Lord;
hear my prayer, and answer me.*

*Virgin Mary, Mother of God,
I pray that you and
your holy husband, St. Joseph,
may obtain for N. and me
the graces needed to restore
and renew our marriage.
Teach us how to strive for perfection,
and help us to imitate
your loving example.
May your Son, Jesus,
show us the way to
lasting happiness and peace.*

Our Father . . . Hail Mary . . . Glory be to the Father . . .

Old Age

Do not cast me off in the time of old age;
forsake me not when my strength is spent.

Psalm 71:9

A woman lived to be one hundred, and the celebration of her birthday was a big event for the entire community. Her pastor stopped by to congratulate her, and as he was leaving, he said, "Now, Millie, I hope I'll be able to see you again at this time next year." Without missing a beat, the new centenarian answered, "I don't see why not; you look healthy enough to me!"

Not many people live for an entire century (and one man who did claimed, "I don't have an enemy in the world — I've outlived them all"), but most of us do reach age seventy or more. What's considered old? Seventy? Eighty? Ninety? Is old age a matter of reaching a certain number of years? Or is it, as some people claim, more a matter of mind and attitude, meaning that any one of us can still be young at heart?

From our Christian perspective, a successful life doesn't depend on how long we live, but on how fully we respond to the Lord during our earthly lives.

There are a number of saints whose achievements in both regards are impressive.

Quite a few of the Church's religious heroes reached the century mark. Pride of place seems to belong to the abbot St. Alferius, who lived to the age of 120. As a young man, he contracted a serious illness and vowed that, if he recovered, he would enter religious life. He did return to health and kept his vow — probably not realizing just how long a monastic life he'd actually have.

St. Alessio Falconieri, who, with six other prosperous noblemen, after receiving a vision of the Virgin Mary, formed the order of the Servites and devoted himself to prayer, penance, and the service of the poor, is said to have reached 110.

In the fourth century, St. Dorotheus of Tyre reached the age of 107. He was a priest and scholar who, during the persecution ordered by the Emperor Julian in 362, had a very unusual experience for someone so old: that of dying not from old age, but as a martyr. Also attaining the age of 107 was the thirteenth-century priest St. Parisio, who served as spiritual director for the nuns of St. Christina for *seventy-seven years.*

The English abbot St. Gilbert of Sempringham lived during the twelfth century and, like the monks under his supervision, lived very austerely — so much so that others wondered how he managed to survive on so little nourishment. Gilbert died in 1189, having reached the age of 106.

Several saints are said to have died in their 105th year, including St. Anthony of Egypt, who's often called the founder of monasticism. He was twenty when Christ's Gospel command to the rich young man to sell his possessions, give to the poor, and follow Him[91] prompted him to do just that; Anthony spent the next eighty-five years in the desert. The desert air must be very healthy, for in the sixth century, St. Theodosius, who lived in the rough Palestinian countryside near Bethlehem, also reached 105, as did the eleventh-century hermit St. Godric.

---

[91] Matt. 19:16-21.

St. Paul of Thebes, venerated as the first Christian hermit, and St. Raymond of Penafort, a great Spanish Dominican known for his work in codifying canon law, both reached the century mark. At the youthful age of sixty, Raymond was appointed archbishop of the Spanish province of Aragon, but he disliked the honor and authority of the position and was able to resign after two years, using illness as an excuse. The following year, however, Raymond was elected Master General of his order by his fellow Dominicans. He fulfilled his duties faithfully and revised the order's constitution so as to allow the Master General to resign. As soon as this was accepted, Raymond — then sixty-five — promptly resigned from office. The saint spent his remaining thirty-five years teaching, opposing heresy, and encouraging the great Dominican scholar St. Thomas Aquinas.

Most people wish to live to a venerable old age, and for many reasons. One of the most unusual was that of St. Katherine Drexel, an American foundress of a religious order. Born in 1858, Katherine belonged to a wealthy Philadelphia family, who encouraged her religious devotion and her generosity to the poor. Her father, however, was concerned that she would spend her entire inheritance in this manner, so in his will he stipulated that only the annual interest would be available for her use; the principal was to remain untouched and revert to the family estate upon her death. Katherine, who devoted her life to ministering to native Americans and blacks and establishing schools for their education, therefore had a reason to continue living as long as possible. After suffering a heart attack at age seventy-seven, she had to retire — but she spent the next nineteen years in prayer and meditation (with interest income accumulating all the while). By the time of her death in 1955 at the age of ninety-six, more than $12 million had been received and used on her charitable activities.

Our society is fortunate in that most people are able to retire at age sixty-five or seventy. But we are never meant to retire from living out our Faith. The saints understood this. St. Boniface, for instance, had spent many years in the service of God — first as a monk until the age of forty, and then as a bishop, charged by the Pope with the task of reforming and strengthening the Church in eighth-century Germany. In fact, he was called the "Apostle to the Germans." Still active in the Faith in his seventies, Boniface and fifty-three companions set out to convert the Frisians, a fierce pagan tribe who lived in modern-day Holland, but they were ambushed and killed by the natives.

Someone once said that "old age isn't for sissies," and this can also be said of our Christian Faith. "Jesus Christ is the same yesterday and today and forever."[92] No matter what our age, we must live out our Faith as best we can, using the wisdom we've gained over the years to influence others and to help them find the way that leads to eternal life.

For Further Reflection

"Let us go to the foot of the Cross and there complain — if we have the courage." — *St. Madeleine Sophie Barat* (*Sometimes retirement or old age gives us more time to relax, to think . . . and to dwell on our problems. Rather than complaining about them, it's far more valuable for us to unite them with Christ's Sacrifice.*)

"Do not seek death. Death will find you. But seek the road which makes death a fulfillment." — *Dag Hammarskjöld*

At age ninety-one, John Quincy Adams, the sixth president of the United States, was asked by a young woman, "How is Mr. Adams today?" The elderly statesman replied, "Mr. Adams is very well, thank you. It is true that his house is falling apart. The foundations have settled, the rafters sag, and the roof leaks a bit. He will be moving out almost any day now. But Mr. Adams

---

[92] Heb. 13:8.

is well, thank you, very well." (*As this great American realized, we as persons are more than just our bodies, and so our lives should be centered on more than just physical and worldly concerns.*)

Something You Might Try

◆ Like many saints before him, St. Paul of the Cross had to cope with the difficulties of growing old. As he explained in a letter, "I have been up now for four days with the help of one of the Religious [brothers] and a cane. I walked a little bit down the corridor, but then I could not hold myself up, I was so weak. I was more tired after this little walk than I used to be after walking thirty miles. But I am content with the Most Holy Will of God." St. Paul's attitude of acceptance is a challenge and an example. It is the Lord who allows many of His children to live to an old age, and, if this is your calling from Him, it can serve a larger purpose; it can also benefit you spiritually, as long as you're willing to surrender your will to Him.

◆ Keep your focus on God. The renowned spiritual author Fr. Henri Nouwen wrote, "Is my growing old making me any closer to God? Am I only getting older, or am I getting more godly?" The passing of years gives you both the opportunity and the responsibility to grow closer to God. Your relationship with the Lord is the key in determining whether you experience the fullness of life. Try, with God's help, to change your focus from "How do I feel today?" to "What opportunities will God give me today to serve Him or suffer for His name?"

Further Reading

Scripture: Psalm 103:2-5; Isaiah 65:20; Psalm 92:12-14.

Contemporary Works: Richard von Stamwitz, *Creative Aging*; Rea McDonnell and Rachel Callahan, *Good News as We Age*; James A. Magner, *Mental Health in a Mad World*.

Saintly Solutions

Lord, You know better than I know myself that
I'm getting older and will someday be old.
Keep me from the fatal habit of thinking I must
say something on every subject and on every occasion.
Release me from the craving to straighten out everybody's affairs.
Make me thoughtful but not moody, helpful but not bossy.
With my vast store of wisdom, it seems a pity not to use it all,
but You know, Lord, that I want a few friends at the end.
Keep my mind free from the recital of endless details;
give me wings to get to the point.
Seal my lips on my aches and pains.
They are increasing, and love of rehearsing them is
becoming sweeter as the years go by.
I dare not ask for grace enough to enjoy the tales
of others' pains, but help me to endure them with patience.
I dare not ask for improved memory, but for a growing
humility and lessening cocksureness when my memory
seems to clash with the memories of others.
Teach me the glorious lesson that occasionally I may
be mistaken. Keep me reasonably sweet;
I do not want to be a saint — some of them are
so hard to live with — but a sour old person is
one of the crowning works of the Devil.
Give me the ability to see good things in unexpected places,
and talents in unexpected people.
And, give me, O Lord, the grace to tell them so. Amen.

Seventeenth century (anonymous)

Pride

*Clothe yourselves, all of you, with humility toward one another, for
"God opposes the proud, but gives grace to the humble." Humble yourselves
therefore under the mighty hand of God, that in due time He may exalt you.*

1 Peter 5:5-6

What deathbed advice would you give to your loved ones as you
were about to leave this world? What one simple lesson would you
want them to hold on to above everything else? This question was
faced by the holy bishop St. Francis de Sales as he lay dying in
1622. He had taken ill returning from a trip and stopped at a convent of the Sisters of the Visitation, asking for a small, simple room
in the gardener's cottage. As the end approached, he was in pain
and lost the ability to speak. When one of the religious sisters gave
him paper and pen and asked him what virtue he especially wished
the sisters to cultivate, the saint carefully wrote one word in large
letters: *humility*.

The virtue of humility is important precisely because it keeps
us from falling into pride, which is one of the *Seven Deadly Sins*. It
was pride that caused the fall of Lucifer, one of the greatest of the
angels. Many scholars believe that the oracle against the king of
Babylon found in the book of the prophet Isaiah is actually a refer-
ence to the Devil: "How you are fallen from Heaven, O Day Star,

son of Dawn! How you are cut down to the ground, you who laid the nations low! You said in your heart, 'I will ascend to Heaven; above the stars of God I will set my throne on high; I will sit on the mount of assembly in the far north; I will ascend above the heights of the clouds, I will make myself like the Most High.' But you are brought down to Sheol, to the depths of the pit."[93]

St. Anthony of Egypt had a vision in which he saw the entire world covered with Satan's snares and traps. In great sadness, he cried out, "O my God, who can ever hope to escape all these snares, for they are everywhere?" A voice came from Heaven: "The one who is humble." St. John Bosco received a similar message in a dream: Satan, represented by a fierce lion, was attacking and killing as many people as he could, but he could not reach those who bowed down humbly before God.

All the saints recognized the importance of being humble. We see numerous examples of this, beginning with the greatest saint of all: the Virgin Mary. On being told by the angel Gabriel that she was to be the mother of the Savior, she humbly answered, "Behold, I am the handmaid of the Lord; let it be [done] to me according to your word."[94] Soon after this, when she visited her cousin St. Elizabeth, Mary praised God by saying, "He has put down the mighty from their thrones, and exalted those of low degree."[95]

Mary's husband, St. Joseph, was also exceedingly humble, being profoundly aware of his unworthiness to live with the divine Son of God and His immaculate mother. Humility, however, isn't a matter of false modesty or of finding excuses to avoid doing what God asks of us. Joseph accepted the fact that, in spite of his sinfulness, he had been chosen by God to be the husband of Mary and

[93] Isa. 14:12-15.
[94] Luke 1:38.
[95] Luke 1:52.

the foster-father of Jesus, and he did everything possible to fulfill this mission as best he could.

There are, of course, some recorded instances of saints who struggled with the virtue of humility. Those who have been greatly blessed by God are sometimes subject to the temptation of thinking that they might be entitled to praise for their good fortune. Scripture tells us that the Apostles were not immune to such thinking. St. John once said to Jesus, "Teacher, we saw a man casting out demons in Your name, and we forbade him, because he was not following us"[96] — in other words, he wasn't part of the "in group." Jesus gently corrected His favorite apostle, explaining that all people who do good in His name should be united in love and acceptance. On another occasion, the mother of St. John and his brother St. James requested of Jesus that her sons might have the places of honor in His kingdom. Again, the Lord had to correct His followers: their task was to glorify God, not themselves.[97]

Even the leader of the Apostles was sometimes motivated by false pride. St. Peter could be humble — he once called himself a "sinful man"[98] — but at the Last Supper, he couldn't admit even the possibility that he might desert His Master. Peter claimed, "Though they all fall away because of You, I will never fall away"; and when Jesus prophesied that Peter would deny knowing Him three times, the apostle insisted, "Even if I must die with You, I will not deny You."[99] Using Peter's pride, the Devil sought to deceive and control him,[100] but Peter's failure was only temporary, and, according to legend, when he himself was about to be crucified more than thirty years later, he asked to be nailed to his cross

---

[96] Mark 9:38.
[97] Matt. 20:20-28.
[98] Luke 5:8.
[99] Matt. 26:33-35.
[100] Luke 22:31.

upside down, for he was not worthy to be hung there in the same manner as his Lord.

The young St. Augustine, before his conversion, spent his life as a student and then as an instructor searching for the truth, but it had to come to him in a way that satisfied his pride. He was certainly aware of Christianity; after all, his mother, St. Monica was a devout follower of Christ. In reading the Bible, however, he was put off by what he considered its harsh and crude language, thinking that truth should be so sublime that only superior intellects such as his own could grasp it. As he later explained, "Reading it, I found the threshold too low and did not wish to bow my head to enter." Only after many years did he discover where wisdom was indeed to be found.

An opposite experience is seen in the life of St. Basil the Great, a member of one of the most remarkable families in the Church's history: his grandmother, parents, older sister, and two brothers were all, like him, eventually canonized. Basil returned home after his excellent education somewhat lacking in humility — a deficiency that his sister St. Macrina took upon herself to remedy. Her blunt honesty helped Basil pursue the path of holiness.

Another saint who needed to be warned against pride was the sixth-century abbot St. Colman; it's said that when he became too satisfied with his own great learning and intellectual achievements, God allowed him to suffer a temporary loss of memory.

God humbles those who are proud, for only through humility can they become and remain faithful servants. Some of the saints learned this from experience, including the eleventh-century monk Bl. Gunther. He was related to St. Stephen of Hungary and to the emperor St. Henry, but holiness didn't come easily or naturally to him. He lived an irreligious life until he was fifty, when St. Gothard aided his conversion and helped him become a monk. After a pilgrimage to Rome, Gunther asked, in light of his royal background, to be made abbot of the monastery. The request was granted, but with unfortunate results: friction between Gunther and the monks disrupted the community. St. Gothard rebuked him. Chastened by this, and by an apparently Heaven-sent illness, Gunther, as a simple monk, strove from then on to be as humble as possible.

The sixth-century abbot St. Senoch once went on a journey, during which he was treated with so much deference and respect that his ego became inflated. He repented only after being rebuked by St. Gregory of Tours.

The great English bishop St. Thomas Becket struggled against pride. Knowing his weakness in this area, he ordered several of his clergy to warn him of any faults they saw in his conduct, for, as he said, "four eyes see more clearly than two."

As a rule, the saints feared becoming proud and thus bore life's problems and humiliations patiently and even gratefully. St. Joseph Calasanz established a religious order in the seventeenth century, but at one point he was demoted within his order. He endured this and other difficulties without complaint.

St. John Leonardi had a similar problem involving the religious order he established. During a time of difficulty, he stayed with his friend St. Philip Neri, who gave him a very important responsibility: caring for his cat! John, being allergic neither to cats nor to humility, didn't complain.

The great thirteenth-century Franciscan theologian St. Bonaventure was informed by messengers that the Pope had appointed him Cardinal of Albano; when they sought to present him with the cardinal's red hat, he asked them to hang it on a nearby tree, as his hands were still greasy from doing the dishes. A similar informality was shown by Pope St. Pius X, who was embarrassed by the pomp of the papal court. He tearfully remarked to a friend, "Look how they have dressed me up." (When Pius was elected, his mother helped keep him in his place. After she had kissed his papal ring, she held out her own hand, on which she wore her wedding band, and said, "Now you kiss *my* ring — for without it, you never would have received yours.")

As many of the saints knew, obedience is often an antidote to pride. St. Ignatius of Antioch stressed the importance of Christians' remaining subject to their lawfully appointed bishops, for this sort of unity is pleasing to God and essential to the Church's continued growth and strength. (A legend about Ignatius, by the way, states that he was the child whom Jesus placed in the midst of His Apostles when they were arguing about which of them was most important.[101])

St. Hippolytus, a brilliant but temperamental scholar who was dissatisfied with several Popes (all canonized saints), had himself elected a rival pope, or antipope. He eventually ended his schism and died as a martyr.

Many other saints would never have dreamed of opposing legitimate authority, let alone seeking authority and power for themselves. St. Francis of Assisi refused to be ordained a priest, believing himself to be unworthy. St. Martin de Porres applied to be a "lay helper" with the Dominican Order, for he thought he didn't deserve the dignity of being a religious brother. After his death, St. Bruno, the founder of the Carthusian Order of monks, was never formally canonized, for he and all the members of his order have made a point of shunning all religious honors and publicity. (Perhaps not coincidentally, the Carthusians are one of the few orders who have never had to change their constitution or undergo significant reforms.)

Another saint known for his humility was the eighteenth-century Franciscan lay brother St. Crispin of Viterbo. He was happy to be assigned to menial tasks, for he called himself "the little beast of burden of the Capuchins." Not only was Crispin personally humble; he was not averse to reminding the many important

---

[101] Cf. Mark 9:33-37.

visitors who came to see him, including cardinals and bishops, of their need to repent of the sin of pride.

Also known for his humility was St. Thomas Aquinas. His silence during classes at the University of Cologne gave rise to his nickname the "Dumb Ox," and a sympathetic classmate offered to explain each day's lesson to him. Thomas, who possessed one of the most brilliant minds of all time, gratefully accepted, and when the "tutor" was stumped by a difficult passage, Thomas amazed him with his clear, concise explanation.

Those who wish to be great in God's eyes must be humble — although not falsely or excessively humble. When a reluctant Cardinal Albani was elected Pope in 1700, his confessor, St. Joseph Tomasi (who was with him in the conclave), ordered him, under pain of sin, to accept — which he did, becoming Pope Clement XI. Twelve years later, the Pope "got even" by forcing the humble Fr. Tomasi to accept the cardinalate, knowing that, in spite of his protestations, he had much to offer the Church. Joseph had once called himself a ne'er-do-well in an uncle's presence; the uncle rebuked him, telling him to be humble but not abject.

St. Elizabeth Ann Seton explains the danger of pride: "The gate of Heaven is low; only the humble can enter it." Humility is essential in our efforts to become virtuous. St. Vincent de Paul states that if we lack humility, all our other virtues will eventually wither away. St. John Vianney expresses the same idea: "Humility is to the various virtues what the chain is to the Rosary; take away the chain and the beads are scattered, remove humility and all virtues vanish." St. John Chrysostom notes, "Humility is the mother, root, nurse, foundation, and center of all other virtues."

Of course, we find it easier to be humble at some times than at others. St. Bernard of Clairvaux observes, "It is no great thing to be humble when you are brought low, but to be humble when you are praised is a great and rare achievement." In this regard, St. Louis of France advises us, "In prosperity, give thanks to God with humility and fear, lest by pride you abuse God's benefits and so offend Him."

How are we to achieve and maintain a humble spirit? The first step is to remind ourselves of our utter dependence on God. Bl. John of Avila suggests, "Say to the Lord, 'I am clay, and You, Lord, the potter. Make of me what You will.' " St. John Vianney presents another helpful image: "Humility is like a pair of scales; the lower one side falls, the higher rises the other. Let us humble ourselves like the Blessed Virgin, and we shall be exalted."

Imitating our Lady and asking for her intercession are the surest and easiest ways of growing in humility or any other virtue. This is the method used by St. Bartholomea, who as a girl wrote in her journal, "I propose to make myself a saint by the practice of three virtues: humility, self-denial, and prayer. Mary, my dear Mother, please help me to become a saint." When we combine these practices with love for our neighbor, our spiritual lives will bear fruit, for as St. Poemen noted, "A living faith consists in thinking little of oneself and having tenderness toward others."

Humility makes us very pleasing to God and, many times, to the people around us. One of the best-loved saints was also one of the most humble. St. Thérèse of Lisieux developed what she called her "little way." Knowing that as a simple Carmelite sister (particularly one in poor health) she would never do "great" things, she decided to become holy by filling every one of her actions, no matter how small or routine, with as much love as possible. This is the essence of humility: loving God and our neighbor as much as we can, and making as much room in our lives as possible for God's grace to enter in.

For Further Reflection

"If you seek an example of humility, look upon the Crucified One, for God wished to be judged by Pontius Pilate and to die." — *St. Thomas Aquinas*

"Humility and charity are the two master-chords: one, the lowest; the other, the highest; all the others are dependent on them." — *St. Francis de Sales*

"The most powerful weapon to conquer the Devil is humility. For, as he does not know at all how to employ it, neither does he know how to defend himself from it." — *St. Vincent de Paul*

Something You Might Try

♦ In his *Admonitions*, St. Francis of Assisi writes, "If you were the most handsome and the richest man in the world, and could work wonders and drive out devils, all that would be something extrinsic to you; it would not belong to you, and you could not boast of it. But there is one thing of which we can all boast; we can boast of our humiliations and in taking up daily the holy cross of our Lord Jesus Christ." Remind yourself that nothing in which you might take pride is truly of your own doing — other than your choice to follow Jesus (and even in this, you need His help to follow through). Take a moment to think of everything you're proud of about yourself and your life. Then ask yourself whether you'd have any of this without God's permission and aid. Give credit where credit is due; praise and thank Him, not yourself.

♦ Use humility to protect your virtues. The fourth-century virgin St. Syncletica wrote, "A treasure is secure so long as it remains concealed; but when once disclosed and laid open to every bold invader, it is presently rifled; so virtue is safe as long as it is secret, but if rashly exposed, it too often evaporates in smoke." So make a point of *not* boasting about your virtues, for the more you boast about them, the more likely they are to grow weak or to disappear.

Further Reading

Scripture: Proverbs 11:2; Sirach 11:12-13; Matthew 11:29; Matthew 18:1-5.

Saintly Solutions

Classics: St. Bernard of Clairvaux, *On the Love of God;* St.
Francis de Sales, *An Introduction to the Devout Life;* St.
Alphonsus Liguori, *The Practice of the Love of Jesus Christ.*

O Lord,
all our powers of body and spirit,
every gift both natural and supernatural,
outward and inward,
comes as a blessing from You
and reveals Your goodness,
generosity, and love,
for You have given us all that is good.
You know what is best to give each one;
and since it is clear
to You what each one's merits are,
it is for You and not for us to decide
why one has less and another more.
And so, O Lord God,
I can even consider it a great blessing
if I do not have much to bring me
praise and glory from man;
for when one does not have much,
he can look at his poverty and worthlessness,
and far from being burdened and sorrowful and dejected,
he can feel comforted and glad,
for it is the poor and humble
and despised in the eyes of the world
that You have chosen,
O God, to be familiar members
of Your household.

Thomas à Kempis

Profanity

Let no evil talk come out of your mouths,
but only such as is good for edifying, as fits the occasion,
that it may impart grace to those who hear.

Ephesians 4:29

One day St. John Bosco, the holy nineteenth-century Italian priest, was returning home by train. A fellow passenger was cursing and blaspheming, so the saint gently reminded him that cursing is a sin. The man excused himself by saying, "I know it is, Father, but it's a habit. I just can't stop." St. John found out that the man was going to the same station as he, so he said, "I'll tell you what I'll do. If you can keep from swearing until we get there, I'll treat you to a bottle of wine." The man agreed, and he kept to the bargain; a few times he was about to swear out of habit, but each time he caught himself. Later, as they shared the bottle of wine, St. John congratulated him on his success and asked, "If you can stop cursing long enough to win a bottle of wine, why not stop altogether and win salvation for your soul?"

St. John's question goes right to the heart of the matter. We can stop ourselves from using profanity if we really want to — so why is it that so many of us don't really want to? It used to be the case that people — men in particular — were very careful not to use crude or vulgar language in the presence of women and children. Nowadays, this courtesy is often neglected or even treated with derision. It was also once the case that profanity was at least reserved for situations in which people were genuinely angry or upset; now many people incorporate it into their normal conversations. Why? What does this gain for us? Or perhaps a better question is, what does this lose for us?

Cursing is a violation of the Second Commandment, and it harms us and other people by lowering standards — not just in communication, but also in our self-esteem. If there are certain things we won't do and certain things we won't say, then a foundation exists on which we can build our character, adding virtues and growing in grace. But if anything goes, we can never hope to make any spiritual progress. Worse, sinful language can lead to sinful thoughts and actions, and even to the loss of God's friendship.

Compared with the many moral problems in our society, profanity may not seem all that important. The saints, however, took it seriously and were careful to use God's name properly and respectfully and to avoid using language that might offend Him or others. For instance, St. Joan of Arc, the holy Maid of Orleans, insisted that the rough soldiers of the French army not speak profanely when they were in her presence. The same thing was true of the holy French king St. Louis IX, who had a strong aversion to blasphemous language; he did not use it himself, nor would he allow others to do so. In fact, he decreed that anyone guilty of using God's name disrespectfully would be branded, and when some complained that this law was too harsh, he said that he himself would gladly undergo this ordeal if it would bring an end to this sin.

In the fourth century, St. Thais, a former prostitute, spent years doing penance for her sinful life. She would not even allow herself to pronounce the name of God, feeling herself unworthy to do so; instead, she would pray, "O Thou, who hast created me, have mercy on me!"

St. Francis of Assisi is said to have advised the members of his order to imitate one of his own habits: that of picking up any pieces of paper on which were written God's name and putting them in a place of safekeeping as a sign of respect for the Creator. Something similar was done by Bl. Louisa of Savoy. She and her husband discouraged profanity in their household by having a poor box into which women had to pay a fine for using vulgar language; men, however, had to kiss the ground after each offense (that being considered a more effective deterrent in their case).

When St. Aloysius Gonzaga was a boy, he spent much time in the company of soldiers; when he repeated some of their vulgar language at home, not knowing what it meant, his tutor reproved him. Aloysius was overcome with sorrow and shame and afterward never ceased trying to make amends for what he considered a great sin on his part.

Bl. Felix of Nicosia, at the age of six, was sent as an apprentice to a shoemaker's shop. He'd frequently stuff his ears with wool so as not to hear the profanity being used there. It's related that a workman once accidentally made a cut across the top of a shoe, ruining it. Felix cringed as the man swore at his mistake, but then the boy worked a miracle: moistening his finger with saliva, he ran it across the slit, then handed the now-undamaged shoe back to the worker. The man and all the other workers were amazed — so much so that from that time on, they avoided using profanity.

We, of course, are unable to combat the use of bad language by performing miracles. It's probably also unwise for us to employ the method sometimes favored by St. John Vianney when he preached against profanity: mentioning the offensive words from the pulpit so his people would have no doubts as to the type of language to avoid. Rather, we should use a simple, gentle approach, along with our good example, to help others to watch their language. For instance, when traveling on a boat one day, St. Louis de Montfort was troubled by the obscene songs being sung by his fellow passengers, and he twice invited them in a friendly manner to join him in praying the Rosary. At first they responded with jeers, but eventually — touched by Louis's manner — they joined in the prayer very reverently and then listened attentively to his impromptu homily. Sometimes prayer, gentleness, and persistence can bring about surprising results.

Language has more of an ability to form our character, and our destiny, than most of us realize. The saints never lacked this awareness. They chose their words carefully, especially when using God's name, and many of our society's problems would be reduced if all of us followed this example. Respectful language manifests (and can even help create) respectful feelings toward others, in turn creating a greater awareness of personal accountability — something that would truly benefit everyone.

For Further Reflection

"If you desire, dear brothers, to be happy in this life, and that God should bless your houses, never swear, and you will see that everything will be well in your house." — *St. John Vianney*

"Fishes have no tongue. In the midst of storms at sea, they swim and glide along in silence. What a great lesson we can draw from them. When we are in the storms of great sufferings, we must lock in this treasure with the golden key of silence and not seek to complain to anyone." — *St. Paul of the Cross (Profanity is often occasioned by setbacks or annoyances, but if we can form the habit of responding to irritations with a simple, silent prayer, rather than with curses or vulgarity, we'll grow in virtue and in peace of mind.)*

"Silence is not always tact, and it is tact that is golden, not silence." — *Samuel Butler (In other words, sometimes the right thing to do is object to profane language in a respectful manner, rather than enduring it silently.)*

Something You Might Try

◆ It was the rule of Bl. Charles the Good, a twelfth-century ruler of Flanders, that any member of his household who used God's name in vain was to be punished by making a fast of forty days on bread and water. Although you don't have to be so severe on yourself, you might impose a penance on yourself each time you use profanity: donating a dollar to charity, praying one decade of the Rosary, watching less TV than you had intended that night, or making another sacrifice that atones for your profane speech and gives you an incentive to avoid such language in the future.

◆ If you have a problem with inappropriate language, try to replace it — perhaps by forming the habit of saying a silent prayer (such as the Hail Mary) after each time you speak profanely. Also, try to be aware of the situations in which you're tempted to speak profanely, and prepare yourself before they occur by praying for God's assistance (for instance, "Lord, help me watch my tongue," or "Dear Jesus, please remind me that You hear everything I say").

◆ Whenever you hear others using God's name carelessly or profanely, say a silent prayer in atonement, such as "Lord, may Your holy name be honored forever."

Further Reading

Scripture: Sirach 23:15; 2 Maccabees 12:14-15; Proverbs 26:2; James 3:10-11.

Classics: St. Francis de Sales, *An Introduction to the Devout Life*.

☞

God, my Father,
I admit that I have a problem in the language I use.
I often find myself cursing or speaking profanely,

sometimes when I'm angry at myself or others,
sometimes when things don't go my way,
and sometimes just to go along with others
who speak in this manner.
I know it's wrong, Lord, and I apologize.
I'm trying, by the way I live, to let my actions
proclaim my love for You.
With Your help, I will try harder to let that
also be true of my words.
Please assist me in my efforts
to speak only in ways that give You glory
and allow me to grow in Your grace.
May Your holy name be
forever praised and blessed,
and may all creation join in an
unending hymn of gratitude and love. Amen.

Self-Indulgence

Do not follow your base desires, but restrain your appetites.
If you allow your soul to take pleasure in base desire,
it will make you the laughingstock of your enemies.

Sirach 18:30-31

Sometimes priests and religious, reflecting on their relatively comfortable lives, are reminded of the old saying "We went out into the world to do good, and we ended up doing well." It's very easy for any follower of Christ — priest, religious, or layperson — to get used to being comfortable, and this can naturally lead to a preoccupation with our own well-being, quite often accompanied by a series of rationalizations: "I deserve the best food and drink, because I've made so many sacrifices for the Church," or "I'm entitled to a lot of vacations and days off, since I work so hard," or "My ministry involves a lot of time on the road, so I really need a car that's comfortable and luxurious."

Enjoyable experiences and valuable possessions aren't wrong in and of themselves, but these things can easily become a trap; those who wrap themselves in luxury can suddenly find themselves in a spiritual straitjacket. God put us here on earth to serve Him, not ourselves. And this means that self-indulgence is a moral issue that requires our careful attention.

Many of the saints practiced great austerities. The Desert Fathers, for instance, lived in remote, forbidding areas, often fasting and performing other acts of penance and self-denial. Other saints were known to perform severe penances, such as wearing uncomfortable garments and going without sleep for prolonged periods. These holy men and women shared a realization that the more we remove human desires and other distractions from our lives, the better we're able to recognize and receive God's presence.

Not every saint began with this insight; there were some who lived rather self-indulgently before taking God's call seriously. For instance, St. John Baptist de La Salle, coming from a noble French family in the seventeenth century, was used to a comfortable lifestyle. After being ordained a priest at twenty-seven, he was assigned to the prestigious city of Rheims — a sign that his life in the Church could well be one of privilege and dignity. This changed, however, when John became aware of the realities faced by poor children: insufficient food, clothing, and, above all, a lack of education. Feeling called to respond (even though the ministry of working with children was at first unappealing), John gave away his share of the family fortune and, having received permission to leave Rheims, gathered a group of young men to teach the poor (this was the origin of the Christian Brothers).

In his early life of self-indulgence and in his later life of service to the poor, John was imitating the example of the great French priest St. Vincent de Paul. Unlike John, Vincent came from a peasant family, but his poor background made a comfortable life within the Church every bit as appealing for him as it would later be for John Baptist de La Salle. For ten years, Vincent was content with an unchallenging, leisurely life as a priest, until he came under the influence of the saintly Fr. Pierre de Berulle. This holy priest helped him become more aware of the needs of the poor and of a calling from God to work among them, and that is what Vincent did for the remainder of his life. The priest who had sought a life of comfort and ease found instead one of hard work and service — and in the process discovered a purpose and a joy beyond his imagining.

A similar transformation occurred in the life of the twelfth-century English priest St. Wulfric. Even after Ordination, his was a carefree life, mainly given to hawking and hunting; but then — possibly because of a chance encounter with a beggar — his life changed. Divine grace broke through his self-indulgence, and from that time on, Wulfric devoted himself to severe penance and to scholarship.

At times the escape from self-indulgence is dramatic. At the beginning of the twelfth century, St. Norbert was ordained to the subdiaconate (a religious office, no longer in existence, marking one of the steps toward priestly ordination) but, because of his noble blood, he desired little more than to lead a life of leisure, and he lived as a courtier at various princely courts until the age of thirty-five. While riding in the open country one day, he was overtaken by a severe thunderstorm and was thrown from his horse and remained unconscious for about an hour. When he came to, he echoed the words of Saul outside Damascus: "What shall I do, Lord?"[102] An inner voice replied, "Turn from evil and do good; seek after peace and pursue it."[103] Norbert was soon ordained a priest and pursued his religious duties with great intensity (even to the point of antagonizing some of the local clergy).

A seventeenth-century religious, St. Hyacintha Mariscotti, experienced a similar conversion. Her noble family forced her to enter the convent (which sometimes happened when a marriage couldn't be arranged). Seeking to remain in the world even though not really a part of it, Hyacintha merely went through the motions for ten years, living a very self-indulgent life and scandalizing the

[102] Acts 22:10.
[103] Cf. Ps. 34:14.

community. A priest severely reproached her for what she was doing, and for a time she seemed to repent, but then reverted to her previous ways. However, a serious illness suddenly came upon her, and Hyacintha looked upon it as a sign from God. She converted and, from then on, proceeded determinedly down the path of virtue.

If we are pliable in God's hands, He can be gentle with us, but when our hearts are set on other things, sterner measures are called for. Bl. Villana of Florence in the fourteenth century was frightened into repenting of a self-indulgent life. After marrying, she devoted herself almost entirely to pleasure. One day, after dressing in a beautiful gown for a party, she stopped to admire herself in a mirror. Rather than seeing her own reflection, Villana discovered a hideous demon staring back at her; the same thing happened when she looked in two other mirrors. Terrified, Villana realized she was seeing the reflection of her own sinful soul; she took off her dress and changed into penitential clothing, went to Confession, and soon afterward entered the Third Order of St. Dominic.

The saints realized the importance of sacrifice and self-discipline in spiritual growth. As St. Vincent de Paul noted, "Mortification is the A, B, C of spiritual life. Whoever cannot control himself in this, will hardly be able to conquer temptations more difficult to subdue." St. Ambrose issued a similar warning: "He who knows not how to command his desires finds himself hurried away with them." And St. Rita of Cascia observed, "The more we indulge ourselves in soft living and pamper our bodies, the more rebellious they will become against the spirit." This war between body and soul, in which we experience a conflict between what we *ought* to do and what we *want* to do, is one of the effects of Original Sin.

Self-deception often plays a role in this experience, for as St. Francis de Sales noted, "Self-love is cunning; it pushes and insinuates itself into everything, while making us believe it is not there at all." Thus, if we are to come closer to the Lord and be of genuine service to Him, we must be completely honest with ourselves, asking God to make known to us our hidden motives and attachments. Then we must use His grace and strength in reordering our priorities. St. Francis advises, "We should enjoy spiritual things but only use corporal things." Achieving this sort of detachment can be a difficult, long-term process, but according to St. Madeleine Sophie Barat, "The more we have denied ourselves during the day, the nearer we are each evening to the Heart of our Lord."

Self-indulgence can be a form of pride and may represent a failure to trust in God. But when we humbly rely on the Lord for our life's purpose and happiness, everything falls into its proper place. As St. Macarius advised, "Receive from the hand of God poverty as cheerfully as riches, hunger and want as readily as plenty; then you will conquer the Devil, and subdue your passions." The legitimate enjoyment of life's pleasures should not interfere with our moral and religious duties, for it is not by doing well that we glorify God, but by doing good.

For Further Reflection

"The way of perfection passes by the way of the Cross. There is no holiness without renunciation and spiritual battle. Spiritual progress entails the ascesis [self-denial] and mortification that gradually leads to living in the peace and joy of the Beatitudes [as described by St. Gregory of Nyssa]: 'He who climbs never stops going from beginning to beginning, through beginnings that have no end. He never stops desiring what he already knows.' " — *Catechism of the Catholic Church*, par. 2015

"When we are commanded not to love the world, it does not mean we should refrain from eating, drinking, or begetting children. But temperance is ordered because of the Creator, so that such things will not enslave you by your love of t
Augustine

"The human heart is constantly seeking good things that will
make it happy; but if it seeks them from creatures, it will never
be satisfied, no matter how many it acquires. If it seeks God
alone, God will satisfy all its desires. Who are the happiest people in this world, if not the saints? And why? Because they desire and seek only God." — *St. Alphonsus Liguori*

Something You Might Try

♦ One of St. Augustine's famous, and often-misunderstood,
sayings is, "Love, and do what you wish." St. Alphonsus Liguori
explains it in these words: "Love God, and do what you wish, because he who loves God tries to avoid displeasing his Beloved and
to do only that which the Beloved wishes." In every decision we
make, no matter how small or insignificant, our starting point
should be "How can I show my love for God right now? What
would please Him?" Controlling our desires, so that they don't interfere with our spiritual growth, is a practical and important way
of demonstrating our love. Try forming this habit: every day, perform one small act of penance of your choice (during Lent, do
more than one each day). Give up one legitimate pleasure — especially in an area in which you tend to overdo things: skip dessert
once a week; on another day, delay turning on the TV for half an
hour; on another day, abstain from alcohol; and so on. Getting
into this habit will strengthen your character and allow God's
grace to be more deeply at work in you.

♦ *Choose* to prepare yourself for eternity, even as you live in
this world. For St. Gregory of Nyssa writes, "The One [Jesus] who
orders us to imitate our Father orders us to separate ourselves from
earthly passions, and this is a separation that does not come about
through a change of place, but is achieved only through choice."
But you can't follow through on such a choice without God's help.
Pray for the Lord's assistance, and renew this request each day. You

may find it helpful to offer a specific prayer every day for this intention (perhaps the one given below or one you compose yourself to fit your particular circumstances).

Further Reading

Scripture: Luke 21:34; Romans 13:14; 1 Peter 2:11-12.

Classics: St. Francis de Sales, *An Introduction to the Devout Life*; St. Alphonsus Liguori, *Thoughts on the Holy Spirit*; St. Thérèse of Lisieux, *The Story of a Soul*.

Dear Jesus,
help me to spread Thy fragrance everywhere I go.
Flood my soul with Thy spirit and life.
Penetrate and possess my whole being so utterly that
all my life may be only a radiance of Thine.
Shine through me, and be so in me that every soul
I come in contact with may feel Thy presence in my soul.
Let them look up and see no longer me but only Jesus!
Stay with me, and then I shall begin to shine as Thou shinest,
so to shine as to be a light to others; the light, O Jesus,
will be all from Thee; none of it will be mine;
it will be Thou shining on others through me.
Let me thus praise Thee in the way Thou dost
love best by shining on those around me.
Let me preach Thee without preaching,
not by words but by my example,
by the catching force of the sympathetic influence
of what I do, the evident fullness of the love
my heart bears to Thee. Amen.

Ven. John Henry Cardinal Newman

Sloth

Slothfulness casts into a deep sleep,
and an idle person will suffer hunger.

Proverbs 19:15

Sloth — also known as laziness or acedia — doesn't refer to legitimate leisure or rest; when we've been working hard, we need to take time to recharge our batteries. Moreover, there should be regular periods when we slow down the pace of life, so as to appreciate God, His creation, and the people around us. This, of course, is part of the meaning of the Third Commandment; Sunday is to be a day of prayer, so as to give to God what's due to Him, and a day of rest, so as to give ourselves what's due to us. Many Americans fall short in both these ways, working too hard while also failing to make room in their lives for God.

Spiritual rest and physical rest are moral and emotional requirements, but it's certainly possible to go to the opposite extreme and become lazy. When we think primarily of our own comfort and convenience, when we're unwilling to exert ourselves on behalf of others, and when, without good cause, we neglect to fulfill our duties — whether physical or spiritual, secular or religious — we're being lazy. This is a sin, and it can lead to other sins. But with God's help and the inspiration of the saints, anyone can overcome sloth.

When we think of the saints, we imagine them as being very energetic and dynamic. St. Paul, for instance, possessed remarkable stamina, for he experienced an inner compulsion to preach the Gospel to as many people as possible. All the saints were willing to take up their cross each day, and sometimes that cross involved physical or emotional tiredness. With God's help, they persevered, but it wasn't always easy.

St. Leo the Great could write, "I am both weak and lazy in fulfilling the obligations of my office. . . ." This outstanding fifth-century Pope accomplished a great deal, but he sought to do even more in Christ's name. This sort of noble attitude didn't come easily for all the saints. The well-loved French priest St. Vincent de Paul, for instance, became known for his tireless service of the poor, but he didn't start out with such dedication. For the first ten years of his priesthood, he was quite content with a quiet, peaceful life, in which the Church provided for his needs and protected him from uncomfortable challenges. It was only after he came under the influence of a wise and holy priest named Fr. de Berulle that Vincent began to hear and respond to a deeper calling from God.

A tendency toward laziness can keep us from responding to God's plan for us and allow us to fall into temptation, for "idleness is the Devil's workshop." According to St. Jane Frances de Chantal, "Hell is full of the talented, but Heaven, of the energetic." In other words, we'll be judged not on how many talents we had, but on how well we used the ones we were given. Seen in this light, an aversion to labor — in both the physical sense of working for a living and the spiritual sense of searching for the truth — can be a serious moral danger. One of the reasons St. Augustine had such a long and difficult path to holiness was that he found himself "detoured" at an early age. Augustine's father was unable to afford to continue his son's education, so the youth returned home at sixteen, with nothing to do. He fell into a lazy, sensual lifestyle, much to the dismay of his mother, St. Monica. Even after he resumed a more active life, his sin of unchastity — begun during his period of indolence — continued for many years, until finally his mother's prayers helped bring about his conversion.

Augustine made up for his youthful sloth by working very hard during his thirty-five years as Bishop of Hippo, in North Africa. In particular, he authored several books and thousands of sermons, scriptural commentaries, and theological treatises. (Keeping busy in this manner also helped him overcome his tendency toward moodiness and depression.)

The Catholic Church has always taught that we can't *earn* our salvation through our own efforts or good deeds. Redemption is a free, undeserved gift offered to us through Jesus Christ. But we must *actively accept* this gift. Instead of floating through life, we must be busily engaged in doing the Lord's will — like faithful servants ready for their Master's return.[104] This sort of committed response on our part obviously includes fulfilling our secular duties within our family or community, rather than taking advantage of the generosity of others; indeed, St. Paul says, "If anyone will not work, let him not eat."[105]

Even more important than this, however, is the fulfillment of our spiritual duties. The *Catechism of the Catholic Church* defines *acedia* as "a form of depression due to lax ascetical practice, decreasing vigilance, [and] carelessness of heart."[106] If we fail to pray and to attend Mass, or if we merely go through the motions, if we neglect to learn more about our Faith and to seek out opportunities for spiritual growth, if we make little or no effort to hear and respond to God's call, we're spiritually lazy. This condition not only offends God, but it also increases the likelihood that we'll prove to be like seed sown among thorns, which fails to produce a

[104] Cf. Luke 12:37.
[105] 2 Thess. 3:10.
[106] Paragraph 2733.

harvest.[107] Combating this situation requires our choice to place God's will ahead of our own and calls for ongoing prayer for the courage, energy, and strength to do what God asks of us.

Hard work is usually part of life, and certainly part of growing in holiness, although, as noted earlier, we must set aside sufficient time for ourselves and for God. This can lead to criticism or misunderstanding. For instance, after being converted to Christianity, Bl. Kateri Tekakwitha refused to work on Sundays, causing her relatives to call her lazy and disrespectful and to treat her with great severity. Nevertheless, we are called to put God first in our lives, in both our laboring and our resting, for nothing we do can bear genuine fruit without Him.

The saint who understood this better than any other, of course, is St. Joseph, honored on May 1 as Joseph the Worker, the patron of all those who labor for a living (and perhaps also of those seeking to overcome laziness). His life was one of hard work, honesty, and humility, with prayer as the foundation of everything he did. If we seek his intercession and try to live by his example, we, too, will one day be welcomed into Heaven, where we will find rest from our labors.[108]

For Further Reflection

"Remember, you will be faulted not because you are ignorant against your will but because you neglect to seek out what it is that makes you ignorant." — *St. Augustine* (*We are responsible for seeking out God's will for us, and then acting on it.*)

"Idleness begets a life of discontent. It develops self-love, which is the cause of all our miseries and renders us unworthy to receive the favors of divine love." — *St. Ignatius of Loyola*

[107] Cf. Matt. 13:22.
[108] Cf. Rev. 14:13.

"Perform faithfully what God requires of you each moment, and leave the thought of everything else to Him. I assure you that to live in this way will bring you great peace." — St. Jane Frances de Chantal

Something You Might Try

◆ St. Benedict Joseph Labre used to say to beggars and the homeless, "Try to work if you can. If you can't work, be good to the people who care for you." In other words, we all have certain responsibilities, regardless of our state in life; this includes showing respect and appreciation to those who help us in any way. This, indeed, can be a motive for work: when you have to do something you'd rather not do, look on it as an opportunity to say "thank you" to God or to your loved ones. (Actions speak louder than words — so if you really *are* grateful, get up and do something to show it!)

◆ If you're having trouble motivating yourself to do a difficult or unappealing task, begin with prayer. St. Benedict advised the members of his order, "Whenever you begin any good work, you should first of all make a most pressing appeal to Christ our Lord to bring it to perfection. . . ." Ask for the Lord's help, and then *get started*. Once you've done your part by getting the project underway, the Lord will help you sustain it.

Further Reading

Scripture: Proverbs 6:9-11; Proverbs 20:13; Matthew 11:28-29; 1 Thessalonians 3:7-10.

Classics: St. Alphonsus Liguori, *The Practice of the Love of Jesus Christ*; St. Francis de Sales, *An Introduction to the Devout Life*.

Contemporary Works: Rudolf Allers, *Self-Improvement*; James A. Magner, *Mental Health in a Mad World*.

Receive me unto the praise and glory of Thy name,
who hast prepared Thy Body and Blood
to be my meat and drink.
Grant, O Lord God my Savior,
that with coming often to Thy mysteries,
the zeal of my devotion may increase.

Thomas à Kempis

Spiritual Dryness

O God, Thou art my God, I seek Thee,
my soul thirsts for Thee; my flesh faints for Thee,
as in a dry and weary land where no water is.

Psalm 63:1

We all have periods in our spiritual lives when praying is difficult, boring, or unfulfilling; we feel as if we're just going through the motions, we have no sense of God's presence, and we wonder whether we're just wasting our time. Our efforts to find God seem like a failure, and we're certainly not aware of His running after us. It seems as if the Lord has withdrawn from us and that the religious devotions and forms of prayer that we used to find helpful or engaging are no longer so. Our spiritual lives seem to be enveloped by a vast grayness, a feeling of unreality, in which we've lost our direction and focus. And we have no sense of being able to do anything to change this.

This experience of spiritual dryness doesn't indicate any sort of failure on our part; it doesn't mean we've offended God and caused Him to turn away from us, or that our previous religious highs were imaginary and that we've finally discovered the normal, unchanging reality of prayer. No, spiritual dryness — because of our imperfect human nature and the lingering effects of Original Sin — is the almost inevitable experience of those who persevere in their efforts to grow closer to God. St. Philip Neri advises, "As a rule, people who aim at a spiritual life begin with the sweet and afterward pass on to the bitter. So now, away with all tepidity, off with that mask of yours, carry your cross, don't leave it to carry you."

God allows us to undergo this period of testing and growth so that we may progress in our spiritual lives. St. Paul writes, "When I was a child, I spoke like a child, I thought like a child, I reasoned like a child; when I became a man, I gave up childish ways."[109] His example of growing and developing as a person applies here: quite possibly the reason our previously satisfying experiences of prayer no longer appeal to us is that the Lord is calling us to a more mature faith, one requiring a deeper foundation.

This experience may be compared to moving from one community to another, which is often difficult; we have to leave behind places and experiences that we enjoyed, in exchange for a setting that's unfamiliar and probably uncomfortable at first. This sort of move, however, might be necessary or beneficial for our career or for other important considerations, and if we give it a chance, it can prove to be a great blessing.

God often calls us in the same way. Sometimes the transition from one stage to another is uncomfortable and confusing; we can experience this process as one of spiritual dryness, but if we persevere, our efforts will be rewarded and our relationship with God will be renewed and enriched.

The saints were no strangers to spiritual dryness. We might assume that, because they were so holy and because they had completely dedicated themselves to God, they must have been constantly aware of His presence. In fact, many times this wasn't the case; they had some of the same spiritual struggles we do. They became saints, however, by radically abandoning themselves to

[109] 1 Cor. 13:11.

God's will in an act of profound trust and by persevering in what they knew to be pleasing to Him — prayer and obedience — even though they found it difficult and lacking in all satisfaction.

St. Ignatius of Loyola speaks of times of consolation, when prayer is easy, joyful, and satisfying, and times of desolation, when prayer is dry, uncomfortable, and unfulfilling.[110] God gives us consolation to renew us and to reward us for our spiritual fidelity; He allows desolation to purify us from our attachments and to remind us of our utter dependence on Him. Consolation is valuable in that it encourages us to continue our prayers and devotions, but it's our faithfulness in times of desolation that allows us to make great spiritual progress. To pray when praying is easy is a good thing, but it doesn't prove that we're not just fair-weather friends to God. To pray when praying is hard greatly pleases the Lord, for it shows that our desire to know Him is deep and genuine. God knows us better than we know ourselves, and He orders all things for our benefit. St. Augustine exclaimed, "O God, You seek those who hide from You, and hide from those who seek You!" If we persevere in this spiritual hide-and-seek, we'll be the winners.

A wonderful description of spiritual dryness, or desolation, and the proper response to it, is given in *The Story of a Soul*, the autobiography of St. Thérèse of Lisieux. She writes, "I must tell you about my retreat for [religious] profession. Far from experiencing any consolation, complete aridity — desolation, almost — was my lot. Jesus was asleep in my little boat as usual. How rarely souls let Him sleep peacefully within them. Their agitation and all their requests have so tired out the Good Master that He is only too glad to enjoy the rest I offer Him. I do not suppose He will wake up until my eternal retreat, but instead of making me sad, it makes me very happy. Such an attitude of mind proves that I am far from being a saint. I should not rejoice in my aridity, but rather

---

[110] See also the chapter on depression.

consider it as the result of lack of fervor and fidelity, while the fact that I often fall asleep during meditation or while making my thanksgiving should appall me. Well, I am not appalled; I bear in mind that little children are just as pleasing to their parents asleep as awake, that doctors put their patients to sleep while they perform operations, and that after all, 'the Lord knoweth our frame. He remembereth that we are but dust.' "

In a letter to her sister Celine, St. Thérèse also writes, "St. Teresa [of Avila] says we must feed the fire of love. When we are in darkness, in dryness, there is no wood within our reach, but surely we are obliged at least to throw little bits of straw on the fire. Jesus is quite powerful enough to keep the fire going by Himself, yet He is glad when we add a little fuel; it is a delicate attention which gives Him pleasure, and then He throws a great deal of wood on the fire; we do not see it, but we feel the strength of Love's heat. I have tried it; when I feel nothing, when I am incapable of praying or practicing virtue, then is the moment to look for small occasions, nothings that give Jesus more pleasure than the empire of the world, more even than martyrdom generously suffered. For example, a smile, a friendly word, when I would much prefer to say nothing at all or look bored, etc. . . . Do you understand? It is not to make my crown, to gain merits, but to give pleasure to Jesus. . . . When I find no occasions, at least I want to keep telling Him that I love Him; it's not difficult and it keeps the fire going; even if that fire of love were to seem wholly out, I should throw something on it and then Jesus could relight it. . . ."

Many of the saints underwent prolonged periods of spiritual dryness, including St. Mary Magdalene de Pazzi, whose five years of dryness included violent temptations and much physical pain; St. Joseph of Cupertino, who was afflicted with a severe melancholy that lasted almost thirteen years; St. Alphonsus Rodriguez, who especially experienced desolation as he became older; St. John of the Cross, whose profound writings on the *Dark Night of the Soul* were based on his own intense suffering; St. Anthony Claret, who at times was unable to pray in any manner other than the recitation of vocal prayers; St. Louise de Marillac, whose fears that her sins had caused her husband's illness led to long spells of aridity and doubt; St. Hilarion, who responded with earnest perseverance when oppressed by anguish because his prayers were seemingly unanswered; and St. Josepha Rossello, who — in spite of depression and the fear that she was damned — held on to her faith, telling the sisters of her religious community, "Cling to Jesus. There are God, the soul, eternity; the rest is nothing."

Based on their hard-won spiritual victories, the saints have valuable advice for us on how to persevere when prayer seems difficult and unsatisfying. First, St. Jane Frances de Chantal assures us, "The great method of prayer is to have none. If, in going to prayer, one can form in oneself a pure capacity for receiving the Spirit of God, that will suffice for all method." Thus, we shouldn't be unduly worried over how to pray, but should focus on why — and St. Alphonsus Liguori reminds us of the reason: "This, then, is your answer whenever you feel tempted to stop praying because it seems to be a waste of time: 'I am here to please God.'" The measure of prayer isn't whether it pleases us, but whether it pleases God; and our willingness to persevere for His glory will, in turn, aid our own spiritual growth. As St. John Eudes notes, "You can advance farther in grace in one hour during this time of affliction than in many days during a time of consolation."

In terms of specific responses to spiritual dryness, St. John Vianney tells us that our Lord, although invisible to human eyes, is always present in the tabernacle. Therefore, silently sitting or kneeling before the Blessed Sacrament in church can be a valuable and effective way of praying, even if nothing seems to be happening. The saint also suggests, "If you find it impossible to pray, hide behind your good angel, and charge him to pray in your stead."

A somewhat different, but complementary, approach is offered by St. Paul of the Cross, who writes, "When you are dry as dust in prayer, don't quit, but keep going. Use little short prayers, especially acts of acceptance of the Most Holy Will of God. For example: 'O dear Will of my God, may You be blessed forever! O most gentle Will! May You be always fulfilled by all.' " Short prayers of this sort follow our Lord's teaching on the need to keep our prayers simple and sincere.[111]

Fidelity in the face of spiritual dryness — whether in our prayers or in our efforts to perform good deeds — is of far more value than commonly supposed. According to St. Francis de Sales, "Our actions are like roses, which when fresh have more beauty but when dry have more strength and sweetness. In like manner, our works performed with tenderness of heart are more agreeable to ourselves — to ourselves, I say, who regard only our own satisfaction. Yet when performed in times of dryness, they possess more sweetness and become more precious in the sight of God."

The saints took this lesson to heart and persevered; they didn't give up either on themselves or on God. In so doing, they show us the proper course through our own troubled spiritual waters. If we can't pray, we can offer God our inability to pray; if we can't sense God's presence, we can make an act of trust that He nevertheless hears us; if we don't feel loved or loving, we can choose to love God (for love is not primarily a feeling, but an act of the will). Consolations will return if we hold on long enough. Heaven awaits those who hold fast in faith. Jesus never abandons us; rather, He blesses those who trust completely in Him.

For Further Reflection

"Dryness belongs to contemplative prayer when the heart is separated from God, with no taste for thoughts, memories, and

[111] Matt. 6:7-13.

feelings, even spiritual ones. This is the moment of sheer faith clinging faithfully to Jesus in His agony and in His tomb. 'Unless a grain of wheat falls into the earth and dies, it remains alone; but if it dies, it bears much fruit.' If dryness is due to the lack of roots, because the word has fallen on rocky soil, the battle requires conversion." — *Catechism of the Catholic Church*, par. 2731

"God values in you an inclination to aridity and suffering for love of Him more than all possible consolations, spiritual visions, and meditations." — *St. John of the Cross*

"There is nothing so profitable, nothing so fruitful in such states of dryness and sterility as not to long for or too strongly desire to be delivered from them. I do not say that we must not even wish for a deliverance, but that we should not set our heart upon it. Thus we yield ourselves up to the pure mercy and special Providence of God, that He may use us to serve Him among these thorns and amid the deserts as long as it may please Him." — *St. Francis de Sales*

Something You Might Try

◆ According to St. Teresa of Avila, "We cannot know whether or not we love God, although there are strong indications for recognizing that we do love Him; but we can know whether we love our neighbor. And be certain that the more advanced you see you are in love for your neighbor the more advanced you will be in the love of God; [and] to repay us for our love of neighbor, He will in a thousand ways increase the love we have for Him." Thus, as long as you try to love other people in practical ways (especially those you dislike and those in need), you're certain to grow in love for God — even if your prayer is dry and unsatisfying.

◆ St. Paul of the Cross advises, "Never leave prayer because of dryness or difficulty. Remain before God entirely plunged in His holy love, detached from all desire for your own pleasure. It might help to send out little darts of love, such as, 'O my God, my true Good, I am yours!' and then remain in peace."

Further Reading

Scripture: Psalm 13:2-4; Psalm 42:1-3; Isaiah 58:9; Mark 13:13.

Classics: St. Alphonsus Liguori, *Conformity to the Will of God* and *The Practice of the Love of Jesus Christ*; St. Francis de Sales, *An Introduction to the Devout Life*.

O supreme and inaccessible Light,
O complete and blessed Truth,
how far You are from me,
even though I am so near to You!
How remote You are from my sight,
even though I am present to Yours!
You are everywhere in Your entirety,
and yet I do not see You;
in You I move and have my being,
and yet I cannot approach You;
You are within me and around me,
and yet I do not perceive You.
O God, let me know You and love You
so that I may find my joy in You;
and if I cannot do so fully in this life,
let me at least make some progress every day,
until at last that knowledge, love, and joy
come to me in all their plenitude.

St. Anselm

Tardiness

Do your work before the appointed time,
and in God's time He will give you your reward.
Sirach 51:30

Angelo Cardinal Roncalli, the future Bl. Pope John XXIII, served as Archbishop of Venice in the 1950s. On one occasion, his friend Stefan Cardinal Wyszynski, returning to Poland after a visit to Rome, stopped by to see him, and Roncalli arranged to take him on a tour of Venice's famous canals by a motor launch. At one point, Cardinal Wyszynski became worried because it was almost time for his train to leave, but Roncalli reassured him, "Don't worry. See that man at the head of the launch? He is station master at the train station. I asked him to join us as a precaution, because no train leaves the station without his permission."

It's nice to have a guarantee that, no matter what happens, we won't be late, but that doesn't occur very often. Most of the time, we have to be ready, or in place, at the proper moment — whether we're leaving on a trip, attending a meeting or a movie, or going to Mass. (Unfortunately, many Catholics seem to show more concern over being on time for sporting events, movies, and other leisure activities than they do over being on time to worship God at Mass.)

Saintly Solutions

Punctuality is generally admirable; it shows our respect for others, because we don't keep them waiting, and it saves us from missing out on worthwhile experiences. It has been said that "God is never late, but seldom early"; in other words, He offers His help and His grace at precisely the right moment. To benefit, however, we must be ready and, if necessary, wait patiently. If God keeps us waiting, it's for our own good, whereas if we keep God waiting, we do so to our own detriment.

Many people have trouble being on time for important events. Fortunately, there are saints to whom we can pray for assistance here. St. Vitus is the patron saint of those who have trouble getting out of bed in the morning; such persons might also pray for the intercession of St. Thérèse of Lisieux, for her father had been a watchmaker (presumably giving his daughter an appreciation of the value of punctuality).

Persons who are often a few minutes late for Mass might ponder the example of Bl. Arnulf of Villers. As a young man, Bl. Arnulf would rise early each day to attend Mass. If he overslept and arrived late, he atoned for this by standing outside the church and taking part from there, regardless of the weather. Those who are in the habit of leaving Mass early might profit spiritually by considering the words of the Portuguese bishop St. Theotonius. He was once about to begin Mass when he received a message from the queen; she was in the church and wanted him to shorten the time he usually took when presiding. The bishop sent back word that he was offering the Liturgy in honor of a Sovereign greater than any earthly one and that Her Highness was free to stay or go, but the Mass would not be rushed.

The Spanish laborer St. Isidore the Farmer was never in a hurry to leave Mass. In fact, after daily Mass, he sometimes became so engrossed in prayer that he showed up late for work. His employer, recognizing Isidore's sanctity (and realizing that he was blessed to have such a man in his employ), allowed him this liberty.

292

Not everyone today has this luxury, but many of us can make at least a little time for prayer each morning, if only we're willing to rearrange our schedules and priorities. Quite often punctuality comes down to the question, "What is it that I value?" If something is important to us, we'll usually manage to be ready for it. St. Augustine admitted to having kept God waiting, although he later repented of this. Even though he eventually came to trust in God, he was in no hurry to reform his sinful life, and as he later described, he prayed in effect, "Presently, by and by, let me alone a little longer." God's voice, of course, finally broke through, and after his conversion, Augustine worked diligently in the Lord's name.

We are given only a certain number of days and hours in this life — time that, once passed, can't be retrieved. St. Teresa of Avila, who even as a child had a deep yearning to be with God, displayed a proper attitude toward this truth. When young Teresa heard a clock strike, she used to exclaim, "Behold me one hour nearer to my country and my eternal reward!" As she and all the other saints realized, time is a gift from God — something to be, not wasted, but invested. Being punctual — particularly in hearing and answering the call of God — will be of great help to us when we finally leave the realm of time and enter into eternity.

For Further Reflection

"The enemy is glad to make you lose time when he cannot make you lose eternity." — *St. Francis de Sales*

"We have so little time to be born to this moment." — *St. John Perse*

"Every moment comes to you pregnant with a Divine Purpose; time being so precious that God deals it out only second by second. Once it leaves your hands and your person to do with as you please, it plunges into eternity, to remain forever whatever you made it." — *Archbishop Fulton J. Sheen*

Something You Might Try

◆ Here's a story that offers a way to help you be on time: A young woman was about to be married, and on the day of her wedding, her home was in an uproar, with everyone hurrying about in a frantic effort to get ready. Finally, after many anxious moments, the family was ready to leave for the ceremony, whereupon the father announced, "Now we can take our time and leisurely drive to the church — for last night I set all the clocks in the house half an hour ahead." This was one man's successful way of handling a situation in which he knew everyone would be running late. If you're habitually tardy, consider trying setting your clock a few minutes ahead; sometimes we can "save" time by tricking ourselves into thinking it's later than it actually is.

◆ Use your time wisely. Someone once said, "Remember, when you kill time, it has no resurrection." Every minute wasted is a minute of time lost to you forever . . . and one less opportunity to express your love for God. Are you ready to die and to be judged by God right now? Are you prepared to leave this realm of time and enter into eternity? If not, you need to begin making better use of each day God gives you. It's not a matter of filling your schedule or of becoming more efficient or productive, but of making more room in your life for God. Spend some quiet time with Him every day, and each morning — before beginning your daily routine — ask Him to guide, order, and bless all your activities during the next twenty-four hours.

Further Reading

Scripture: Ecclesiastes 3:1; Sirach 18:21-22; Habakkuk 2:2-3; 2 Peter 3:8-9.

Classics: St. Alphonsus Liguori, *The Practice of the Love of Jesus Christ.*

Contemporary Works: Rudolf Allers, *Self-Improvement;*
Rev. John Hampsch, *Timely Tips on the Use of Time.*

Lord Jesus, You were here on earth for a
relatively short time — only thirty-three years —
but You made every moment count.
Not an instant of Your life was wasted,
because You offered to Your Father every single
thing You did and everything You experienced.
Help me to make each of my days and moments holy.
There's always so much to do,
and I can't seem to fit everything in.
I get tired and discouraged, sometimes trying
to do too much, other times not feeling
like doing anything at all.
Please give me a sense of energy and diligence,
of purpose and order, so that I may do all
the things that are truly necessary (by Your standards,
not mine) in the proper manner and at the proper moment.
May I not keep anyone waiting, but may I instead inspire
others to place all their hours and moments in Your hands.
To You be all glory forever and ever. Amen.

Temptations

God is faithful, and He will not let you be tempted beyond your strength,
but with the temptation will also provide the way of escape,
that you may be able to endure it.

1 Corinthians 10:13

What is the one thing *every* human being throughout history who has reached the age of reason has shared in common? It isn't the reality of sin, either Original Sin or personal sin. Jesus and Mary never sinned, and neither was touched by the sinful inheritance of Adam and Eve. No, the one reality we all share is the experience of being tempted to sin.

Even Jesus (and surely Mary, although Scripture doesn't record it) experienced temptation. Three times the evil one approached Jesus during His forty days of fasting and prayer in the desert: "If You are the Son of God, command these stones to become loaves of bread. . . . If You are the Son of God, throw Yourself down [from the pinnacle of the Temple]. . . . All these [the splendors of the world's kingdoms] I will give You if You will fall down and worship me."[112] In each case, Jesus rejected the Devil's suggestions. Not only did He wish to remain true to the will of His Father, but He

[112] Matt. 4:3, 6, 9.

also desired to provide us with encouragement to face and, with His help, to overcome our own temptations to sin.

The saints, too, faced many types of temptations. St. Paul, after telling the Corinthians that he had been blessed with a vision of Heaven, said, "To keep me from being too elated by the abundance of revelations, a thorn was given me in the flesh, a messenger of Satan, to harass me."[113] We don't know what sort of affliction he was referring to; it's entirely possible that Paul was suffering from a violent temptation of some sort — something he begged the Lord to take away from him. Instead, God responded, "My grace is sufficient for you, for my power is made perfect in weakness."[114] Whether or not Paul was speaking of an actual temptation, the idea expressed in this passage applies: God's power can help us overcome every obstacle to holiness (and indeed, *only* the power of God can help us achieve this).

St. Anthony of Egypt, during his long years in the desert, experienced many severe temptations; evil spirits frequently assaulted him, but God's grace kept him safe from harm. Even someone with firsthand knowledge of the Devil's existence, however, realized that not all temptations can be ascribed to the evil one. St. Anthony said that Satan came to him one day with a complaint: "I want to know why it is that you Christians are always cursing me. For at the first misfortune that comes to you, you always say, 'Cursed be the Devil!' " Anthony insisted, "We have great reason to curse you, for you are always tempting us and laying snares to drag us into sin." To this the Devil responded, "I am often not so much to blame as you think, for people are often the cause of their own ruin, by seeking the occasions of sin, hoping they will not fall, although they know how frail they are. I never could overcome them if they only used the weapons God has put into their hands.

[113] 2 Cor. 12:7.
[114] 2 Cor. 12:9.

So they need not blame me, nor curse me so much, since it is entirely their own fault that they are lost."

Although we should never take the Devil at his word, in this instance as described by St. Anthony, Satan seems to be speaking the truth. We're responsible for some of the many temptations that assault us, and none of them could ever overcome us if we'd only use the spiritual resources and defenses God gives us. The Lord is present to sustain those who wish to conquer sin and temptation, even though we often forget this.

St. Anthony himself had to be reminded of this. Once he was so distressed after being tempted that he cried aloud, "O my good Jesus! Where were You all this while?" Jesus answered him, "I was here beside you; I saw your conflict and struggle. By my permission you were tempted, but fear not; fight bravely, for I am always near to help you!" Quite understandably, these words gave Anthony renewed peace and strength. God will give us, too, the grace we need, whether our temptation comes from the Devil, from within, or from others.

Other people — sometimes even those we love — can seek to divert us from the path of holiness. This was the case for St. Thomas Aquinas, who as a young man sought to enter the Dominican Order. His family objected, for in the thirteenth century, the order was new and not wealthy or prestigious. When Thomas persisted, his mother arranged for him to be kidnaped and imprisoned by one of his brothers. Hoping to use temptations of the flesh against him, the family paid a naked young woman to enter his cell, but Thomas rejected her vigorously: he used a red-hot iron poker from the fireplace to chase her out of the room. In light of such a determined rejection of sin, it's not surprising that Thomas's will prevailed and that he was able to enter the Dominican Order soon afterward.

All the saints experienced temptation of one sort or another; only a few can be mentioned here: St. Margaret of Cortona, who, even after repenting of an immoral relationship, remained subject to temptations of the flesh for another three years; St. Mary Magdalene de Pazzi, who experienced violent temptations during a five-year period of spiritual anguish; St. Jane Frances de Chantal, who was frequently tempted with doubts against the Faith; St. John of the Cross, who, during his "Dark Night of the Soul,"[115] was tempted to believe that God had abandoned him; St. Rose of Lima, who is said to have suffered not only temptations by the Devil, but also physical assaults and beatings from him; St. Euphrasia, who was tempted to return to the world after withdrawing to the desert, and whose abbess helped her persevere by assigning her difficult and humbling tasks (such as moving a pile of stones from one place to another, back and forth, thirty times); Bl. Christina of Stommeln, whom the Devil — disguised as St. Bartholomew — unsuccessfully tempted to suicide; Bl. Helen of Udine, whose steadfast resistance to frequent suicidal temptations was always rewarded by spiritual consolations; and St. Mary of Egypt, who suffered many temptations during her forty-seven years in the desert, but found relief in prayer, especially to the Virgin Mary.

Praying to Mary for her intercession and assistance can be a very powerful means of combating temptation. The saints offer us other helpful suggestions.

St. John Bosco was well aware that idleness increases the Devil's opportunities to lead us astray, so in his ministry to boys, this holy Italian priest always emphasized the importance of keeping busy in wholesome activities. This consideration still applies to us today; we need quiet time with God and time for relaxing, but we also need to make sure that boredom doesn't lead us into morally dangerous activities.

St. Ignatius of Loyola said that sometimes we can be tempted by *good* things. We should develop our natural talents and abilities,

---

[115] A time of intense and prolonged spiritual desolation.

but, Ignatius warned, we must be careful that pride in these gifts doesn't cause us to ignore our debt to God or to neglect our spiritual duties. Brilliant, talented people are in as much danger of damnation as anyone else. Ignatius also recognized that mystical gifts can, if misused or overemphasized, lead us astray. (St. Paul had faced this same situation when a squabble over the different gifts of the Spirit threatened to divide the Christian community of Corinth.[116]) Ignatius was richly blessed with spiritual gifts, but he was also an eminently practical man; he realized that the great consolations he received sometimes distracted him from his duties, and when his doctor told him his eyesight was threatened by the gift of tears,[117] the saint prayed to have this gift taken away, so that he might be able to continue laboring on behalf of the Church and his order.

As a former soldier, St. Ignatius realized that the Devil is like a shrewd military commander who will assault an enemy fortress at its weakest point; thus, wise defenders will concentrate their greatest efforts at that location. In spiritual terms, this means honestly admitting our faults and weaknesses and seeking to grow not only in ways we find comfortable and enjoyable, but especially in those areas that are challenging and frequently sources of temptation. To prevent Satan from breaking into our souls, we should give our primary attention to our areas of moral weakness, while not neglecting to guard those approaches where we're morally strong.

When it comes to resisting temptation, all the saints emphasize the importance of prayer. St. Bernard of Clairvaux reminds us that prayer is more powerful than the Devil and his enticements, and St. John Chrysostom says, "As water extinguishes fire, so prayer extinguishes the heat of the passions."

[116] Cf. 1 Cor. 12:28-31.

[117] A profound sensitivity manifested by the ability to cry very easily and readily.

St. Paul of the Cross advises us, "Be valiant in fighting tempta-tions, but in fighting, maintain a peaceful spirit. The humble heart will be victorious." Humility is also stressed by St. Francis de Sales, who describes how a little child runs to his father's arms when he sees a threatening bear or wolf. In the same way, we must turn in-stantly to God when assaulted by temptations. In like manner, St. Alphonsus Liguori warns us, "When you are tempted, do not trust yourself, and do not trust all the good resolutions and promises you have made, but rely completely on divine assistance. Have imme-diate recourse to God and the Blessed Virgin."

Someone once wryly observed that most of us, when fleeing temptation, leave a forwarding address. This, of course, is a mis-take. Temptations should be given as little attention as possible. St. Anselm tells us, "Do not argue with perverse thoughts or evil desires, but when they attack you, occupy your mind vigorously with some profitable meditation or plan until they vanish. No thought or intention is ever expelled from the heart except by some other thought or intention incompatible with it."

Quite often temptations involve other people — particularly those we dislike. In this regard, St. John Vianney suggests, "The way to overcome the Devil when he excites feelings of hatred for those who injure us is immediately to pray for their conversion." Once temptations gain a foothold in our consciousness, they can quickly grow in strength or attraction. That's why St. Alphonsus states, "As soon as we become aware of a thought that has an evil look about it, we must dismiss it immediately. We must, as it were, slam the door in its face, denying it admittance into the mind, without stopping to decipher its meaning or intention. We must shake off such wicked suggestions as quickly as we would shake off fiery sparks that landed on our clothes."

In addition to resisting temptations, we must remember what they signify — that we are involved in a spiritual war, from which we can choose to emerge victorious, with God's help. St. Francis of Assisi tells us, "No one ought to consider himself a true servant of God who is not tried by means of temptations and trials."

St. John Vianney says that it's actually a *good* sign if we're experiencing temptations: "Blessed are they who are tempted! It is when the Devil sees that a soul is tending toward union with God that he redoubles his efforts." By the same token, the saint says, "The greatest of all evils is *not* to be tempted, because there are then grounds for believing the Devil looks upon us as his property." He also observes that farm workers don't complain about long hours at harvest time, for it's then that they earn good money by their hard work; similarly, temptation is the season of spiritual harvest — for each time we successfully use God's help in rejecting sin, we grow in grace and become morally stronger.

Finally, St. Paul of the Cross advises, "Don't be afraid of temptations. God permits them to refine your humility and to lay deep foundations for the lofty spiritual edifice that He has planned to build in your soul."

Temptations are opportunities to prove our love for God and to become holier by exercising our spiritual muscles. Both the Devil and our own imperfect human nature are formidable opponents to us as we try to grow in grace, but the Lord will never allow us to be tempted beyond our strength. Those who persevere with God's grace will not only triumph in the short term, but will make great progress along the narrow path that leads to everlasting life.

For Further Reflection

"As the pilot of a vessel is tried in the storm, as the wrestler is tried in the ring, the soldier in the battle, and the hero in adversity, so is the Christian tried in temptation." — *St. Basil the Great*

"A man who governs his passions is master of the world. We must either command them or be enslaved by them. It is better to be a hammer than an anvil." — *St. Dominic*

"In time of peace, that is, when temptations to the sin to which you are most inclined do not molest you, make several acts of the contrary virtue. If occasions to do so do not present themselves, endeavor to seek them out. By this means you will strengthen your heart against future temptations." — *St. Francis de Sales*

Something You Might Try

♦ St. Paul of the Cross advises, "Pay no attention to any assaults of temptations you may encounter, no matter how filthy and disgusting they may be. Say that you would rather die than consent to them, and then don't be afraid. Leave the thoughts alone, and don't worry about them." God wants you to reject temptations, but not to worry about them. St. Philip Neri used to encourage his penitents not to grieve over the temptations they suffered, saying that when the Lord intends to bestow a particular virtue on us, He often permits us first to be tempted by the opposite vice. Therefore, look upon every temptation as an invitation to grow in a particular virtue and a promise by God that you'll be successful, if only you stand fast.

♦ St. Augustine suggests, "Emulate the tiny ant; be an ant of God. Listen to the word of God, and hide it in your heart. Collect plenty of food during the happy days of your spiritual summers. You will then be able to endure the difficult days of temptations during the winters of your soul." In other words, when things are going well, make extra efforts to pray for strength and an increase of virtue, especially in areas of personal weakness or regarding sins to which you've been tempted in the past.

Further Reading

Scripture: James 1:12-15; Hebrews 2:18.

Classics: St. Ignatius of Loyola, *Spiritual Exercises*; St. Francis de Sales, *An Introduction to the Devout Life*; St. Alphonsus

Liguori, *Conformity to the Will of God* and *The Practice of the Love of Jesus Christ.*

⌒

O God, by Thy mercy,
strengthen us who lie exposed to the
rough storms of troubles and temptations.
Help us against our own negligence and cowardice,
and defend us from the treachery of our unfaithful hearts.
Succor us, we beseech Thee, and bring us
to Thy safe haven of peace and felicity.

St. Augustine

Timidity and Aggressiveness

When they bring you before the synagogues and the rulers and
the authorities, do not be anxious how or what you are to answer
or what you are to say; for the Holy Spirit will teach you
in that very hour what you ought to say.

Luke 12:11-12

Many legends, stories, and fairytales talk about finding that proper balance between boldness and timidity, between zealousness and indifference, or between having too little and having too much. We have a saying "He who hesitates is lost" — to which it has been truthfully rejoined that "sometimes he who *doesn't* hesitate is lost." Too soon or too late, too little or too much, too strong or too soft: how do we find the proper balance?

The ancient Greeks advised "moderation in all things," and in terms of human relationships, this proper balance can be summed up in the word *assertiveness*. Unlike the extremes of aggressiveness (in which we show too much respect to ourselves and not enough to others) and timidity (in which we show too much respect to others and not enough to ourselves), assertiveness is a way of standing up for ourselves and our own rights, while accepting and respecting the needs and rights of others. In religious terms, however, being assertive isn't so much a matter of defending ourselves, as it is of upholding Christ's truth, through which we obtain our deepest identity. As Jesus said, "He who loses his life for my sake will find it."[118] This is something the saints understood and practiced in a powerful way. They didn't insist on their own rights and dignity, but they respected the rights and dignity of others, and they were willing to do anything — even to give their lives — to uphold the honor and authority of God.

The Bible gives us several powerful examples of this. The same St. Paul who urged prayers on behalf of earthly kings and authorities[119] also asserted that every knee on earth shall bend at the name of Jesus;[120] moreover, Paul never hesitated to preach the Gospel, in season or out of season, welcome or unwelcome — and he frequently found himself in trouble with the authorities as a result. Some years earlier St. John the Baptist had risked the displeasure of King Herod Antipas by rebuking him for living with his sister-in-law,[121] knowing full well that doing so might cost him his freedom and his life. After Christ's Resurrection and Ascension, the Apostles chose seven men as deacons, and one of them — St. Stephen — soon became known for fearlessly proclaiming Jesus as Lord. He, too, paid for speaking the truth with his life, becoming the first Christian martyr.[122]

But finding the right balance between strength and weakness can be an ongoing challenge. After a lifetime of experience, the eleventh-century abbot St. Odilo said that of the two extremes, he chose to offend by being too tender, rather than too harsh. The great Father of the Church St. Irenaeus strongly defended the true Faith against heresy, but in doing so, rather than condemning his

[118] Matt. 10:39.
[119] 1 Tim. 2:1.
[120] Phil. 2:10.
[121] Mark 6:18.
[122] Acts 7:58-60.

opponents, he sought to persuade them, and he was always concerned for their spiritual well-being.

We certainly don't have to threaten or shout at others to gain their attention; gentleness can be just as effective, if not more so. Someone who had to learn this lesson was the great sixth-century Irish missionary St. Columba; as one commentator wrote, "Of all qualities, gentleness was precisely the one in which Columba failed the most." The saint was very demanding in his youth, but — as happens with many of us — his character mellowed as he grew older. Eventually Columba became known for his kindness, although he remained quite capable of defending his flock fiercely.

Throughout the Church's history, there have been powerful shepherds who have provided tender leadership to the flock while protecting it from danger, particularly among the successors to St. Peter. For instance, it was said of Pope St. Fabian that the Roman emperor Decius would have preferred coping with a political rival than facing him.

In the mid-fifth century, Pope St. Leo the Great saved Rome from Attila the Hun. When the civil authorities fled in fear, Leo, virtually alone and unarmed, rode out to meet the barbarian warrior chief and persuaded him to withdraw without harming the city. (It should be noted, however, that Leo had supernatural assistance. When Attila was later asked why he agreed to the Pope's request, he spoke of seeing a fierce angel staring at him menacingly while standing protectively at Leo's side.)

Some 150 years later, St. Gregory I — another Pope given the title "the Great" — defended the Church and the common people during a time of societal crisis and government collapse. Later popes such as Gregory VII, Pius V, and Pius X — all canonized saints — provided the Church with strong leadership in the face of worldly hostility.

Many bishops were unyielding in their defense of the Church's rights. St. Athanasius insisted on the true teaching of the Church that Jesus is both divine and human, even when the emperor and most of the bishops fell into heresy and denied Christ's divinity; as a result, he was exiled for many of his forty-six years as bishop.

In the fourth century, St. Ambrose, Bishop of Milan, refused an imperial decree to turn over one of the city's churches to a group of heretics for their own use; later he publicly denounced the emperor for massacring several thousand people and demanded that he do penance — and the emperor submitted.

In twelfth-century England, King Henry II appointed his friend Thomas Becket Archbishop of Canterbury, expecting that Thomas would cooperate in his efforts to gain control over the Church. Thomas surprised him by taking his spiritual duties seriously, and his vigorous defense of the Church's rights led to his martyrdom.

Even laypersons have at times been vigorous in the exercise of their Christian calling. St. Catherine of Siena, for instance, was outspoken in giving advice to popes and kings — advice that was usually carefully considered and often heeded.

It can be prudent and noble to set aside our desires or preferences for the sake of harmony, but we don't have that option when it comes to defending the Gospel. The best way to share the truth with others is by lovingly bearing witness to it. Christians needn't fear a reputation of being pushy in standing up for the Faith, for God's truth is eternal and unchanging, and sharing it boldly and respectfully is the most loving gift we can give to those around us.

For Further Reflection

"Humble gentleness is the virtue of virtues that God has recommended to us; therefore, we must practice it always and everywhere." — *St. Francis de Sales*

"I have tried many methods of governing, but I have found none better than gentleness and tolerance." — *St. Jane Frances de Chantal*

"What fine edification a soul gives who, when greeted with scorn, answers gently to conciliate the offensive individual; or perhaps makes no reply at all, nor complains to others, but maintains a placid expression and shows no bitterness." — *St. Alphonsus Liguori* (*This sort of response, contrary to our society's understanding, is not a sign of weakness, but of strength; we are asserting that, because we love God, we will not allow anyone to make us respond to an offense in a non-Christian way.*)

Something You Might Try

♦ It can be especially difficult to practice assertiveness when we need to correct others. How do we avoid the extremes of ignoring or downplaying the offense, and of overreacting to it? St. Alphonsus Liguori advises, "Even when correcting faults, superiors [and parents, teachers, employers, and anyone else with authority] should be kind. It is one thing to reprove forcefully, and another to rebuke harshly. Sometimes one must deliver a firm admonishment when the fault is serious, and especially if it be repeated after the subordinate's attention has been called to it. But let us always beware of harsh and angry rebukes; the person who chides with anger does more harm than good. . . . On some rare occasion it may be necessary to say a harsh word, to make the offender realize the gravity of the fault; still we should always leave the offender with a gentle expression and a few kind words. . . . And if the person being corrected becomes disturbed, the reproval must be put off until his anger subsides, or else we will only make things worse."

♦ It's impossible to satisfy everyone, so limit yourself to trying to satisfy God. He is your Father, and it should be a matter of family pride for you to defend His name and authority.

Further Reading

Scripture: Psalm 23:4; Isaiah 12:2; 2 Timothy 4:1-2.

Saintly Solutions

Classics: St. Alphonsus Liguori, *The Practice of the Love of Jesus Christ*; St. Francis de Sales, *An Introduction to the Devout Life*.

Contemporary Works: Harry A. Olson, *Power Strategies of Jesus*.

Father of gentleness and strength,
help me to find the proper balance
in all my dealings with the world
and in all my relations with other people.
Sometimes I am headstrong and stubborn;
other times I am fearful and submissive.
I overreact to some things;
others I fail to take seriously.
I value my faith and my membership
in Your family,
but I don't always show it.
Give me wisdom and strength,
courage and prudence,
boldness and compassion,
so that I may proclaim Your truth to a world
that often follows bright, shining lies.
Let me know Your will, and help me to follow it —
humbly, confidently, and lovingly —
so that my life will witness to Your truth and
Your kingdom may break into our world.
Blessed be Your name forever and ever. Amen.

Uncertainty

When the Spirit of truth comes,
He will guide you into all the truth.

John 16:13

Wouldn't it be great if we had a direct connection to Heaven — a phone line by which we could call God Himself and ask questions such as "Lord, what's the easiest way for me to solve this problem?"; or "Father, how much longer do I have to put up with this situation?"; or "God, I really don't know what it is that You want me to do; will You please show me?" There have been such cases recorded; the Old Testament hero Moses, for instance, used to talk to God face-to-face,[123] and the Apostles were able to question Jesus whenever they wanted. Many mystics and visionaries throughout the centuries have allegedly held conversations with Jesus or one of the saints, and there are hundreds (perhaps thousands) of persons today who claim to be in contact with Heaven.

It seems as if life would be so much easier if, after praying to God for guidance or assistance, we could hear His answers directly. As most of us know, however, it usually doesn't work that way; we listen for God, hoping to hear His voice in a powerful wind, in an

---

[123] Exod. 33:11.

313

earthquake, or in a blazing fire — but instead, we hear only a tiny whispering sound.[124] The answers to our questions are sometimes vague and confusing. We have to discover what God wants of us; we have to figure out which path He wants us follow.

This process of discovering God's will for us is called *discernment*. Discernment doesn't mean choosing between something morally right and something morally wrong; obviously we must avoid anything sinful. Discernment involves deciding between two or more courses of action that are morally good or at least morally neutral.

The saints often had just as much need for discernment as the rest of us do. Some of them found that the Lord's will for us is revealed by other people. In the twelfth century, St. William of Vercelli wanted to make a pilgrimage to Jerusalem, but his friend St. John of Matera assured him that God had a different plan in mind. Ignoring John, William set out, but soon afterward he was attacked by robbers. Taking this as a sign that John was right after all, William returned home to his true calling: living for a time as a hermit and later becoming the abbot of a monastery.

God's will for our life is sometimes revealed very dramatically, but usually it's made known in a simpler, more ambiguous way. The fifth-century bishop St. Hilary of Arles, for instance, was torn between the possibility of a successful worldly career, for which he was well-trained, and the possibility of a religious vocation, which his friend and mentor St. Honoratus strongly suggested. Writing later about this period of his life, Hilary stated, "On the one side, I felt that the Lord was calling me, while on the other hand, the seductions of the world held me back. My will swayed backward and forward, now consenting, now refusing. But at last Christ triumphed in me." Having discovered and accepted God's will for him, St. Hilary gave his money to the poor and followed his friend Honoratus into religious life.

[124] Cf. 1 Kings 19:11-13.

Many of the saints had to choose between several paths; their holiness lay not in having a direct line to God, but in being completely open to doing His will once they had discerned it.

Each of us is called to do the Lord's will, for as St. Ambrose says, "The will of God is the measure of all things." Moreover, St. Basil the Great tells us, "It is the duty of those who are zealous for God's good pleasure to make inquiry as to what is right for them to do."

According to St. Rose of Lima, "When God is consulted sincerely, He gives a clear answer" — but in what form will this answer come? St. John Vianney assures us, "God speaks to us without ceasing by His good inspirations," but it's still necessary for us to listen attentively. "In important matters especially," writes St. John of the Cross, "we must seek clear lights from God. It happens often that we do not do the will of God, but our own, since we don't seek to know God's will by much prayer, seeking counsel, and much reflection." Prayer is very important; as St. Theophane Venard advised his younger brother, "Pray simply, humbly, and fervently to know God's will, and your path will be made clear. Then you must follow the inspiration Divine Mercy puts into your heart."

It is, of course, essential that we truly seek to do the Lord's will, instead of our own. But how do we know for sure what the Lord is asking us to do?

This was a major concern of St. Ignatius of Loyola, one of the great spiritual geniuses of history, so he created what he called a set of "Rules for the Discernment of Spirits." Very simply, Ignatius states that if we receive a direct, unmistakable revelation from God as to His will for us, we should obey as completely and wholeheartedly as possible. Such a revelation, however, is relatively rare, and usually we will be required to discern the proper course of action using the abilities and gifts God has given us. (Again, this is a matter of choosing, not between good and evil, but between two or more potentially good courses of action on an issue of some importance — for instance, whether to remain in our job or to accept a new position elsewhere.) This involves using our God-given intellect, feelings, and imagination:

• *Intellect.* Analyze the situation logically. What are the advantages and disadvantages of each course of action? Do the advantages of one choice substantially outweigh the other choices? Which decision seems best from a rational point of view?

• *Feelings.* What feelings, if any, are raised as you consider each possibility? Is there a strong sense of desire or excitement involved in one option (which may be an indication it should be chosen) or a sense of dread or unhappiness over another (which may indicate that this choice is not God's will for you)?

• *Imagination.* If someone came to you for advice about the situation you're facing, what would you say or urge that person to do? If you imagined yourself on your deathbed, looking back at all the choices and actions of your lifetime and knowing that you'd soon be reviewing them with God, what decision — from that perspective — would you want to have made?

St. Ignatius tells us that, after going through one or more of these steps, a course of action will usually begin to stand out from the others. After additional prayer and reflection, we may make this our choice. Ignatius warns that, once we've prayerfully made our decision and offered it to God and feel a sense of inner peace over the results, we may have second thoughts — in particular, an experience of doubt, restlessness, anxiety, and temptation, which he calls *desolation*.[125] Quite often this feeling is not from God, but

---

[125] See also the chapter on depression.

from the Devil, for it's natural that Satan would try to dissuade and upset us if we've made a choice that's pleasing to God. Ignatius stresses that we must *never* change our decision (or make our decision in the first place) during an experience of desolation. Our response to any doubts or second thoughts should be "Lord, if You want me to change this decision, I will — but not now; I'll do so only when I feel completely at peace in Your presence." When we've followed this process honestly and humbly, we can be sure that God is pleased with us and that the results will aid our growth in holiness.

For Further Reflection

"Man has the right to act in conscience and in freedom so as personally to make moral decisions. 'He must not be forced to act contrary to his conscience. Nor must he be prevented from acting according to his conscience, especially in religious matters.' " — *Catechism of the Catholic Church*, par. 1782

"Reflect that your guardian angel does not always move your desire for an action, but he does always enlighten your reason. Hence, in order to practice virtue, do not wait until you feel like it, for your reason and intellect are sufficient." — *St. John of the Cross*

"Every Christian must refer always and everywhere to the Scriptures for all his choices, becoming like a child before it, seeking in it the most effective remedy against all his various weaknesses, and not daring to take a step without being illuminated by the divine rays of those words." — *Pope John Paul II*

Something You Might Try

◆ Prayer is at the heart of discernment. When one of her students asked her, "Can you advise me about my future?" St. Edith Stein replied, "Let us pray together to get an answer from God. We must ask Him to let us know what He wants from you." It's unlikely we'll ever know God's will for us unless we take the time to ask Him. Once you've prayed about a decision or situation, you'll be ready to use St. Ignatius's "Rules for the Discernment of Spirits," described above.

◆ According to Thomas à Kempis, a fifteenth-century monk known as the author of the *Imitation of Christ*, "We should not trust every word we hear or every feeling in our hearts; rather, we should bring such matters before God and carefully ponder them at our leisure. . . . Instead of following your own notions, consult someone who is wise and conscientious, and seek to be guided by one who is better than you." Thus, we need to make important decisions prudently — by not rushing them and by seeking advice from someone wiser and holier than we.

Further Reading

Scripture: Wisdom 9:10-11; Psalm 25:4-5; Psalm 143:8.

Classics: St. Ignatius of Loyola, *Spiritual Exercises*; St. Alphonsus Liguori, *Conformity to the Will of God.*

Contemporary Works: Pierre Wolff, *Discernment: The Art of Choosing Well*; Thomas H. Green, *Weeds Among the Wheat — Discernment: Where Prayer and Action Meet*; Rev. John Hampsch, *Speak Up, Lord, I Can't Hear You.*

☞

Be kind to Your little children, Lord.
Be a gentle teacher,
patient with our weakness and stupidity.
And give us the strength and discernment
to do what You tell us,
and so grow in holiness.

May we all live in the peace
that comes from You.
May we journey toward Your city,
sailing through the waters of sin
untouched by the waves,
borne serenely along by the Holy Spirit.
Night and day may we give You praise and thanks,
because You have shown us that
all things belong to You
and all blessings are gifts from You.
To You, the essence of wisdom,
the foundation of truth,
be glory for evermore. Amen.

St. Clement of Alexandria

Unforgiveness

For if you forgive men their trespasses, your heavenly Father
also will forgive you; but if you do not forgive men their trespasses,
neither will your Father forgive your trespasses.

Matthew 6:14-15

If, immediately after the Last Judgment, a vote were to be taken among all the residents of Heaven as to which teaching of the Gospel had been the most challenging or difficult to obey, a majority in all likelihood would say the need to forgive our enemies so as to receive God's forgiveness. It goes against our sinful human nature to renounce vengeance and to leave our malefactors unpunished, but this is what is expected of us. " 'Vengeance is mine; I will repay,' says the Lord."[126] This very difficult teaching was obeyed by the saints — although in some cases, not without much struggle — and we must also heed it.

The first Christian martyr, St. Stephen, gives us a powerful example of Christian forgiveness. The Acts of the Apostles tells how he was stoned to death for his fearless proclamation of the Gospel. His last words were "Lord, do not hold this sin against them."[127]

---

[126] Rom. 12:19.
[127] Acts 7:60.

Other saints and martyrs are also known for their amazing charity toward their persecutors. For instance, St. Wenceslaus, king of Bohemia, was murdered for political purposes by supporters of his brother Boleslav, who lured the king into an ambush under the pretense of meeting him for Mass. As Wenceslaus fell at the door of the chapel, his final words were, "Brother, may God forgive you."

This was also the sentiment expressed by the virgin and martyr St. Maria Goretti, who was murdered in 1902 when she was only twelve. Maria was assaulted by a neighboring youth named Alessandro Serenelli; when she resisted his sexual advances, the enraged youth repeatedly stabbed her. Before dying in a hospital the following day, Maria expressed her forgiveness of Alessandro. (It was eight years before he accepted it; Alessandro was unrepentant in prison, until he had a dream of Maria gathering flowers and presenting them to him.)

St. John Vianney noted, "The saints have no hatred, no bitterness; they forgive everything, and think they deserve much more for their offenses against God." For example, St. Louis IX, who reigned as King of France for thirty-five years, was known for his mercy and impartial justice and even forgave members of the nobility who unsuccessfully rebelled against his rule.

The founder of the Society of Jesus, St. Ignatius of Loyola, once walked a hundred miles during the winter to nurse a man who had fallen ill — a man who, only a few weeks earlier, had stolen Ignatius's meager savings.

During the persecution of the Church by Queen Elizabeth I of England, the priest and martyr St. Edmund Campion was betrayed and arrested; while in prison, he was visited by the man who had betrayed him. Not only did Edmund forgive his betrayer; he also urged him to leave England, where he might be in danger himself, and gave him a letter of safe-conduct to a Catholic nobleman in Germany.

How is it possible for sinners like us to follow the wonderful example of these and other saints? Precisely by reflecting on the fact that we *are* sinners greatly in need of God's mercy. Our Lord's parable of the unforgiving servant[128] reminds us that if we insist on strict justice in the cases of those who've sinned against us, we will also be held fully liable for our own far greater offenses against the infinite majesty of God. Because the saints were so honest in admitting their own sins, it became very easy and natural for them to forgive the offenses of others.

How can we learn to control our natural tendency to lash out against those who hurt us? After all, our sincere desire to practice Christian forgiveness can, under certain circumstances, easily be overwhelmed by strong feelings of rage or personal affront. The sixteenth-century priest St. Philip Neri suggested that we practice controlling our emotions: we pretend that we've just suffered terrible insults or misfortune and then imagine ourselves imitating Christ's example by bearing these burdens with patience and charity. This sort of rehearsing will eventually make it easier for us automatically to respond in a more loving way to real affronts.

Also, as St. Augustine notes, "There are many kinds of alms, the giving of which helps us to obtain pardon for our sins; but none is greater than that by which we forgive from our heart a sin that someone has committed against us." Thus, as soon as someone offends us, we might tell ourselves, "I have the right to be angry at this person, but I freely renounce it as an act of charity performed in Christ's name." Then we can console ourselves with the reminder that this sort of almsgiving is very pleasing to God and will be richly rewarded.

Moreover, we might remind ourselves of the words of St. Faustina Kowalska: "We resemble God most when we forgive our neighbors."

[128] Matt. 18:23-35.

Many times we are overly concerned with preserving our dignity and reputation, and this can make us quick to retaliate against those who wrong or insult us. But the saints realized that in God's eyes the most dignified or noble response to an injury is to turn the other cheek. In the twelfth century, some workmen were repairing a city wall next to the vineyard of St. Ubald, Bishop of Gubbio. When the saint gently pointed out that they were damaging his vines, the foreman became abusive and pushed the bishop into a pool of liquid mortar. Ubald got up, covered with lime and dirt, but said nothing and calmly went inside to clean himself off. Horrified onlookers expected and desired the foreman to be severely punished, and they dragged him before the city magistrate, but Ubald appeared in court and took control of the situation, announcing that offenses committed against Church officials were under his jurisdiction as bishop. Then he gave the fearful offender a kiss of peace and ordered him released.

One night two thieves stole the oxen that belonged to the hermit St. Philip of Zell, but in trying to escape, they got lost in the woods, and at sunrise, to their great dismay, they found themselves back in front of Philip's hermitage. The saint emerged, knowing what had happened, and the confused and frightened thieves begged his forgiveness. Philip welcomed and reassured them, and let them go — but only after feeding them.

As these examples show, true Christian forgiveness isn't meant to be only a religious concept, but a way of life.

Sometimes forgiving those who wrong us can set the stage for miracles of grace. As St. John of the Cross said, "Where there is no love, pour love in, and you will draw out love," and several examples verify the truth of this observation. For instance, the thirteenth-century priest St. Peregrine Laziosi was quite irreligious as a youth and actively involved himself in a political movement against the Church. The Pope sent St. Philip Benizi to mediate a dispute, but he was accosted by Peregrine, who struck him in the face. When St. Philip responded simply by obeying our Lord's teaching to turn the other cheek,[129] the future St. Peregrine immediately repented of what he had done and converted to Catholicism.

In the following century St. Frances of Rome was held in contempt by Mobilia, her daughter-in-law, who complained about her and ridiculed her in public. Nevertheless, when Mobilia was struck by a serious illness, Frances cared for her lovingly and attentively. So moved was Mobilia by the saint's kindness that her contempt turned to love, and from then on she tried to imitate Frances's virtues.

Not all such incidents result in conversion, however. The great bishop of Geneva, St. Francis de Sales, was intensely hated by a lawyer there, who had sworn lifelong enmity toward the saint and used every opportunity to injure and insult him. One day Francis said to him, "You are my enemy, I know; yet if you were to pluck out one of my eyes, I would still behold you with the other in all kindness." These loving words had no effect, for the man later drew a revolver and shot at the saint; he missed Francis, but struck a priest who was standing with him. Accordingly, the would-be assassin was sentenced to death. Francis, however, pleaded on his behalf, and his death sentence was commuted. Even so, the lawyer showed no gratitude, but actually spat in Francis's face. The saint responded sadly, "I have been able to save you from human justice, but unless you change your dispositions, you will fall into the hands of Divine Justice, from which no power can save you." As St. Francis shows us, the fact that not everyone will accept our offer of forgiveness doesn't excuse us from the obligation of extending it.

Is it always easy to forgive others? Certainly not. Anger is a powerful emotion, and even saints can be tempted by a desire for

[129] Luke 6:29.

revenge, but they simply try harder to use the help God provides to overcome these feelings. When his father and brothers were murdered, Bl. Peter of Pisa wanted to leave his monastery and avenge their deaths, but his sister Bl. Clare Gambacorta aided him in rising above this temptation. By fervent prayer and with the help of his sister's example, Peter arrived at the point where he could sincerely forgive the murderers.

An even more dramatic conversion and act of mercy involved St. John Gualbert. John's older brother Hugh was murdered by someone pretending to be a friend. John swore vengeance, and one day encountered his unarmed enemy in a narrow passage that allowed no room for escape. Drawing his sword, John advanced, but was surprised when the murderer fell to his knees and crossed his arms on his breast. This posture reminded John of how Christ forgave His enemies while on the Cross. Profoundly moved, John put away his sword, embraced his enemy, and left him in peace. (It's said that John then went to a church to pray, and the image of Christ on the crucifix there miraculously bowed its head in recognition of John's sincere repentance and his act of forgiving his enemy.)

John Gualbert, like every other saint before and after him, came to realize the absolutely essential need to forgive our enemies, for Christ will reign only in a heart that seeks to be at peace.

For Further Reflection

"If you are suffering from a bad man's injustice, forgive him, lest there be two bad men." — *St. Augustine*

"Pardon one another so that later on you will not remember the injury. The recollection of an injury is itself wrong. It adds to our anger, nurtures our sin, and hates what is good. It is a rusty arrow and poison for the soul. It puts all virtue to flight." — *St. Francis of Paola (Forgiving and forgetting is very hard to do; indeed, it can be done successfully only with the help of God's grace; and we must never hesitate to ask for this help.)*

"I cannot believe that a soul which has arrived so near to Mercy itself, where she knows what she is, and how many sins God has forgiven her, should not instantly and willingly forgive others, and be pacified and wish well to everyone who has injured her, because she remembers the kindness and favors our Lord has shown her, whereby she has seen proofs of exceeding great love, and she is glad to have an opportunity offered to show some gratitude to her Lord." — *St. Teresa of Avila (Thus, saying "I forgive you" to another person is also a very valuable and practical way of saying "I love You" to God.)*

Something You Might Try

♦ In his *Admonitions*, St. Francis of Assisi wrote, "Our Lord says in the Gospel, 'Love your enemies.' A man really loves his enemy when he is not offended by the injury done to himself, but for love of God feels burning sorrow for the sin his enemy has brought on his own soul, and proves his love in a practical way." Thus, remind yourself that the person who sins against you is in the weaker, less desirable position. Rather than joining that person by giving in to anger or thoughts of revenge, show your love in a practical way — by speaking kindly to him, by speaking kindly of him, by doing a favor for him, or at the very least by praying for him.

♦ Forgiving someone who has betrayed or hurt you very badly can be terribly difficult, but it's possible with God's help. To forgive doesn't mean to approve of what happened or to act as if it didn't really matter. Nor does forgiveness prevent you from seeking justice, as in the case of forgiving from your heart a drunk driver who killed a family member, even as you go ahead with prosecuting him. Nor does forgiveness prevent you from taking reasonable steps to protect yourself in the future, as in being very careful about trusting someone who has betrayed you or lied to you. Forgiving simply means wishing the other person well in a spiritual sense — as in praying that he or she will be blessed by God. If you can offer this prayer, God will be very pleased with you. If this is too hard to do, do this instead: ask Jesus to forgive the person on your behalf. Imagine yourself and your enemy standing together before Jesus. Ask Jesus to forgive the person for you; imagine Him turning to your enemy and saying, "You are forgiven."

Further Reading

Scripture: Proverbs 25:21; Sirach 28:1-7; Matthew 18:21-35; James 2:12-13.

Classics: St. Francis of Assisi, *Admonitions*; St. Francis de Sales, *Introduction to the Devout Life*.

Contemporary Works: Matthew, Sheila, and Dennis Linn, *Don't Forgive Too Soon*; Rev. Robert DeGrandis, *To Forgive Is Divine*; James A. Magner, *Mental Health in a Mad World*.

⌒

Lord, Jesus,
I thank You for forgiving my sins,
time and again, without limit.
Now I need Your help in forgiving someone else.
I have been badly hurt, Lord,
and I'm not sure I'm ready to forgive just yet;
I don't know if I have it in me to forgive at all.
I know, however, that I must forgive
if I am to be forgiven by You and
welcomed into Your kingdom.
Therefore, I ask You to help me, Lord.

Extend Your mercy to my enemies,
to those who hate me and those who have hurt me;
bless them in whatever way You choose.
Give them a sense of Your peace
and a desire to live in Your grace,
and help them find and follow
the path that leads to eternal life.
You are Mercy itself, O Lord;
I thank You, I praise You, and
I beg for Your forgiveness.
Touch the hearts of all people,
that we may live always in Your peace. Amen.

Unpopularity

Do not wonder, brethren, that the world hates you.
1 John 3:13

In 1818, St. John Vianney, the patron saint of parish priests, was sent to the remote French town of Ars, whose residents were largely indifferent to the Faith. By means of prolonged prayer, frequent fasting, powerful preaching, and saintly example, St. John set into motion the spiritual transformation of his parish. During his forty years there, he became known throughout France as a holy, insightful confessor, seemingly able to read minds and remind penitents of sins they had forgotten, and people came from many miles away to confess to him (requiring him to spend up to sixteen hours a day in the confessional). Late in his life, John was worn out from his unending efforts to save souls, and three times he tried to leave the parish for a monastery, but the people would not allow it.

John was extremely popular and beloved, but not everyone appreciated him. Some of the neighboring priests were jealous of his success and accused him of being overly zealous, ignorant, and perhaps even deranged. (To this the bishop replied, "I wish, gentlemen, that all my clergy had a touch of the same madness.")

There were also several women in the parish who approached St. John soon after his arrival there and asked him to begin saying

Mass each week for "a special intention." This went on for fourteen years; finally the saint's curiosity got the better of him, and he asked the women what sort of intention it was that hadn't been granted after all that time. The women replied, "We've been praying that you'd be sent to a different parish."

It's impossible to be universally popular and appreciated; even someone as successful and beloved as St. John Vianney had his own experience of unpopularity. Human affections are, by their very nature, fickle and unpredictable. People can be attracted to or dislike someone for the most trivial reasons. Adding a religious element further complicates the picture: because religion can be such a controversial subject, those who take their Faith seriously are always at risk of being misunderstood and treated with contempt. Jesus frequently warned His followers that, because they were not of this world, they would be hated and persecuted. Christians and others who seek to live out their moral values will frequently provoke anger and criticism. The world never rewards those whose actions call into question its values and beliefs or who proclaim a message it doesn't want to hear. Unpopularity is sometimes a milder form of this opposition, and not surprisingly, many of the saints experienced it.

St. John of Kanty eventually became as beloved by his parishioners as was St. John Vianney, but at first he was quite unpopular. This fifteenth-century Polish priest had been quite successful as a preacher and university professor, but the jealousy of his rivals led to his being assigned to a parish in the poor, unimportant town of Olkusz. He wasn't welcome there, and he himself doubted his qualifications to be a pastor; however, John worked very hard and, after a number of years, became much loved by his parishioners.

In the sixth century, the great monk St. Benedict found that unpopularity could be dangerous. As a young man, he decided to live as a hermit; soon afterward, some monks sought him out and asked him to serve as their leader. This arrangement didn't work out, though. The monks were upset by Benedict's high standards, and they expressed their displeasure in a rather unmistakable way: they attempted to poison him. (Taking the hint, Benedict went elsewhere, but he remained committed to the idea of monks' working, living, and praying together.)

Unpopularity can have a number of causes, such as a person's seeming strange or different. This happened to St. Joseph of Cupertino when he was a young man; his unhappy childhood caused him to become withdrawn and absentminded, and he tended to wander aimlessly through his village with his mouth agape and a blank expression on his face. Although lazy, Joseph had a strong temper, which added to his unpopularity. Only after several failures and setbacks did he find his calling as a Franciscan priest, and eventually he became renowned for the many alleged miracles associated with him.

Unpopularity can also result from failure. Pope St. Gregory VII strongly upheld the authority of the Church against Emperor Henry IV of Germany. At first it seemed as if Gregory would prevail, but Henry went back on his word and besieged and conquered Rome in 1084. The city was recaptured on Gregory's behalf by a Catholic prince from Normandy, but the cost in human life and property damage was so great that the furious Roman citizens forced the Pope to flee. The following year Gregory died in Salerno, having remarked, "I have loved righteousness and hated iniquity; that is why I die in exile."

We can also suffer unpopularity because of our honest efforts to serve God and oppose wickedness. This was the experience of the great fourth-century defender of the Faith St. Athanasius. He almost singlehandedly preserved the Church from the heresy of Arianism, which denied the divinity of Christ. Because many bishops and important laypeople (including some emperors) favored Arianism, Athanasius frequently found himself under attack and was exiled for many of his forty-six years as bishop. The same thing happened to St. Eusebius of Vercelli, who experienced much abuse from the Arians when he was exiled, and to St. Cyril of Jerusalem, who, ironically, was falsely accused of Arianism himself. These three fourth-century bishops helped preserve the true Faith of the Church; their immediate reward was to be vilified, condemned, and punished. Only toward the end of their lives was their contribution recognized and applauded by their contemporaries.

Christ commanded us to love our enemies and pray for our persecutors,[130] and this command includes our loving response to those with whom we're unpopular. According to St. Alphonsus Liguori, "The saints bear no malice against those who mistreat them, but love them all the more; and the Lord, as a reward for their patience, heightens their inner peace." While the saints loved everyone, they were completely indifferent to human approval. St. John Vianney reminds us, "You cannot please both God and the world at the same time. They are utterly opposed to each other in their thoughts, their desires, and their actions." This being the case, we must choose Christ, and as Christians, we must renew this choice regularly — indeed, in every moral decision we make — even at the cost of unpopularity. The Cure d'Ars advises us, "Do not try to please everybody. Try to please God, the angels, and the saints — *they* are your public," and he also offers us these blunt words: "If you are afraid of other people's opinion, you should not have become a Christian."

There's a price to be paid for following Jesus; committed Christians must expect a certain amount of unpopularity. However, as St. Gerard Majella asks, "Who except God can give you peace? Has the world ever been able to satisfy the heart?" The measure of a successful life is not fame and popularity, nor is it the judgment of history (although, in the end, history will look with favor on all servants of Christ). The only judgment that matters is God's. If we

[130] Matt. 5:44.

please Him, we'll experience everlasting popularity in Heaven, and this goal is well worth whatever it costs us here and now.

For Further Reflection

"Finding no resting-place without, [the one who strives for righteousness] cleaves more intensely to God within. All his hope is fixed on his Creator, and amid all the ridicule and abuse, he invokes his interior witness alone. One who is afflicted in this way grows closer to God the more he turns away from human popularity." — *St. Gregory the Great*

"The aversions that you experience, the ridicule, the scorn, the jokes, etc., should be received with great gratitude toward God. These serve as the pyre of love on which the victim of love is burned. Gently drive away all aversions, and show yourself cordial to everyone." — *St. Paul of the Cross*

"We must practice patience and show our love for God by peacefully suffering the scorn we receive from others. As soon as souls give themselves completely to God, God Himself causes or permits others to despise and persecute them." — *St. Alphonsus Liguori*

Something You Might Try

♦ When asked by his wife how he always remained so calm and patient when he was mocked or insulted, the fourteenth-century nobleman St. Elzear answered, "I turn and look on Jesus, who was despised and rejected, and I see that the affronts to me are nothing compared with what He suffered for me; so God gives me strength to bear it all patiently." This is a simple but effective method you can use, too. When you experience any form of unpopularity or derision, remind yourself of all that Jesus suffered for you, and consciously choose to unite your insignificant sufferings with His.

Saintly Solutions

◆ Learn to rejoice in your unpopularity. According to Archbishop Fulton J. Sheen, "The acceptance of the fullness of Truth will have the unfortunate quality of making you hated by the world. Forget for a moment the history of Christianity, and the fact that Christ existed. Suppose there appeared in this world today a man who claimed to be Divine Truth; and who did not say, 'I will teach you Truth,' but, 'I am *the Truth.*' Suppose he gave evidence by his works of the truth of his statement. Knowing ourselves as we do, with our tendency to relativism, to indifference, and to the fusing of right and wrong, how do you suppose we would react to that Divine Truth? With hatred, with obloquy, with defiance; with charges of intolerance, narrow-mindedness, bigotry, and crucifixion. That is what happened to Christ. That is what our Lord said would happen to those who accept His Truth." Archbishop Sheen's insight suggests that if you're unpopular, it may be because you're doing something *right*, and if that's the case, you should wear your unpopularity and nonconformity with the world's values as a badge of honor. Indeed, a willingness to do what's right without worrying about what others think can be a powerful form of evangelization, and so you can console yourself by remembering that your willingness to persevere even in the face of unpopularity can be a way of proclaiming the Gospel.

Further Reading

Scripture: Psalm 69:4; Matthew 24:9; John 15:18-19.

Classics: St. Alphonsus Liguori, *The Practice of the Love of Jesus Christ.*

*Lord Jesus, You experienced unpopularity, criticism,
and even hatred to the fullest extent possible,
and so I turn to You to be strengthened*

and consoled in my own troubles.
For reasons that aren't entirely clear to me, Lord,
I am unpopular; there are more people willing
to be my persecutors than to be my friends.
Sometimes I get into trouble simply for
trying to live out my Faith and do what's right;
other times I'm unpopular for less noble reasons:
because of the way I look or speak,
because of my stupid mistakes and failings,
and because of who I am and where I come from.
It's all so unfair, Lord Jesus.
I want to be liked and accepted and welcomed.
I need to be understood and valued,
loved and appreciated.
I know You understand;
I know You had some of these same human feelings
and that You suffered terribly because of
the hatred You experienced.
Please help me with my own cross, dear Lord.
I am not brave or strong;
I would never willingly
choose to be unpopular or controversial.
But I choose to follow You and to accept
whatever that means and whatever that costs.
I only ask that You help me, Lord,
and that You walk with me each step of the way.
Send me friends to assist me and loved ones to console me,
and fill me with grace and wisdom and courage,
so that I may truly offer You all my experiences
and continue trusting in Your loving care.

Appendix

Recommended Reading

The following books may be particularly helpful to those seeking additional stories about the saints or insights from their writings applicable to daily life.

A Year with the Saints (Sisters of Mercy, 1891; TAN Books and Publishers, Inc., 364 pp.). Although written more than a century ago, this work is easily understandable and of great spiritual value. It focuses on a different virtue for every month of the year, with individual entries for each day, including a quotation from a saint and a story or insight showing you how to further your spiritual and moral growth.

An Introduction to the Devout Life, St. Francis de Sales (TAN Books and Publishers, Inc., 1942, 1994, 318 pp.). This classic by St. Francis de Sales is one of the greatest works on practical spirituality ever written. It stresses the idea (re-emphasized by the Second Vatican Council) that *all* Christians are called to holiness and provides a wealth of information and advice on how to live out this call. If you can read only one book from this list, *An Introduction to the Devout Life* should be your choice.

Lessons from the Lives of the Saints, Rev. Joseph M. Esper (Basilica, 1999, 260 pp.). This book offers a brief biography of each saint in the Church's liturgical calendar, along with two or three lessons for Christian living taken from that saint's life.

Modern Saints: Their Lives and Faces, Ann Ball (TAN Books and Publishers, Inc., 1983; Book One: 435 pp.; Book Two: 489 pp.). The lives of more than one hundred contemporary (from the eighteenth, nineteenth, and twentieth centuries) saints and servants of God are presented here, along with artistic renderings or, in many cases, photographs of them.

Saint of the Day, Leonard Foley, O.F.M. (St. Anthony Messenger Press, 1990, 347 pp.). A revised and updated edition of the 1974 original, this work offers a short biography of each saint in the Church's liturgical calendar, along with an appropriate reflection, quotation, or story.

Secular Saints, Joan Carroll Cruz (TAN Books and Publishers, Inc., 1989, 751 pp.). This book provides brief biographies of more than two hundred lay men, women, and children who have been canonized or beatified by the Church, along with an extensive index listing saints by their state in life (married, widowed, or unmarried), life experiences and challenges, and occupations and hobbies.

The Little Way of Saint Thérèse of Lisieux, John Nelson (Liguori, 1997, 140 pp.). St. Thérèse of Lisieux, the Little Flower, is surely one of the most popular saints in history, and this short book is a delightful collection of passages from *The Story of a Soul* (her spiritual autobiography), interspersed with scriptural quotations and other reflections. This is a perfect introduction to St. Thérèse's writings.

Bibliography

Augustine Day by Day, edited by John E. Rotelle, O.S.A. (Catholic Book Publishing Co., 1986).

The Avenel Dictionary of the Saints, Donald Attwater (Avenel Books, 1965).

Butler's Lives of the Saints, edited by Herbert J. Thurston, S.J. (Christian Classics, 1990).

The Complete Book of Christian Prayer (Continuum Publishing Company, 1996).

Conversations of the Saints, Bernard-Marie, O.S.F., and Jean Huscenot, F.E.C. (Liguori, 1999).

Fifty-Seven Saints, Eileen Heffernan, F.S.P. (Pauline Books and Media, 1994).

How to Live a Holy Life, St. Alphonsus Liguori, edited by Thomas M. Santa, C.Ss.R. (Liguori, 1999).

Imitation of Christ, Thomas à Kempis, edited by William C. Creasy (Ave Maria Press, 1989).

An Introduction to the Devout Life, St. Francis de Sales (TAN Books and Publishers, Inc., 1942, 1994).

Irish Saints, Robert T. Reilly (Avenel Books, 1964).

Saintly Solutions

John Paul II's Book of Saints, Matthew Bunson, Margaret Bunson, Stephen Bunson (Our Sunday Visitor, 1999).

The Ladder of the Beatitudes, Jim Forest (Orbis Books, 1999).

Lessons from the Lives of the Saints, Rev. Joseph M. Esper (Basilica, 1999).

The Little Way of Saint Thérèse of Lisieux, John Nelson (Liguori, 1997).

Lives of the Saints for Every Day of the Year, Rev. Hugo Hoever (Catholic Book Publishing Co., 1993). Two volumes.

Living Wisdom for Every Day, edited by Rev. Bennet Kelley, C.P. (Catholic Book Publishing Co., 1991).

Modern Saints: Their Lives and Faces (Books One and Two), Ann Ball (TAN Books and Publishers, Inc., 1983).

A New Dictionary of Saints, compiled by Donald Attwater, edited and revised by John Cumming (Liturgical Press, 1994).

The Practice of the Love of Jesus Christ, St. Alphonsus Liguori (Liguori, 1997).

Prayers and Heavenly Promises, Joan Carroll Cruz (TAN Books and Publishers, Inc., 1990).

Purgatory Explained by the Lives and Legends of the Saints, Rev. F. X. Shouppe, S.J. (TAN Books and Publishers, Inc., 1973).

Saint Anthony of Padua, edited by Rev. Cassian A. Miles, O.F.M. and Janet E. Gianopoulos (Catholic Book Publishing Co., 1991).

Saint of the Day, Leonard Foley, O.F.M. (St. Anthony Messenger Press, 1990).

Saint-Watching, Phyllis McGinley (The Thomas More Press, 1969).

The Saints and the Sunday Gospels, Msgr. Arthur J. Tonne (Didde Printing Company, 1951).

Saints for All Seasons, edited by John J. Delaney (Doubleday and Company, Inc., 1978).

The Saints, Humanly Speaking, Felicitas Corrigan, O.S.B. (Servant Publications, 2000).

Saints: Their Cults and Origins, Caroline Williams (St. Martin's Press, 1980).

Secular Saints, Joan Carroll Cruz (TAN Books and Publishers, Inc., 1989).

Selected Writings and Prayers of Saint Alphonsus, edited by John Steingraeber, C.Ss.R. (Liguori, 1997).

Stories from The Catechist, Rev. Canon G. E. Howe (TAN Books and Publishers, Inc., 1989).

Thoughts of the Curé d'Ars (TAN Books and Publishers, Inc., 1967).

Touching the Risen Christ: Wisdom from the Fathers, edited by Patricia Mitchell (The Word Among Us Press, 1999).

The Treasury of Catholic Wisdom, edited by John A. Hardon, S. J. (Ignatius Press, 1987).

The Voice of the Saints, edited by Francis W. Johnston (TAN Books and Publishers, Inc., 1965).

The Wisdom of the Saints, Jill Haak Adels (Oxford University Press, 1987).

The World's Greatest Catholic Literature, edited by George N. Shuster (Roman Catholic Books, 1942).

A Year with the Saints (Sisters of Mercy, 1891; TAN Books and Publishers, Inc.).

Saints Mentioned and Quoted

St. Aelred of Rievaulx (1110-1167), Cistercian abbot and writer of several treatises (March 3).

St. Agatha, virgin martyred in Sicily (February 5).

St. Agnes (d. c. 304), Roman martyr (January 21).

St. Agnes of Assisi (d. 1253), sister of St. Clare and first abbess of the Poor Clare convent of Monticelli in Florence (November 16).

St. Albert the Great (c. 1200-1280), medieval theologian, philosopher, and scientist (November 15).

St. Albert of Montecorvino (d. 1127), bishop (April 5).

St. Aldegund (d. 684), Abbess of Maubeuge (January 30).

St. Aldetrude (d. 696), daughter of St. Waudru, niece of St. Aldegund, and Abbess of Maubeuge.

St. Alessio Falconieri (d. 1310), one of the Seven Founders of the Order of Servites, who established a Servite community in Siena (February 17).

St. Alferius (d. 1050), founder and Abbot of the Abbey of La Cava (April 12).

St. Aloysius Gonzaga (1568-1591), young Jesuit who cared for plague victims (June 21).

St. Alphonsus Liguori (1696-1787), bishop, Doctor, writer, and founder of the Redemptorists (August 1).

St. Alphonsus Rodriguez (d. 1617), Spanish wool merchant and Jesuit lay brother (October 30).

St. Ambrose (c. 340-397), Bishop of Milan and Doctor (December 7).

St. Ammonas the Hermit (d. c. 350), hermit monk of the Nitrian desert (October 4).

Bl. Andre Bessette (1845-1937), Canadian Holy Cross brother who built St. Joseph's Oratory in Montreal (January 6).

St. Andrew Bobola (d. 1657), Jesuit of Vilna known for his success in reconciling dissident Orthodox with the Holy See (May 21).

St. Andrew Corsini (1302-1373), bishop and papal emissary (February 4).

St. Andrew of Fiesole, ninth-century Irish archdeacon (August 22).

St. Angadrisma (d. c. 695), Abbess of Oroër-des-Vierges, near Beauvais (October 14).

St. Ann, mother of the Blessed Virgin Mary (July 26).

Bl. Anne-Marie Jahouvey (1779-1851), foundress of the Congregation of St. Joseph of Cluny (July 15).

St. Anselm (c. 1033-1109), Archbishop of Canterbury and Doctor (April 21).

St. Ansgar (801-865), bishop (February 3).

St. Anthony (251-356), desert monk and father of Western monasticism (January 17).

St. Anthony Claret (d. 1870), bishop and founder of the congregation of Missionary Sons of the Immaculate Heart of Mary, also known as the Claretians (October 24).

St. Anthony of Padua (1195-1231), Franciscan friar and Doctor (June 13).

Bl. Antonia Mesina (1919-1935), virgin who was murdered by a young man whose advances she resisted (May 17).

St. Antoninus (1389-1459), Archbishop of Florence, moral theologian, and writer on local and international law (May10).

Bl. Antony Grassi (d. 1671), priest of the Oratory of Fermon in the Italian Marches (December 13).

St. Apollo (d. c. 395), abbot at Hermopolis (January 25).

St. Apollonia (d. 249), deaconess of Alexandria whose teeth were knocked out by rioting heathens (February 7).

Bl. Arnould Jules Reche (1838-1890), French religious brother and member of the Brothers of Christian Schools (October 23).

Bl. Arnulf of Villers (c. 1180-1228), lay Cistercian brother who practiced severe penances (June 30).

St. Arsenius (d. c. 449), deacon in Rome who later lived as a hermit in Egypt (July 19).

St. Athanasius (c. 297-373), Bishop of Alexandria and Doctor (May 2).

St. Augustine (354-430), Bishop of Hippo and Doctor (August 28).

St. Augustine of Canterbury (d. c. 605), Bishop (May 27).

St. Barnabas, early Christian apostle (June 11).

St. Bartholomea Capitanio (1807-1833), foundress of the congregation of the Sisters of Charity at Lovere and spiritual writer (July 26).

St. Bartholomew, one of the Twelve Apostles, also known as Nathanael (August 24).

St. Bartholomew of Farne (d. 1193), Benedictine hermit (June 24).

St. Basil the Elder, husband of St. Emmelia and father of St. Basil the Great, St. Macrina, St. Peter of Sebaste, and St. Gregory of Nyssa.

St. Basil the Great, Bishop of Cappadocia and Doctor (January 2).

St. Bavo (d. c. 655), convert who became a hermit (October 1).

St. Benedict (c. 480-c. 547), abbot who founded the monastery of Monte Cassino (July 11).

St. Benedict Joseph Labre (1748-1783), pilgrim and mendicant saint.

St. Benildus (1805-1862), member of the Brothers of the Christian Schools (August 13).

St. Bernadette (1844-1879), Sister of Notre Dame who, in 1858, received eighteen apparitions of the Blessed Virgin Mary (April 16).

St. Bernard of Clairvaux (1090-1153), abbot and Doctor (August 20).

Bl. Bernard of Offida (d. 1694), Capuchin lay brother known for his wisdom and miracles (August 26).

St. Bertilia (seventh century), wife of St. Walbert and mother of Sts. Waudru and Aldegund.

St. Bertilla Boscardin (1885-1922), postulant of the Sisters of St. Dorothy of Vicenza who lived according to the "little way" of holiness (October 20).

St. Blase (d. c. 316), Bishop of Sebaste and martyr (February 3).

St. Blesilla (d. 383), young widow and daughter of St. Paula (January 22).

St. Bogumilus (d. 1182), Archbishop of Gniezno who later became a Camaldolese hermit (June 10).

St. Bonaventure (1221-1274), Franciscan mystical theologian and scholastic, writer, bishop, and Doctor (July 15).

Saintly Solutions

St. Boniface (c. 680-754), bishop, Primate of Germany, and martyr (June 5).

St. Boniface of Lausanne (d. 1260), bishop who spent his later years as chaplain to the Cistercian nuns at La Cambre and in pastoral work (February 19).

St. Brendan (d. 577 or 583), monk who founded a monastery at Clonfert in Ireland (May 16).

St. Bridget of Sweden (1304-1373), foundress of the Brigittine Order (July 23).

St. Brigid (c. 450-c. 525), Abbess of Kildare (February 1).

St. Bruno (1030-1101), founder of the Carthusian Order (October 6).

St. Cajetan (1480-1547), founder of the Theatine Order (August 7).

St. Callistus (d. c. 222), Pope from c. 217 and martyr (October 14).

St. Camillus de Lellis (1550-1614), reformed soldier and gambler who directed a hospital and founded the nursing congregation of the Ministers of the Sick (July 14).

Bl. Caroline Kozka (1898-1914), young woman who was killed by a Russian soldier when she resisted his advances (November 18).

St. Casimir (1461-1484), son of King Casimir IV of Poland and patron saint of Poland and Lithuania (March 4).

St. Catherine of Genoa (1447-1510), mystic and writer who ministered to the sick at a Genoese hospital (September 15).

St. Catherine of Siena (1347-1380), Dominican tertiary (April 29).

St. Celestine V (c. 1210-1296), Benedictine hermit who founded the Celestines and Pope from 1294 (May 19).

St. Ceowulf (d. 764), king of the Northumbrians and later a monk at Lindisfarne (January 15).

St. Charles Borromeo (1538-1584), bishop who established the Confraternity of Christian Doctrine (November 4).

St. Charles Garnier (d. 1649), French missionary to North America and martyr (October 19).

Bl. Charles the Good (d. 1127), son of King St. Canute of Denmark, defender of the poor, and martyr (March 2).

St. Charles Lwanga (d. 1886), martyr during the persecution by King Mwanga in Uganda (June 3).

St. Charles of Sezze (d. 1670), lay brother of the Observant branch of the Franciscans (January 19).

Bl. Christina of Stommeln (1242-1312), virgin who experienced ecstasies and other astonishing phenomena (November 6).

Bl. Christopher of Mexico (c. 1514-1527), teenage convert and martyr.

St. Clare of Assisi (c. 1193-1253), foundress of the Poor Clares (August 11).

Bl. Clare Gambacorta (1362-1419), Dominican nun (April 17).

Bl. Clare of Rimini (d. 1346), widow and Franciscan tertiary who led a life of penance and almsgiving (February 10).

St. Clement of Alexandria (c. 150-c. 215), Church Father and theologian (December 4).

St. Clement Hofbauer (d. 1820), Redemptorist who established an orphanage and schools and established a Redemptorist congregation in Warsaw (March 15).

St. Clement of Rome (d. c. 99), third successor to St. Peter and martyr (November 23).

St. Clotilda (c. 474-545), wife of the Frankish king Clovis who spent her later years as a widow serving the poor and the suffering (June 3).

St. Colette (1381-1447), foundress of the Colettines, a branch of the Poor Clares (March 6).

St. Colman (555-611), abbot who founded a monastery at Lann Elo (September 26).

St. Columba (c. 521-597), Irish abbot (June 9).

St. Columban (d. 615), Abbot of Bobbio (November 23).

St. Conrad of Piacenza (d. 135), hermit of the Third Order of St. Francis (February 19).

St. Cosmas (d. c. 283), physician and martyr; brother of St. Damian (September 26).

Bl. Crescentia of Kaufbeuren (d. 174), Franciscan tertiary (April 6).

St. Crispin of Viterbo (d. 1750), Capuchin lay brother (May 19).

St. Cyprian (c. 200-258), Bishop of Carthage and martyr (September 16).

St. Cyril (d. 869), priest and Apostle of the Slavs, with his brother St. Methodius (February 14).

St. Cyril of Alexandria (c. 376-444), bishop and Doctor (June 27).

St. Cyril of Jerusalem (c. 315-386), bishop and Doctor (March 18).

St. Damasus (c. 304-384), Pope from 366 (December 11).

St. Damian (d. c. 283), physician and martyr; brother of St. Cosmas (September 26).

St. Deicolus (d. c. 624), bishop and founder of the abbey of Lure (January 18).

St. Dentilin, seventh-century seven-year-old confessor, son of St. Waudru and St. Vincent Madelgarus (March 16).

St. Didacus (c. 1400-1463), Spanish Franciscan lay brother (November 13).

St. Dismas, the repentant criminal crucified with Christ and known as the "Good Thief" (March 25).

St. Dominic (c. 1170-1221), founder of the Dominican Order, also known as the Order of Preachers (August 8).

St. Dominic Savio (1842-1857), student of St. John Bosco known for doing even the smallest things out of love for God (March 9).

St. Dominic of Silos (d. 1073), abbot and monastic reformer (December 20).

St. Dorotheus of Tyre (d. c. 362), priest of Tyre exiled by Diocletian and later martyred under Julian the Apostate (June 5).

St. Dositheus (d. c. 530), wealthy young man who was converted in Jerusalem and became a monk at Gaza (February 23).

St. Drogo (d. 1189), Flemish hermit, pilgrim, and shepherd (April 16).

St. Dymphna (d. c. 620), young woman martyred by her father for defending her purity (May 15).

St. Ebba the Elder (d. 683), foundress of the monastery of Coldingham (August 25).

St. Edith Stein (1891-1942), Jewish convert to the Catholic Faith who became a Carmelite nun and was martyred in Auschwitz (August 9).

St. Edmund (d. 870), Martyred king of the East Angles (November 20).

St. Edmund Campion (c. 1540-1581), Jesuit priest martyred at Tyburn (December 1).

St. Edward the Confessor (1004-1066), English king (October 13).

St. Elizabeth, mother of St. John the Baptist (November 5).

Bl. Elizabeth Canori Mora (1774-1825), third order Trinitarian (February 4).

St. Elizabeth of Hungary (1207-1231), daughter of King Andreas II of Hungary, niece of St. Hedwig, and widow who became a third order Franciscan (November 17).

St. Elizabeth of Portugal (1271-1336), wife of King Denis of Portugal who became a Poor Clare tertiary after her husband's death (July 4).

St. Elizabeth Ann Seton (1774-1821), the first American-born saint, who founded a school and the congregation of the Sisters of Charity of St. Joseph (later known as the Daughters of Charity of St. Joseph), of which she was Superior (January 4).

St. Elzear (1285-1323), husband of Bl. Delphina of Glandèves, Baron of Ansouis, Count of Ariano, tutor to Prince Charles of Naples, and diplomat (September 27).

St. Emeric (1007-1031), son of Hungary's first Christian king, St. Stephen (November 4).

Bl. Emmanuel Domingo Y Sol (1836-1909), priest and founder of the Sacred Heart Fraternity of Diocesan Priests (January 25).

St. Emmelia, wife of St. Basil the Elder and mother of St. Basil the Great, St. Macrina, St. Peter of Sebaste, and St. Gregory of Nyssa.

St. Ephrem (c. 306-373), theologian, preacher, Doctor, and writer of poems, hymns, and biblical commentaries (June 9).

St. Euphrasia (d. c. 240), virgin who spent her life in a convent in Egypt in austerity and humility (March 13).

St. Eusebius of Vercelli (c. 283-371), bishop and martyr who fought Arianism (August 2).

St. Fabian (d. 250), Pope and martyr under Decius (January 20).

St. Fabiola (d. 399), Roman patrician who, after the death of her second husband, did public penance for their illicit marriage, devoted her time and money to charity, and established the first Christian public hospital in the West (December 27).

St. Faustina Kowalska (1905-1938), Sister of Our Lady of Mercy who spread devotion to the Divine Mercy.

St. Felicity, early Roman martyr (March 7).

Bl. Felix of Nicosia (d. 1787), Capuchin lay brother who had the gift of healing (June 1).

St. Fiacre (d. c. 670), Irish hermit who spent his later years in France (September 1).

St. Fidelis (1577-1622), Capuchin who wrote and preached against Calvinism and was martyred (April 24).

St. Finnian of Moville (d. c. 579), bishop who established the monastery of Moville in Ireland (September 10).

St. Flora of Beaulieu (d. 1347), hospitaller nun of the order of St. John of Jerusalem (October 5).

St. Frances Xavier Cabrini (1850-1917), Italian-born foundress of the Missionary Sisters of the Sacred Heart at Codogno in Lombary and of orphanages and hospitals in North and South America; first United States citizen to be canonized (November 13).

St. Frances of Rome (1384-1440), foundress of the Benedictine Oblates of the Tor de' Specchi (March 9).

St. Francis of Assisi (1182-1226), founder of the Franciscan Order, also known as the Order of Friars Minor (October 4).

St. Francis Borgia (1510-1572), Duke of Gandia who became a Jesuit, established the order throughout western Europe, and sent missionaries to the Americas (October 10).

St. Francis de Sales (1567-1622), Bishop of Geneva, writer, and Doctor (January 24).

Bl. Francis Palau Y Quer (1811-1872), discalced Carmelite priest, preacher, journalist, and hermit who founded two religious institutes (March 20).

St. Francis of Paola (1416-1507), founder of the order of Minim friars (April 2).

St. Francis Xavier (1506-1552), Jesuit missionary to the East Indies (December 3).

St. Gabriel Possenti (1838-1862), Passionist who sought to attain perfection in and through small things (February 27).

St. Gaspar Bertoni (1777-1835), Italian priest who served as chaplain to the sisters of Saint Magdalen Canossa, established the Marian Oratories, organized free schools for the poor, and founded the

Congregation of the Sacred Stigmata of Our Lord Jesus Christ, also known as the Stigmatines (June 12).

St. Gerard Majella (d. 1755), Redemptorist lay brother known for miracles of healing and for bilocation (October 16).

St. Gerlac of Valkenburg (d. c. 1170), Dutch soldier who, after his wife's sudden death, repented of and did penance for his disorderly life (January 5).

St. Gertrude (1256-c. 1302), German mystic (November 16).

St. Gilbert of Sempringham (d. 1189), founder of the Gilbertine Order (February 16).

St. Giles, Provençal hermit or monk in the sixth or eighth century (September 1).

Bl. Giles of Assisi (d. 1262), early follower of St. Francis of Assisi (April 23).

St. Gothard (d. 1038), Abbot of Niederaltaich in Bavaria and Bishop of Hildesheim (May 4).

St. Gregory VII (c. 1020-1085), Pope from 1073 (May 25).

St. Gregory the Great (d. 604), Pope from 590, writer, and Doctor (September 3).

St. Gregory of Nazianzus (c. 329-390), Bishop of Constantinople, theologian, and Doctor (January 2).

St. Gregory of Nyssa (d. c. 395), bishop and writer (March 9).

St. Gregory of Tours (d. 594), bishop, historian, and hagiographer (November 17).

St. Gummarus (d. c. 774), husband who exemplified heroic virtue in dealing with his troublesome wife and who, when his wife became too much for him and they separated, became a hermit (October 11).

Bl. Gunther (d. 1045), worldly nobleman who became a monk at Niederaltaich at age fifty and later began an eremetical life and made amends for his earlier excesses (October 9).

St. Guy of Anderlecht (d. c. 1012), lay sacristan who lost all his money in an investment, became a pilgrim, and led a hidden life of simplicity and mortification (September 12).

St. Helen of Skovde (d. c. 1160), widow of a Swedish nobleman, who gave her goods to the poor and was unjustly executed after being accused of being involved in the death of her son-in-law (July 31).

Bl. Helen of Udine (d. 1458), widow who became an Augustinian tertiary, gave to the needy, and practiced great austerities (April 23).

St. Helidorus (d. c. 400), Bishop of Altino who helped fund St. Jerome's work.

St. Henry (972-1024), Holy Roman emperor and husband of St. Cunegund (July 13).

St. Henry Morse (1595-1645), Jesuit priest martyred at Tyburn (February 1).

Bl. Henry of Treviso (d. 1315), laborer who dedicated his life to God and through whose relics many miracles have occurred (June 10).

St. Hermenegild (d. 585), son of the Visigothic Spanish king Leovigild who was killed by his father for converting from Arianism to Christianity (April 13).

St. Hilarion (c. 291-371), abbot and first hermit of Palestine (October 21).

St. Hilary of Arles (d. 449), bishop (May 5).

St. Hilary of Poitiers (d. c. 368), bishop and Doctor who fought Arianism (January 13).

St. Hippolytus (d. c. 235), Roman priest and theological writer who became an antipope, but was later reconciled to the Church and martyred (August 13).

St. Honoratus (d. 429), Bishop of Arles and founder of the abbey of Lerins (January 16).

St. Hormisdas (d. 523), Pope from 514 and author of the confession of Faith known as the Formula of Hormisdas, which led to the end of the Monophysite Acacian schism in 519 (August 6).

St. Hugh of Grenoble (1052-1132), bishop who was canonized only two years after his death (April 1).

St. Hyacintha Mariscotti (d. 1640), religious who was unfaithful to her rule, converted, relapsed, and finally converted and attained heroic virtue (January 30).

St. Ignatius of Antioch (d. c. 107), disciple of John the Evangelist, bishop, and martyr (October 17).

St. Ignatius of Loyola (1491-1556), founder of the Jesuit Order, also known as the Society of Jesus (July 31).

St. Irenaeus (c. 125-c. 203), student of St. Polycarp, missionary, Bishop of Lyons, and Church Father (June 28).

St. Isidore the Farmer (d. 1130), Spanish farm worker and example of Christian perfection (May 15).

St. James, one of the Twelve Apostles and brother of St. John; known as St. James the Greater (July 25).

St. Jan Sarkander (1576-1620), parish priest in Moravia, who, during the Thirty Years War, was ordered to disclose the confession of his penitent and was tortured and martyred when he refused (March 17).

St. Jane Frances de Chantal (1572-1641), foundress of the Visitation Order (August 18).

St. Jerome (c. 342-420), Doctor who translated the Bible into Latin (September 30).

St. Jerome Emiliani (1481-1537), founder of the congregation of clerks regular known as the Somaschi, primarily to care for orphans (February 8).

St. Joachim, father of the Blessed Virgin Mary (July 26).

St. Joan of Arc (1412-1431), French heroine who led the French army against English invaders and was burned to death for alleged heresy, but later declared innocent (May 30).

St. Joan Delanoue (1666-1736), foundress of the Sisters of St. Anne of Providence in Saumur, an order dedicated to caring for orphans and the elderly (August 17).

Bl. Joanna Beretta Molla (1922-1962), pediatrician who developed a cancerous tumor during her fourth pregnancy, underwent a successful surgery to remove the tumor, but died of a painful infection in her womb days after giving birth to her daughter (April 28).

St. John, Evangelist and one of the Twelve Apostles (December 27).

Bl. John XXIII (1881-1963), Pope from 1958, who opened the Second Vatican Council.

St. John of Avila (d. 1569), Spanish secular priest, writer, adviser of saints and sinners, and missionary in Andalusia (May 10).

St. John the Baptist, forerunner of Christ (Birth: June 24; Martyrdom: August 29).

St. John Baptist de La Salle (1651-1719), founder of the Institute of the Brothers of Christian Schools (April 7).

St. John Berchmans (1599-1621), Jesuit who followed the "little way" (November 26).

St. John Bosco (1815-1888), priest who founded the Salesian Order (January 31).

St. John Chrysostom (c. 347-407), Archbishop of Constantinople and Doctor; named Chrysostom, or "Golden Mouth" for his eloquent preaching (September 13).

St. John Climacus (d. c. 649), abbot of the monastery of Mount Sinai and author of the mystical work *Ladder to Paradise* (March 30).

Bl. John Colombini (d. 1367), avaricious merchant who underwent a conversion, separated from his wife, and formed the Gesuati, a society of men dedicated to prayer, mortification, and works of charity (July 31).

St. John of the Cross (1542-1591), Spanish Carmelite mystic, and reformer of the Carmelite Order (December 14).

St. John Eudes (1601-1680), priest who tended to victims of the plague and who founded the Sisters of Our Lady of Charity of the Refuge and a congregation for the sanctification of the clergy and those aspiring to the priesthood (August 19).

St. John of God (1495-1550), founder of the order of Brothers Hospitallers (March 8).

St. John Gualbert (d. 1073), founder of the Vallombrosan congregation of the Benedictines (July 12).

St. John of Kanty (d. 1473), priest and professor at the University of Cracow who gave his goods to the poor (December 23).

St. John Leonardi (c. 1550-1609), priest who founded the congregation of Clerks Regular of the Mother of God and reformed the monks of Vallombrosa and Monte Vergine (October 9).

St. John of Matera (d. 1139), monk who faced persecution because of his austerity and who founded a monastery at Pulsano (June 20).

Ven. John Henry Newman (1801-1890), convert from Anglicanism to Catholicism who became a cardinal.

St. John Perse (1887-1975), French poet and diplomat awarded the Nobel Prize for Literature in 1960.

St. John of Vercelli (1205-1283), Master General of the Order of Preachers who drew up the schema for the second ecumenical council of Lyons and promoted devotion to the Holy Name of Jesus (December 1).

St. John Vianney (1786-1859), patron saint of parish priests; known as the Curé d'Ars (August 4).

Bl. Jordan of Saxony (d. 1237), second Master General of the Dominican Order known for his eloquent preaching (February 15).

St. Joseph, husband of Mary and foster-father of Jesus (March 19; Joseph the Worker: May 1).

St. Joseph Cafasso (1811-1860), priest known for his selfless devotion to others and to the needs of criminals and convicts (June 23).

St. Joseph Calasanz (1556-1648), priest who founded the congregation of the Clerks Regular of the Religious Schools, also known as the Piarists, for the free schooling of poor and neglected children (August 25).

St. Joseph Cottolengo (d. 1842), canon who established in Turin a small hospital for the poor, which grew into a great medical institution, and who founded the Daughters of Compassion, the Daughters of the Good Shepherd, the Hermits of the Holy Rosary, and the Priests of the Holy Trinity (April 29).

St. Joseph of Cupertino (1603-1663), Franciscan tertiary (September 18).

St. Joseph Moscatti (1880-1927), Italian physician noted for his medical research and for caring for his patients free of charge (November 16).

St. Joseph Tomasi (1649-1713), learned Theatine clerk regular and confessor of Cardinal Albani, the future Pope Clement XI (January 1).

St. Josepha Rossello (1811-1880), foundress of the Daughters of Our Lady of Mercy (December 7).

St. Julian the Hospitable, penitent who founded an inn and hospital for the poor after he accidentally killed his parents (February 12).

Bl. Julian of Norwich (d. c. 1423), recluse whose book, Revelations of Divine Love, in which she recounts her visions, speaks of God's loving dealings with man (May 13).

Bl. Junipero Serra (1713-1784), Spanish Franciscan priest and missionary in Texas, Mexico, and California (August 28).

Bl. Kateri Tekakwitha (1656-1680), Native American Christian known as the "Lily of the Mohawks."

St. Katherine Drexel (1858-1955), wealthy Philadelphia native who founded the Sisters of the Most Holy Sacrament, numerous catechetical centers, and sixty schools and colleges (March 3).

St. Katherine of Vadstena (d. 1381), daughter of St. Bridget of Sweden who, with her mother, devoted herself to charitable works, pilgrimages, and the Brigittine Order (March 24).

St. Landericus (seventh century), Benedictine bishop of Meaux, Abbot of Soignies, and son of Sts. Vincent Madelgarus and Waudru (April 17).

Bl. Laura Vicuna (1891-1904), virtuous young girl of the Sodality of the Children of Mary who died from an illness after being beaten by her mother's common-law husband (January 22).

St. Lawrence (d. 258), deacon and martyr (August 10).

St. Leo IX (d. 1054), Pope from 1048 (April 19).

St. Leo the Great (d. 461), Pope from 440 and Doctor (November 10).

St. Leodegarius (d. 679), Bishop of Autun who was murdered by the mayor of the royal palace (October 2).

St. Leopold Mandic (1866-1942), Capuchin who devoted much of his time to spiritual direction and hearing confessions (July 30).

St. Louis IX (1214-1270), King of France (August 25).

St. Louis Bertrand (1526-1581), Spanish Dominican who was sent to South America to preach the gospel and became noted for his preaching (October 9).

St. Louis de Montfort (1673-1716), secular priest who founded the Sisters of the Divine Wisdom and the Missionary Priests of Mary and is known for his book *True Devotion to Mary* (April 28).

Bl. Louisa of Savoy (d. 1503), daughter of Bl. Amadeus IX of Savoy who was admitted to a Poor Clare convent after her husband died (September 9).

St. Louise de Marillac (1591-1660), cofoundress of the Daughters of Charity (now known as the Sisters of Charity of St. Vincent de Paul) (March 15).

St. Lucian of Antioch (d. 312), Scripture scholar who was martyred under Diocletian (January 7).

St. Lucy (d. c. 304), virgin and martyr (December 13).

St. Luke, Evangelist and physician (October 18).

St. Lull (d. 786), monk and Bishop of Mainz.

St. Lutgardis (d. 1246), Benedictine nun and mystic who took on the more austere Cistercian life (June 16).

St. Lydwina (1380-1433), virgin who bore patiently the painful symptoms of an illness that resulted from a skating accident and who later received visions (April 14).

St. Macarius the Elder (c. 300-390), priest who lived an austere life and ministered to his fellow hermits (January 15).

St. Macrina (d. 379), director of a community of women in Pontus and sister of Sts. Basil the Great and Gregory of Nyssa (July 19).

St. Madelberte (d. 706), Benedictine abbess and daughter of Sts. Vincent Madelgarus and Waudru (September 7).

St. Madeleine Sophie Barat (1779-1865), foundress of the Society of the Sacred Heart for the education of girls (May 25).

St. Malachy (1095-1148), Abbot of Bangor, Bishop of Connor, and Primate of Armagh who arranged for the first Cistercian foundation in Ireland (November 3).

St. Marcella (d. 410), widow who gave her life to prayer and almsdeeds after the early death of her husband (January 31).

St. Marculf (d. c. 558), founder of a monastery of hermit monks at Nanteuil and patron saint against skin diseases (May 1).

St. Margaret, virgin of Antioch who was disowned by her father and later martyred for becoming a Christian (July 20).

St. Margaret Mary Alacoque (1647-1690), Visitation nun who received revelations of and promoted devotion to the Sacred Heart of Jesus (October 16).

St. Margaret of Cortona (d. 1297), mother who repented of an illicit relationship with a young nobleman when he died suddenly, became a Franciscan tertiary, received visions, and was the instrument of marvelous healings (February 22).

St. Margaret of Scotland (c. 1046-1093), wife of King Malcolm Canmore of Scotland who ministered to the spiritual and temporal needs of her people (November 16).

Bl. Marguerite d'Youville (1701-1771), first native-born Canadian saint and foundress of the Sisters of Charity of the General Hospital (December 23).

Bl. Maria Clementine Annuarite Nengapete, religious sister in Upper Zaire whose efforts to safeguard her virtue caused an enraged officer to kill her.

St. Maria Goretti (1890-1902), twelve-year-old girl who was killed while resisting a young man's advances (July 6).

St. Mark, Evangelist (April 25).

St. Martha, friend of Jesus and sister of Mary and Lazarus (July 29).

St. Martin I (d. c. 656), Pope from 649 and martyr (April 13).

St. Martin de Porres (1579-1639), South American lay brother and infirmarian at the Dominican friary of the Rosary in Lima, Peru, and friend to the poor (November 3).

St. Martin of Tours (c. 315-397), founder of a community of hermit monks and Bishop of Tours (November 11).

St. Martinian the Hermit, hermit of Caesarea (February 13).

Blessed Virgin Mary, Mother of Jesus (Immaculate Conception: December 8; Birth: September 8; Mary, the Mother of God: January 1; Presentation of Mary: November 21; Assumption: August 15; Coronation: August 22; Seven Sorrows: September 15; Visitation: May 31; Our Lady of Lourdes: February 11; Our Lady of Mount Carmel: July 16; Holy Rosary: October 7).

St. Mary of Egypt (c. fifth century), actress who retired to the desert to atone for her sins (April 2).

St. Mary Magdalene, follower of Jesus and the first to whom He appeared after His Resurrection (July 22).

St. Mary Magdalene Bentivoglio, founder of the Poor Clares in America.

St. Mary Magdalene de Pazzi (1566-1607), Carmelite nun who patiently bore grievous trials of body and spirit (May 25).

St. Mary Soledad (1826-1887), foundress of the Handmaids of Mary Serving the Sick (October 11).

St. Matilda (d. 968), wife of King Henry I of Germany and mother of St. Bruno (March 14).

St. Matrona (d. c. 350), virgin and martyr (March 15).

St. Matthew, Evangelist and one of the Twelve Apostles (September 21).

Ven. Matthew Talbot (1856-1925), alcoholic who gave up drinking and gave his life to daily Mass, prayer, penance, and hard work.

St. Mechtildis (d. 1160), Abbess of Diessen and of Edelstetten (May 31).

St. Melania the Older (c. 342-410), patrician woman who founded a monastery on the Mount of Olives in Jerusalem (June 8).

St. Melania the Younger (d. 439), married woman who joined a community of women in Jerusalem, where her husband had become a monk, and, with her husband, devoted herself to caring for the poor and copying books (December 31).

St. Methodius (d. 885), monk, bishop, and Apostle of the Slavs, with his brother St. Cyril (February 14).

Bl. Miguel Pro (1891-1927), Jesuit priest who secretly ministered to the people of Mexico and was martyred (November 23).

St. Monegundis (d. 570), hermitess of Tours (July 2).

St. Monica (332-387), mother of St. Augustine (August 27).

St. Moses of Ethiopia (330-405), slave and thief who converted to Christianity and became a priest (August 28).

St. Nathalan (seventh century), bishop who founded churches in Scotland (January 19).

St. Nathanael, see St. Bartholomew.

St. Nemesius (d. 250), Alexandrian who was acquitted of theft, but condemned and executed for being a Christian (December 19).

St. Nicholas (d. c. 346), Bishop of Myra (December 6).

St. Nicholas of Flue (1417-1487), father of ten who, with the consent of his family, spent nineteen years as a hermit (March 22).

St. Nicholas of Tolentino (1245-1305), Augustinian friar known for his patience, humility, and selfless work (September 10).

St. Noel Chabanel (d. 1649), Jesuit missionary to North America who was martyred (September 26).

St. Norbert (1080-1134), Bishop of Magdeburg and founder of the Premonstratensians, or Norbertines (June 6).

North American Martyrs, Jesuit missionaries who were killed by American Indians between 1642 and 1649 (October 19).

St. Odilo (d. 1049), Abbot of Cluny (January 1).

St. Olaf (d. 1030), King of Norway and martyr (July 29).

St. Opportuna (d. c. 770), Abbess of the Benedictine convent at Almenèches (April 22).

Bl. Padre Pio (1887-1968), Capuchin priest and stigmatist known for bilocation, reading of souls, and miracles of healing.

St. Pammachius (d. 410), Roman senator and friend of St. Jerome who married St. Paula's daughter Paulina and, as a widower, with St. Fabiola, founded the first pilgrims' hostel in the West (August 30).

St. Paphnatius (d. c. 350), Egyptian bishop who was left lame and without an eye after the persecution under Maximinus (September 11).

St. Parisio (d. 1267), Camaldolese monk and spiritual director near Treviso (June 11).

St. Paschal I (d. c. 824), Pope from 817 who moved the relics of many martyrs from the catacombs to various Roman churches (February 11).

St. Patrick (c. 389-c. 461), patron saint and apostle of Ireland (March 17).

St. Paul, Apostle and author of several New Testament letters (June 29).

St. Paul of the Cross (1694-1775), founder of the Passionist Order, who had gifts of prophecy and healing (October 19).

St. Paul the Simple (d. c. 339), married man who left his wife because of her unfaithfulness and became a disciple of St. Anthony (March 7).

St. Paul of Thebes (d. c. 342), first hermit (January 15).

St. Paula (347-404), wife and mother of five — among them Sts. Blesilla and Eustochium — who, after her husband's death, formed a community of religious women and helped St. Jerome in his biblical work (January 26).

St. Paulinus of Nola (c. 354-431), wealthy convert to Christianity who became a bishop and built churches, an aqueduct, and other public works in Nola, Italy (June 22).

St. Pelagia the Penitent, beautiful, wealthy actress of Antioch who repented of a disordered life, was baptized, and became a hermit (October 8).

St. Peregrine Laziosi (1260-1345), convert to the Faith who became a Servite priest (May 1).

St. Perpetua, young married woman who was martyred in the third century (March 6).

St. Peter, one of the Twelve Apostles and first Pope (June 29; Chair of Peter: February 22).

St. Peter of Alcantara (1499-1562), mystic and founder of a reformed order of Franciscans known as the Alcantarines (October 19).

St. Peter Armengol (d. 1304), converted brigand and thief who became a Mercedarian who worked tirelessly to ransom hostages (April 27).

St. Peter Canisius (1521-1597), Jesuit who worked to rebuild the Church after the Reformation and spent his time preaching, teaching, arbitrating, writing catechisms and other works, and reforming and establishing schools (December 21).

St. Peter Claver (1580-1654), Jesuit who ministered to the slaves in South America (September 9).

St. Peter Damian (1007-1072), abbot, Cardinal-bishop of Ostia, and Doctor devoted to writing, preaching, and working against clerical abuses of his time (February 21).

St. Peter Julian Eymard (1811-1868), founder of the congregation of Priests of the Blessed Sacrament and writer (August 1).

Bl. Peter of Pisa (1355-1435), founder of the Poor Brothers of St. Jerome, a small community of hermit monks (June 17).

St. Peter of Sebaste (d. c. 391), abbot and Bishop of Sebaste (January 9).

Bl. Peter of Siena (d. 1289), widower who became a Franciscan tertiary (December 11).

St. Peter of Verona (1205-1252), Dominican who became a popular preacher, was murdered by a heretical assassin, and was canonized the year after his death (April 29).

St. Philip, one of the Twelve Apostles (May 3).

St. Philip Benizi (1233-1285), Servite priest who worked for peace between the Guelphs and the Ghibellines and assisted at the second general Council of Lyons (August 23).

St. Philip Neri (1515-1595), Italian priest who founded the Congregation of the Oratory (May 26).

St. Philip of Zell (d. c. 770), Benedictine hermit and founder of the monastery of Zell (May 3).

Bl. Pierre Toussaint (1766-1853), slave who worked as a hairdresser to support his late owner's widow until he was granted his freedom, after which he gave his earning to philanthropic causes.

St. Pius V (1504-1572), Pope from 1565 (April 30).

St. Pius X (1835-1914), Pope from 1903 (August 21).

Saintly Solutions

Bl. Placid Riccardi (d. 1915), Benedictine monk of the
monastery of St. Paul Outside the Wall in Rome (March 14).

St. Poemen (fourth century), abbot of a group of desert
hermits (August 27).

St. Raphael, archangel whose name means "God heals" and
who is known for his healing, particularly in the Old Testament
book of Tobit (September 29).

Bl. Raymond of Capua (d. 1399), Master General of the
Dominicans and spiritual director and biographer of St.
Catherine of Siena (October 5).

St. Raymond Lull (1232-1316), founder of the first "missionary
college" and martyr who was stoned to death in one of several
attempts to convert the Moors (September 5).

St. Raymond Nonnatus (d. 1240), Mercedarian who succeeded
St. Peter Nolasco in ransoming slaves in Algeria and who was
later made a cardinal (August 31).

St. Raymond of Penafort (1175-1275), Master General of the
Dominicans (January 7).

St. Remigius (d. c. 530), Bishop of Rheims known for his
learning, his eloquence, and his miracles (October 1).

St. Richardis (d. c. 895), wife of Emperor Charles the Fat who
was cleared of an accusation of unfaithfulness by ordeal by fire
and who then retired to a convent (September 18).

St. Rita of Cascia (1381-1457), widow who became an Augustinian
nun who experienced ecstasies while meditating on our Lord's
Passion (May 22).

St. Robert Bellarmine (1542-1621), Jesuit Cardinal, teacher,
writer, and Doctor (September 17).

St. Roch (1295-1327), French pilgrim to Rome who cared for
plague victims and mistakenly accused of and imprisoned for
espionage (August 16).

St. Romuald (c. 950-1027), founder of the Camaldolese Order (June 19).

St. Rose Philippine Duchesne (1769-1852), member of the Society
of the Sacred Heart who established a school for the poor in
France, hid priests during the French Revolution, and was sent
as a missionary to the Louisiana Territory (November 18).

St. Rose of Lima (1586-1617), third order Dominican and first canonized saint of the New World (August 23).

St. Scholastica (d. 543), sister of St. Benedict and head of a convent at Plombariola, under her brother's direction (February 10).

Bl. Sebastian Valfre (1629-1710), Oratorian priest and spiritual director (January 30).

St. Senoch (d. 576), Benedictine abbot and hermit (October 24).

St. Seraphim of Sarov (1759-1833), Russian priest, hermit, and spiritual director (January 2).

St. Seraphina (d. 1253), young girl who bore patiently and cheerfully complications from painful and repulsive diseases (March 12).

St. Severinus of Noricum (d. c. 480), hermit and later missionary to Austria who founded monasteries (January 8).

St. Silverius (d. c. 537), Pope from 536 and martyr (June 20).

Bl. Simon of Todi (d. 1322), preacher of the Austin friars who kept silence under false accusation so as not to cause scandal and dissension in his order (April 20).

St. Sisoes (fourth century), Egyptian monk (July 6).

St. Stanislaus Kostka (1550-1568), model Jesuit who died during his novitiate (November 13).

St. Stephen, first Christian martyr, spoken of in the Acts of the Apostles, chapters 6 and 7 (December 26).

St. Stephen of Hungary (969-1038), King of Hungary who helped build churches and defended the rights of the Holy See (August 16).

St. Stephen of Rieti (d. c. 560), abbot of a monastery near Rieti (February 13).

St. Sylvester (d. 335), Pope from 314 (December 31).

St. Syncletica (d. c. 400), wealthy Macedonian woman who gave away her fortune and lived as a hermitess (January 5).

St. Tarasius (d. 806), Patriarch of Constantinople (February 25).

St. Teresa of Avila (1515-1582), Spanish Carmelite nun and mystic who reformed her order (October 15).

Bl. Teresa Bracco (1924-1944), young woman who was killed while resisting a soldier's advances.

Bl. Teresa Grillo Michel (1855-1944), foundress of the congregation of the Little Sisters of Divine Providence.

Saintly Solutions

St. Thais (fourth century), converted prostitute who lived as a recluse in a convent (October 8).

St. Theodosius (423-529), hermit given oversight of all the monasteries in Palestine (January 11).

St. Theophane Venard (d. 1861), priest of the Missions Étrangères of Paris who was sent to Western Tonking, where he suffered persecution, imprisonment, and martyrdom (February 2).

St. Theophanes (d. 817), founder and abbot of two monasteries and author of a short history of the world (March 12).

St. Theotonius (d. 1166), Portuguese priest who worked tirelessly for the good of the people (February 18).

St. Thérèse of Lisieux (1873-1897), Carmelite nun and Doctor (October 1).

St. Thomas, one of the Twelve Apostles (July 3).

St. Thomas Aquinas (c. 1225-1274), Dominican philosopher, theologian, and Doctor (January 28).

St. Thomas Becket (1118-1170), Archbishop of Canterbury and martyr (December 29).

Bl. Thomas of Cori (d. 1729), shepherd who became an Observant Franciscan (January 19).

St. Thomas More (1478-1535), Lord Chancellor of England and martyr (June 22).

St. Thomas of Villanova (d. 1555), Augustinian Archbishop of Valencia and writer who had a great love for the poor (September 22).

St. Ubald (c. 1100-1160), Bishop of Gubbio (May 16).

Bl. Urban V (d. 1370), Pope from 1362 (December 19).

St. Veronica Giuliani (1660-1727), Capuchiness who experienced visions and other mystical phenomena (July 9).

Bl. Villana of Florence (d. 1360), Dominican tertiary (February 28).

St. Vincent de Paul (1580-1660), founder of the Lazarist Fathers and the Sisters of Charity (September 27).

St. Vincent Ferrer (1350-1419), Dominican mission preacher who helped mend the Great Schism of the West (April 5).

St. Vincent Madelgarus (d. c. 687), husband of St. Waudru who became a monk and founded the Abbey of Soignies (September 20).

St. Vitus (d. c. 303), Italian martyr (June 15).

St. Walbert (d. c. 665), Abbot of Luxeuil who introduced the Rule of St. Benedict there (May 2).

St. Waudru (d. c. 688), wife of St. Vincent Madelgarus who founded a convent; also known as Waldetrudis (April 9).

St. Wenceslaus (d. 929), leader of Bohemia and martyr (September 28).

St. William Firmatus (d. c. 1090), physician who gave his wealth to the poor and lived as a hermit in France (April 24).

St. William of Vercelli (1085-1142), pilgrim and hermit who organized a community of hermit monks under a severe rule (June 25).

St. Wulfric (d. 1154), hermit at Haselbury (February 20).

St. Wulfstan (d. 1095), monk and Bishop of Worcester who helped suppress the slave trade in Bristol (January 19).

Bl. Zdislava (d. 1252), Dominican tertiary (January 1).

St. Zechariah, father of St. John the Baptist (November 5).

Bl. Zeferino Agostini (1813-1896), Italian founder of the Ursuline Daughters of Mary Immaculate.

Fr. Joseph M. Esper

Joseph Esper studied at Sacred Heart Seminary in Detroit and at St. John's Provincial Seminary in Plymouth, Michigan, and was ordained a priest of the Archdiocese of Detroit in 1982.

Fr. Esper has lectured at Marian conferences, spoken on Catholic radio, and written more than a dozen articles for *Fidelity*, *This Rock*, *Signs and Wonders*, *The Priest*, and *Homiletic and Pastoral Review*. He's the author of three other books: *After the Darkness*, *Lessons from the Lives of the Saints*, and *Why Is God Punishing Me?*

From his experience as a parish priest and his vast knowledge of and devotion to the saints — and of their strengths and weaknesses — Fr. Esper offers today's readers practical, encouraging, and inspiring wisdom to help them follow the countless holy men and women who have preceded them on the path to Heaven.

Index of Saints Mentioned
and Quoted

Index of Saints Mentioned and Quoted